The idea of history, and especially the idea that history is goal-directed, has figured prominently in Western thought since the Renaissance, providing the conceptual foundation for philosophies and theologies of history as well as of a variety of social theories. Therefore an extensive scholarly literature has come into existence in the past century which discusses the origin and early history of the idea. It is widely held that in ancient Greek and Roman thought history is understood as circular and repetitive (a consequence of their anti-temporal metaphysics) in contrast with Judaeo-Christian thought, which sees history as linear and unique (a consequence of their messianic and hence radically temporal theology).

This account of the idea of history in antiquity exemplifies a more general view: that the Graeco-Roman and Judaeo-Christian cultures were fundamentally alien and opposed cultural forces and that, therefore, Christianity's victory over paganism included the replacement or supersession of one intellectual world by another.

In this study Dr. Press shows that contrary to this belief there was substantial continuity between "pagan" and Christian ideas of history in antiquity, rather than a striking opposition between cyclic and linear patterns. He finds that the foundation of the Christian view of history as goal-directed lies in the rhetorical rather than the theological motives of early Christian writers.

Gerald A. Press is a member of the Western Culture Program at Stanford University.

McGill-Queen's Studies in the History of Ideas

Richard H. Popkin, Editor

2

THE DEVELOPMENT OF
THE IDEA OF HISTORY
IN ANTIQUITY

Gerald A. Press

McGill-Queen's University Press
Kingston and Montreal

© McGill-Queen's University Press 1982
ISBN 0-7735-1002-8

Legal deposit 4th quarter 1982
Bibliothèque nationale du Québec

Printed in Canada

Canadian Cataloguing in Publication Data

Press, Gerald A., (Gerald Alan), 1945-
The development of the idea of history in antiquity

(McGill-Queen's studies in the history of ideas,
ISSN 0711-0995 ; 2)
Bibliography: p.
Includes index.
ISBN 0-7735-1002-8

1. History - Philosophy.   2. History, Ancient -
Historiography.   I. Title.   II. Series.
D16.8.P74   901   C82-094246-4

To My Parents
for teaching me to
seek understanding

and to Vida
for helping me
to understand
what I find

Contents

Acknowledgments

I wish to express my gratitude to all those who, in various ways, have helped to make this book possible. In particular I would like to thank Jason L. Saunders and Paul Henry, S.J., whose teaching most directly led to and guided this work, and Richard H. Popkin, Herbert Marcuse, and Stephen Crites, who have been inspirations both as teachers and as creative thinkers. I would also like to thank Steven L. Goldman, Thomas Seebohm, and W. Kendrick Pritchett for reading earlier versions and providing much-needed encouragement, Paul Psoinos for invaluable help with the notes and indexes, Vida Pavesich for aid, counsel, and solace from first to last (but not for typing the manuscript), and David Fate Norton, over many years teacher, editor, adviser, friend.

Abbreviations

I N THE NOTES, classical Greek and Latin authors are cited according to the standard abbreviations of the *Oxford Classical Dictionary*, 2nd ed. (Oxford: Clarendon Press, 1970). Occasionally I have adopted the abbreviations of the Liddell-Scott-Jones *Greek-English Lexicon* (Oxford: Clarendon Press, 1966), or Lewis and Short's *Latin Dictionary* (Oxford: Clarendon Press, 1966). Early Christian authors not included in any of the foregoing are cited according to the abbreviations in Du Cange's *Glossarium Mediae et Infimae Latinitatis* (Paris, 1840–50). In some cases I have had to construct abbreviations or I have chosen to construct one more consistent with the others than are Du Cange's. For a tabulation and explanation of all the abbreviations, see the Index Locorum (pp. 151–64). Wherever possible, authors are cited according to standard numbering systems, although I have uniformly used Arabic numerals rather than the mixtures of Arabic and Roman often found. Citations by page ("p.") refer to the pagination of a particular edition, usually standard, listed in the Index Locorum. A citation of the form "1.345, 1–8" refers to Volume 1, page 345, lines 1–8.

In addition, the following abbreviations are used for series, journals, and collections:

ACW *Ancient Christian Writers: The Works of the Fathers in Translation.*

ANF *The Ante-Nicene Fathers.* Translations of the writings of the fathers down to A.D. 325. Ed. Alexander Roberts and James Donaldson.

CJ	*Classical Journal.*
CP	*Classical Philology.*
CSEL	*Corpus scriptorum ecclesiasticorum latinorum.*
Diels, *DG*	Hermann Diels, *Doxographi graeci*. Berlin: de Gruyter, 1879.
D–K[7]	Hermann Diels, *Die Fragmente der Vorsokratiker*. 7th ed., revised by Walther Kranz. Berlin: Weidmann, 1954. 3 vols.
GCS	*Die griechischen christlichen Schriftsteller der ersten Jahrhunderte*. Berlin: Akademie der Wissenschaften, 1897–1969.
GRBS	*Greek, Roman and Byzantine Studies.*
H & Th	*History and Theory.*
JbAC	*Jahrbuch für Antike und Christentum.*
JHI	*Journal of the History of Ideas.*
JHS	*Journal of Hellenic Studies.*
NPNF	*A Select Library of the Nicene and Post-Nicene Fathers of the Christian Church*. Ed. Philip Schaff. New York: The Christian Literature Co., 1886–90.
PG	J.-P. Migne, *Patrologiae Cursus Completus, Series Graeca.*
PL	J.-P. Migne, *Patrologiae Cursus Completus, Series Latina.*

THE DEVELOPMENT OF
THE IDEA OF HISTORY
IN ANTIQUITY

I

Introduction

MODERN WESTERN THOUGHT exhibits a striking preoccupation with history. The resecularization of history writing in the four-teenth-century Florentine chronicles and the Renaissance rediscovery of the value of knowing something about the human terrestrial past contributed to making history,[1] for the first time in Western civiliza-tion, an independent part of the educational curriculum. Francis Ba-con, for example, divides all human learning into history, poesy, and philosophy.[2] Since then histories have been written not only with the traditional subject matters of nations and wars (including the medie-val variant, ecclesiastical history), but also with subject matters both wider and narrower. Histories have been written of continents, civili-zations, and the world; but they have also been written of institutions, languages, and cultures. There are histories of the arts (liberal, fine, mechanical, domestic, and martial), of aesthetics, art criticism, and taste, as well as of the sciences and technology. Histories have also been written of images, themes, problems, and ideas that recur in the folklore, art, and intellectual culture that unite a civilization, of schools and movements of thought, and of entertainments, sports, and games. There are also histories of history writing, one part of an extensive literature of historiography. A variety of political and social theories have found in history the evidence both for analyses of prevailing systems and for predictions or prescriptions about the future. Meta-physical analyses of the whole course of history have issued in a variety

[1] See Beatrice Reynolds "Shifting Currents in Historical Criticism," *JHI* 14 (1953):471–92; Louis Green, "Historical Interpretation in the Fourteenth Century Florentine Chronicles," *JHI* 28 (1967):161–78; and Donald J. Wilcox. *The Development of Florentine Humanist Historiography in the Fifteenth Century,* Harvard Historical Studies, 82 (1969).

[2] Bacon, *Advancement of Learning,* Bk. 2, Pt. 1, para. 1.

of philosophies of history; and history has been taken to be the proof of Christianity as well as its innermost essence, its difference from and superiority to all other religions. It is not an exaggeration to say that the idea of history is one of the most widely influential and formative ideas in the modern Western intellectual world.[3]

The idea of history that has informed the distinctively modern social theories, philosophies, and theologies is that history is telic, or goal-directed: there is an end or goal—a *telos*—toward which history is (inevitably) moving, which may be known either by rational inquiry into the facts or by revelation, and in relation to which all prior actions and events have both their meaning and their value. In the past hundred years this idea has been extensively discussed, its origins sought in early Jewish or Christian thought, its variants classified, its consequences praised or criticized, and it has been compared with other and earlier ideas of history. In the succeeding chapters I shall try to determine the development of the idea of history in antiquity, taking as my horizon this influential and modern idea of history as goal-directed. But this is only a "horizon" because, despite the weight of previous discussion, the evidence shows that the idea of history as going somewhere is not found in antiquity.

There is, as I have just suggested, a widely accepted account[4] of the idea of history in antiquity, and it presupposes that there was an opposition between the Graeco-Roman and Judaeo-Christian cultures. Although this opposition was already adumbrated in Hegel,[5] the most influential study of it for the discussion of the idea of history

---

[3] Hajo Holborn ["Greek and Modern Concepts of History," *JHI* 10 (1949):3] says: "Only in Hellenic and western civilization did historical thought acquire a truly fundamental role for the whole structure of culture." Similarly, Kostas Papaioannou, "The Consecration of History," *Diogenes* 3 (1960):29–35. Paul Henry, S.J., says [*St. Augustine on Personality* (New York: Macmillan, 1960), n. 35] that the ideas of creation, personality, and history are fundamental in modern Western thought and entirely unknown in these forms to the ancient world. Karl Reinhardt ["Philosophy and History among the Greeks," *Greece and Rome*, n.s. 1 (1954):82–90] undertakes to explain why Greek thought, unlike modern, experienced no problem about the relationship between philosophy and history. And Oswald Spengler [*The Decline of the West*, 2 vol. (New York: Knopf, 1920), 1:132] denies historical consciousness to the "Classical soul."

[4] The following discussion exhibits passages from various scholars and thinkers illustrative of the view that is widely accepted and particular points in it. A more extensive list of works that expound or invoke this view will be found in the Appendix.

[5] See, for example, Hegel, *Lectures on the Philosophy of History*, trans. J. Sibree (New York: Colonial Press, 1900), Pt. 3, Sec. 3, Chap. 2, pp. 318–36.

was Lucien Laberthonnière's *Le réalisme chrétien et l'idéalisme grec*;[6] the theme of the book is that Greek philosophy is

> in radical opposition to Christianity.
>
> But although they carefully preserved the Greek philosophy and its language and its dialectical procedures and even its theories, they introduced here something else. It is a different spirit that flows in their speculations. Under their pen, words change meaning and concepts take on a different content. Far from being alleviated, I should say rather that in their thought the opposition explodes: for, to be definite, it is not a conciliation that they are bringing about, it is a substitution; they substitute one doctrine for another doctrine and one attitude for another attitude. And that remains true of all the great doctors of the Greek church and of the Latin church. . . .
>
> . . . This combination, rather than producing a stable equilibrium in which one might have hoped to settle down, finally came to the point of manifesting even more completely the opposition that we point out. . . .
>
> It is this opposition that we would like to try to make plain.[7]

Note the claims here: there is a different "spirit," in accordance with which "words change meaning and concepts take on a different content"; it is "a substitution [of] . . . one doctrine for another," a "radical opposition." And from this opposition follows the basic move in the usual account of the idea of history in antiquity: the contention that the Judaeo-Christian idea of history differs radically from the Graeco-Roman.

This move was already made in 1891 by Wilhelm Windelband, the historian of philosophy. He writes:

> The fundamental tendency of Christian thought . . . was to portray the historical drama of fall and redemption as a connected series of events taking place once for all, which begins with a free decision of lower spirits to sin, and has its turning point in the redemptive revelation, the resolve of divine freedom. In contrast with the naturalistic concepts of Greek thought, *history is conceived of as the realm of free acts of*

---

[6] Laberthonnière, *Le réalisme chrétien et l'Idéalisme grec* (Paris, 1904; reprinted Paris: Edition de Seuil, 1966).

[7] *Ibid.*, pp. 245–46. J. Guitton [*Le Temps et l'Éternité chez Plotin et St. Augustine* (Paris: Bovin, 1933), p. 357] cites Laberthonnière in the course of arguing for the replacement of cycles by a historical world "with spiritual significance."

personalities, taking place but once, and the character of these acts, agreeably to the entire consciousness of time, is of essentially religious significance.[8]

A. O. Lovejoy, later the founder of the study of the history of ideas, made similar observations about Christianity and the idea of history just after the turn of the century.[9] Discussion of the matter increased around the middle of the century, and one of the most influential participants in that discussion was Oscar Cullmann, the theologian and opponent of Albert Schweitzer and Rudolf Bultmann. In *Christus und die Zeit* Cullmann argues that history is the very essence of Christianity, that "all Christian theology in its innermost essence is Biblical history,"[10] that is, revelatory or redemptive history. For him "the unique Christian conception of time as the scene of redemptive history is of a two-fold character. . . . In the first place, salvation is bound to a *continuous time process* which embraces past, present and future. . . . And in the second place, all parts of this line are related to one *historical fact* at the mid-point."[11] And this, it is believed, is radically different from Greek and Roman views.

Graeco-Roman thought focused on the study of the natural world in which what is real is what is repeatable; not the individual but the species is of interest. The Graeco-Roman mind was devoted to realities and truths outside time (for example, Parmenides, Plato, and Plotinus), to abstractions and ideas, rather than individuals. "It is *abstraction* that is for them the instrument of truth and the instrument of salvation. . . . [the individual] is for them the scandal of thought."[12] The natural world is eternal and the natural species are

[8] Windelband, *History of Philosophy*, trans. James H. Tufts (New York: Macmillan, 1893), p. 257.

[9] Lovejoy, "Religion and the Time Process," *American Journal of Theology* 6 (1903):488ff.; "The Entangling Alliance of Religion and History," *Hibbert Journal* 6 (1907):261ff. On his view, however, this constitutes a flaw in Christian ethics, which ought to be removed.

[10] Cullmann, *Christus und die Zeit* (Zurich, 1946) = *Christ et le Temps* (Neuchâtel, 1947) = *Christ and Time, The Primitive Christian Conception of Time and History*, trans. Floyd Filson (Philadelphia: Westminister Press, 1950), p. 23. Similarly, C. N. Cochrane, *Christianity and Classical Culture* (New York: Oxford University Press, 1944), p. 225.

[11] *Christ and Time*, p. 32. Cf. Gerhart Ladner, "The Impact of Christianity," in *The Transformation of the Roman World*, ed. Lynn White (Berkeley: University of California Press, 1966), Chap. 2.

[12] Laberthonnière, *Le réalisme chrétien*, pp. 248–50.

eternal by virtue of the repeated life cycles of the individual members. Thus, on the usual view, time, which is the number or measure of change in nature, is understood as a circle (for example, Arist. *Phys.* 229b). Rectilinear motion is "imperfect and perishable," circular is "perfect and eternal."[13] Like all natural species the human being is also eternal; and just as each individual undergoes the developmental cycle of the species, so events in the human social and political world were believed to recur in cycles (for example, the Stoic theory of the cyclic destruction and recreation of the world). "For the Greeks, what has been is what shall be, what is done is what shall be done again."[14] The idea of history is logically dependent upon the idea of time; it too, therefore, is circular. "The ancients . . . were impressed by the visible order and beauty of the cosmos, and the cosmic law of growth and decay was also a pattern for their understanding of history. According to the Greek view of life and the world, everything moves in recurrence, like the eternal recurrence of sunrise and sunset, of summer and winter, of generation and corruption."[15]

History, then, is taken to be circular and repetitive. Therefore, neither history as a whole nor any individual historical event can have any particular meaning or value; since if a thing or an event comes to pass over and over again in just the same way, then no one instance of the type can have any more or less meaning than any other. None of them has any meaning in itself; only the type or form of the thing, which is eternal. "When a man lives with the certainty of the finality and excellence of the world, he feels no need whatsoever to confer upon the passing and fortuitous event a privileged status destined to fortify his faith in his own autonomy or to calm his fears over his capacity to form his life according to the desires of his own will."[16]

Since history and historical events in Graeco-Roman thought were meaningless, there could be for them no philosophy of history. "To the Greeks a *philosophy* of history would have been a contradiction in

[13] Kostas Papaioannou, "Nature and History in the Greek Conception of the Cosmos," *Diogenes*, no. 25 (1959), p. 9. Likewise Robert E. Cushman, "Greek and Christian Views of Time," *Journal of Religion* 33 (1953):256.

[14] Papaioannou, "Cosmos," p. 26.

[15] Karl Löwith, *Meaning in History* (Chicago: University of Chicago Press, 1957), p. 4.

[16] Wilhelm Dilthey, *Einleitung in die Geisteswissenschaften*, trans. L. Sauzin (Paris: Presses universitaires, 1942), p. 25.

terms,"[17] Löwith wrote. And Kostas Papaioannou said, "A philosophy of this kind, with the rigid oppositions which it implies between
Nature and mind, between objectivity and subjectivity, between
necessity and freedom, as well as the value emphasis which it places
on all the generative faculties of history runs counter to the deepest
aspirations of the Greek mind."[18] Moreover, on the usual account,
this repetitious, meaningless circularity of time and history "must be
experienced as an enslavement, as a curse. . . . everything keeps
recurring. . . . that is why the philosophical thinking of the Greek
world labors with the problem of time and also why all Greek striving for redemption seeks as its goal to be freed from this eternal,
circular course and thus to be freed from time itself."[19] The pessimism, "the eternal desperate pessimism of the eternal circle of
events,"[20] generated by this explains, finally, both the "failure" of
classical culture to satisfy the spiritual needs of human beings and
the consequent decline of the ancient world.[21]

Graeco-Roman thought, characterized in this way, is then contrasted with Judaeo-Christian thought. The latter, it is said, has a
fundamentally different conception of time, and thus brings into existence a fundamentally new idea of history. Jewish and Christian
thought begins from the createdness of the world, of the natural species, and of human beings. For it time, and therefore history, has a
beginning and an end—Creation and Day of Judgment—although
Jews and Christians differ over the relationship between the present
age in history and the decisive event in history. As against the cyclic
views of classical antiquity, they "saw time as the linear process of
the purpose of God. Initiated by a divine act of creation, it moved
towards a definite τέλος or end, which would mark the achievement
of the divine purpose."[22] Time and history are here understood to be

[17] Löwith, *Meaning in History*, p. 4.
[18] Papaioannou, "Cosmos," p. 3.
[19] Cullmann, *Christ and Time*, p. 53.
[20] R. L. P. Milburn, *Early Christian Interpretations of History* (London: A. and C.
Black, 1954), p. 7.
[21] E.g., Anton-Hermann Chroust, "The Relation of Religion to History in Early
Christian Thought," *The Thomist* 18 (1955):67; John Baillie, *The Belief in Progress*
(New York: Scribners, 1950), p. 50; and James M. Connolly, *Human History and the
Word of God* (New York: Macmillan, 1963–64), p. 4. For an earlier version of the
"failure and decline" model, see Jacob Burckhardt, *The Age of Constantine* (1852),
trans. Moses Hadas (New York: Random House, 1949), Chaps. 5 and 6.
[22] S. G. F. Brandon, "B.C. and A.D.: The Christian Philosophy of History," *History
Today* 15 (1965):197. Likewise, Cullmann, *Christ and Time*, pp. 52ff. N. H. Snaith

rectilinear, once and for all, and directed toward the end or goal of the Messianic Age. In contrast with Graeco-Roman theories of "purposeless cycles, history was now seen to be linear, progressing in a straight line from the six days of creation to a single day of Judgment."[23] Thus, "to the Jews and Christians . . . history was primarily a history of salvation."[24] There is but one history, that of the Divine Economy: "the Biblical conception of the unfolding of God's plan for the creation, and particularly for man's redemption in history."[25] As understood in Judaeo-Christian thought, "terrestrial history is a forward-moving process of a very special kind. It has an *exortus*, a *centrum*, and a *finis*, a definite beginning, a middle or focal point, and a definite end."[26] Each event is thus unique, playing its unique role in the economy, and therefore meaningful.

This new conception of history, so it is thought, can be seen in the development of Christian historiography. On the one hand, the new importance attached to history is seen in the invention of altogether new forms of historical composition, ecclesiastical history and the biography of saints. But more significantly, in the confidence of the early church historians—Eusebius, Socrates Scholasticus, Sozomen, and Evagrius—it is seen that Divine Providence guides all events: "The Church historians' task had a basic unity, for all the historians and their readers would agree that church history was properly and essentially a record of the power of God and of the action of God in human affairs. Thus church history was a test of the truth of the faith. . . . Hence the church historian had a special vocation within the church, not only as a narrator of events, but as a channel through which the truth of the faith was proclaimed."[27]

It is widely agreed, then, that for Judaeo-Christianity, history— that is, the eschatological history of salvation—is linear, once and for all, and therefore meaningful in the goal-directed sense of fulfilling

---

["Time in the Old Testament," in *Promise and Fulfillment*, ed. F. F. Bruce (Edinburgh: T. & T. Clark, 1963), pp. 175–86] distinguishes among circular, horizontal, and vertical time.

[23] Constantinos A. Patrides, *The Phoenix and the Ladder* (Berkeley: University of California Press, 1965), p. 6.

[24] Löwith, *Meaning in History*, p. 5.

[25] R. A. Markus, "Pleroma and Fulfillment. The Significance of History in St. Irenaeus' Opposition to Gnosticism," *Vigiliae Christianae* 8 (1954):213.

[26] Baillie, *Belief in Progress*, p. 84. Likewise Cushman, "Views of Time," p. 254.

[27] Glanville Downey, "The Perspective of the Early Church Historians," *GRBS* 6 (1965):69.

Idea of History

God's promise of salvation for his people, whereas for Graeco-Roman culture history is circular, repetitive, and therefore meaningless. Since philosophy of history is inconceivable apart from history understood as meaningful, it is fair to say that this fundamentally new philosophic pursuit is a consequence of Judaeo-Christianity. "The very existence of a philosophy of history and its quest for a meaning is due to the history of salvation; it emerged from faith in an ultimate purpose. . . . History . . . is meaningful only by indicating some transcendent purpose beyond the actual facts," wrote Löwith.[28] And it is in this sense that Augustine's *De civitate Dei* is often said to be the first treatise on the philosophy of history. "The Christian philosophy of history was first enunciated by Augustine in response to pagan claims that this new religion was responsible for the sack of Rome by Alaric's Goths in 410."[29] Again, "Augustine may rightly be called the father of the Christian 'philosophy' of history. His major work on the subject, *De civitate Dei contra paganos* . . . was written in the apologetic and polemic vein typical of most of his writings."[30]

The widely accepted view of the idea of history in antiquity that I have been outlining is, as is clear, a part of a more general discussion of the relationship between Graeco-Roman and Judaeo-Christian influences on the formation of Western thought and civilization. It is a commonplace that Western thought is Christian (or Judaeo-Christian).[31] But although it is generally and vaguely agreed that

[28] Löwith, *Meaning in History*, p. 5. The view that Judaeo-Christianity is responsible for the invention of philosophy of history is sometimes carried to the extreme of supposing that only a Christian can really understand history at all. J. N. Figgis, for example, writes: "The historical temperament, or whatever you call it, to be genuine must be deeply impregnated with the Christian story" [*Christianity and History* (London: Finch, 1905), p. viii]. And A. N. Wilder [*Early Christian Rhetoric* (London: S.C.M., 1964), p. 136] goes even further and claims "no peoples have a history in the true sense except Israel and those that have entered into its understanding of man. The reality-sense of other human groups is prehistorical and prepersonal by comparison." Émile Bréhier ["Quelques traits de la philosophie de l'histoire dans l'antiquité classique," *R. d'Histoire et Philosophie Religieuses* (1943), p. 38–40], however, holds that the Stoics and Polybius, with their notion of the unity of mankind, created philosophy of history; Christianity did not.

[29] Brandon, "BC. and A.D.," p. 191. Jean Daniélou ["St. Irenée et les origines de la théologie de l'histoire," *R. de science religieuse* 34 (1947):227–31] finds the origin in Irenaeus' explanation of the relation between the Old and New Testaments in terms of a progressive education of humanity.

[30] Patrides, *Phoenix*, p. 13.

[31] See, for example, Lynn White, "Christian Myth and Christian History," *JHI* 2 (1942):145; Franklin La Van Baumer, ed., *Main Currents of Western Thought* (New York: Alfred A. Knopf, 1961), p. 20; and *Basic Writings of Saint Augustine*, ed. with

Christianity *did* decisively transform Western thought, accounts of the rise of Christianity as a distinctly intellectual phenomenon usually set forth the differences between "pagan" and Christian Western civilization rather than showing (in detail) how the transformation came about. Very often studies of the relationship between the Graeco-Roman and Judaeo-Christian intellectual worlds interpret the period of their confluence in terms either of the "decline" of the ancient world or else of the Christian heritage from "pagan" thought, the "classical heritage of the Middle Ages."[32]

In the perspective of historiography generally, this tradition has the effect of depriving late antiquity—the period in which the fusion took place—of a character of its own. It is seen either as the end of what came before or as the beginning of what came later; in terms either of what went in or of what came out, but not in its own terms. In the narrower perspective of the historiography of ideas there is the parallel tradition of opposing the Graeco-Roman and Judaeo-Christian thought-worlds.

This tradition, as the historiographical framework, brings to light another problem with the usual account of the idea of history in antiquity: it is static, nondevelopmental. The different "ideas" of his-

---

introduction by Whitney J. Oates (New York: Random House, 1948), p. v.

[32] It has been customary to give short shrift to the period in studies of cultural history because it is "wholly religious," "superstitious," or "decadent." Typical is A. H. M. Jones [*The Decline of the Ancient World* (New Hork: Holt, Rinehart, and Winston, 1966), 2:957–70], who characterizes the age generally as "religious" and asserts that its only great intellectual achievement was the elaboration of systematic theologies.

Studies of the "decline": Ferdinand Lot, *The End of the Ancient World and the Beginnings of the Middle Ages* (New York: Alfred A. Knopf, 1931), Charles Corbière, *Le Christianisme et la fin de la philosophie antique* (Paris: Fischbacher, 1921); Otto Seeck, *Geschichte des Untergangs der Antiken Welt*, 2 vols. (Berlin: Siemenroth and Troschel, 1901); R. A. Lafferty, *The Fall of Rome* (New York: Doubleday, 1971), a literary treatment of the facts; Solomon Katz, *The Decline of Rome and the Rise of Medieval Europe* (Ithaca: Cornell University Press, 1955); F. W. Walbank, *The Decline of the Roman Empire in The West* (London: Cobbett Press, 1946); K. Pfister, *Der Untergang der Antiken Welt* (Berlin, 1941); Roger Rémondon, *La crise de l'Empire romain* (Paris: Presses Universitaires, 1964). The notion of a "decline" is rejected altogether by Richard Mansfield, *The Myth of Rome's Fall* (New York: Thomas Y. Crowell, 1958).

Studies of the "heritage of the Middle Ages": W. G. de Burgh, *The Legacy of the Ancient World*, 2nd ed. (New York: Barnes and Noble, 1960); H. St. L. B. Moss, *The Birth of the Middle Ages, 395–814* (London: Oxford University Press, 1947); Stewart Perowne, *The End of the Roman World* (New York: Thomas Y. Crowell, 1966); R. R. Bolgar, *The Classical Heritage* (Cambridge: Cambridge University Press, 1954); Christopher Dawson, *The Making of Europe* (London: Sheed & Ward, 1932); Henry Osborn Taylor, *The Classical Heritage of the Middle Ages*, 4th ed. (New York: Ungar, 1957).

tory are presented as deductions, respectively, from a metaphysical and a theological system understood as complete and unchanging. There is the metaphysical thought of the Greeks; and there is the theology of the Christians. Each has its own starting points, and each comes to its own conclusions.

> It is commonly agreed that the Christian doctrine of the Word made Flesh gives to history a significance it did not already possess for classical Greek thought. Time ceases to be circular and acquires directionality. Directionality is constituted not only by *telos* but by *finis*. Time has beginning with Creation, receives its *telos* through the Incarnation, and has its *finis* with the Last Judgment. Time thus acquires meaning as the interval between creation and redemption. . . . In such a perspective history becomes *heilsgeschichte*, or saving history. But this perspective would be quite impossible for the Greek mind in so far as it did not attain to the conception of teleological or historical time.[33]

Just as the two thought-worlds are taken to be complete and unchanging, so their ideas are taken to be complete and unchanging, the result of no process of development, independent from and opposed to one another.[34] The transformation of the idea of history,

---

[33] Cushman, *"Views of Time,"* p. 254. Even J. B. Bury, whose *History of the Later Roman Empire* [2 vols. (London: Macmillan, 1889)] considers the connections between Christianity and paganism, sees the Christian religion as "entirely opposed to the Roman spirit which it was destined to dissolve" (1:26).

[34] That this opposition of static views is a fashion in historical interpretation has been recognized by W. den Boer ("Some Remarks on the Beginnings of Christian Historiography," *Studia Patristica* 4:348). And at least as regards the idea of time, it has been soundly criticized by Arnaldo Momigliano ["Time in Ancient Historiography," *H & Th.*, Beiheft 6 (1966), pp. 1–23; reprinted in Momigliano, *Quarto Contributo alla Storia degli Studi Classici* (Rome: Edizioni di storia e letteratura, 1969), pp. 13–41], who concludes that there are no neat and mutually exclusive views about time to be found in the writings of the ancients. For some examples of this pluralism, see John Callahan, *Four Views of Time in Ancient Philosophy* (Cambridge, Mass., 1948). Besides Momigliano, there are also tendencies to focus on the continuities among patristic scholars; see, for example, C. Fabricius, "Der sprachliche Klassizismus der griechischen Kirchenväter. Ein philogisches und geistesgeschichtliches Problem," *Jb.A.C.* 10 (1967):187–99, and M. Fuhrmann, "Die lateinische Literatur der Spätantike. Ein literarhistorischer Beitrag zum Kontinuitätsproblem," *Antike und Abendland* 13 (1967):56–79. Typical is F. D. McCloy's argument ["The Sense of Artistic Form in the Mentality of the Greek Fathers," *Studia Patristica* 9:69–75] that the fathers have a sense of beauty and that it is an aspect of the old paideia that has been continued in Christian culture. S. MacCormack ["Roma, Constantinopolis, The Emperor, and his Genius," *Classical Quarterly* 25 (1975)] "seeks to contribute to the discussion on change and continuity, and, more specifically, to the problem of what may be understood by conversion from paganism to Christianity in late antiquity" (p. 131).

which I hope to make clear in this study, was on this view not a transformation at all, but only a substitution or supersession of one idea by a wholly different, alien, and oppposed one bearing the same name. For a transformation requires a self-same entity, which undergoes the transformation.

Insofar as those who hold this orthodox view profess to be accounting for the interaction of Graeco-Roman and Judaeo-Christian thought, of course they affirm continuity and genuine transformation; but fundamentally, they believe that Christianity brought something entirely new into the cultural world. W. G. de Burgh, for example, states that Christianity "revolutionized the entire fabric of Mediterranean civilization";[35] but his footnote to that statement says: "This assertion is perfectly compatible with the recognition of the historic continuity between Christianity and pre-Christian Jewish and Hellenic thought. A fair mind can hardly fail to be impressed by the disparity between the Christian faith . . . and any other creed known to history. Affinities in points of detail would not be so arresting, were not the differences of spirit and influence so profound."

While it is certainly true that Graeco-Roman and Judaeo-Christian ways of thinking are very different, it is no less true that the one passed into the other, and not all at once ("with the conversion of Constantine"), but gradually and over a long period of time. So it was that Christianity had such evident social effects on the institutions of the Roman Empire long before it became the official religion that Gibbon could attribute partially to its influence the decline of the empire. So it was, too, that the cultural ferment occasioned by the presence of a large and affluent Jewish community in Alexandria, the cultural center of the Hellenistic world, produced the first attempted philosophical fusions of the Judaeo-Christian and Graeco-Roman cultures in the writings of Philo and the first Greek version of the Pentateuch, the Septuagint, so called after the alleged number of the translators.

The accepted account of the idea of history, then, is nondevelopmental. It is an account of substitution or supersession, not of transformation, and it is rooted in an equally nondevelopmental view of the relationship between Graeco-Roman and Judaeo-Christian thought as the sources of our own intellectual tradition. But to understand our own tradition we shall have to seek a developmental and

[35] De Burgh, *Legacy*, p. 280.

historical account of the ideas or modes of thought that we consider
distinctively Christian or Judaeo-Christian. We shall have to examine changes in ideas within the context of political, social, religious,
and intellectual or cultural movements.[36] From the cultural historian's point of view, the rise of Christianity must be not a miracle
or a divine intervention the decisiveness of which is settled from the
beginning. Christianity is one among many historical processes. And
just as it influences (eventually) the ways in which Western people
think and feel and act, so too it is influenced by the cultural forms
and movements of the world into which it was born, such as, not only
Greek philosophy, but also Greek and Roman rhetoric, politics, and
education. And just as Christianity influences culture in the early
centuries of our era, so do other cultural movements, such as those of
religious innovation. Rather than looking at the rise of Judaeo-
Christianity as the replacement of one cultural world by another, we
need to understand the processes by which the changes occurred.
And to the extent that we fail to understand them, we shall also fail
to understand ourselves; for our intellectual tradition over the many
centuries has been, in large part, determined by just such transformations, and we are creatures of our own tradition.

The accepted view of the idea of history in antiquity is faulted in
the first place for being nondevelopmental, but there is a deeper
problem: the whole literature uses an idea of history that is defined
beforehand—namely, history as the whole temporal process of the
world (or, at least, of the human world), or, more simply, the past.[37]

---

[36] As early as 1904 F. J. Dölger found it unsatisfactory to study the early Christian
writings with a view solely to the history of dogma. What interested him, instead, was
"the process by which the classical civilization, as it existed in the first three centuries, was transformed into the Christianised culture of the four centuries beginning
with Constantine" [E. A. Judge, "'Antike und Christentum.' Some Recent Work from
Cologne," *Prudentia* (Auckland) 5 (1973):2]. His own studies were published in his
personal journal, *Antike und Christentum*; his program has been carried out in the *Reallexikon für Antike und Christentum* and the *Jahrbuch für Antike und Christentum*. But these
publications have not been widely reviewed, and the overall enterprise of which they
are a part has, as a result, had little influence on the fashions in scholarly work on
late antiquity. For a comprehensive critical study of Dölger and the current state of
the enterprise, see Edwin A. Judge, "'Antike und Christentum': Towards a Definition
of the Field. A Bibliographical Survey," in *Aufstieg und Niedergang der römischen Welt*, H.
Temporini and W. Haase (Berlin: De Gruyter, 1979), Pt. 2, Vol. 23:1, pp. 2–58.

[37] That Cullmann, at least, means something different by "history"—namely, the
past—than does Augustine is recognized by R. A. Markus, *Saeculum: History and Society
in the Theology of St. Augustine* (Cambridge: Cambridge University Press, 1970), pp.
231–32.

And then it proceeds within this context to examine "pagan" and Christian ideas of history. But since the content is assumed to be the same for the two ideas, it is more accurate to call these "patterns" or "views" than "ideas" of history. They oppose "linear" or "progressive" to "circular" or "cyclic" patterns of history; but it is not doubted that the "history" of which these are alternative patterns is the whole temporal process. They oppose, in other words, different patterns or views of the same thing. Such a procedure is little likely to reveal what the ancients themselves thought history was if they happened to think that it was something other than the whole temporal process. Rather than adequate studies of the development of the idea of history, this extensive literature is to be read as an account of ancient attitudes toward the past.

The definition problem can also, and more productively, be seen in terms of the question that is asked. The question about the idea of history raised in previous studies has been: What thoughts (opinions, views, attitudes, visions, theories) have other or earlier cultures had about that for which the idea is history? The attempt has been, in the philosophical and theological discussions, to understand different ideas of history by moving from things to ideas, to get at the idea by starting from the reality of which it is the idea. The procedure in general has been to attempt to understand previous ideas of a reality by comparing what was thought and said about that reality, assumed to be the stable, permanent object, referent, or content of the idea in question. And the result here is that, far from understanding any idea of what history is that is really *different* from history understood as the whole temporal process, we can only come to see what other cultures thought about our idea of what history is.

It may be interesting to understand what other cultures thought about the past or the whole temporal process, but it is not to the point. If we want to understand better the impact of Judaeo-Christianity on Western civilization it would be necessary to reexamine the cultural sources of later Western tradition; and this is possible only to the extent that we are able to stand outside the framework of assumptions of Judaeo-Christian Western civilization. In particular, it will be possible to grasp the impact of Judaeo-Christian thought on the idea of history only if we first grasp what history was thought to be before this impact occurred. It should be observed that the fashion of considering Graeco-Roman culture over against Judaeo-Christian reflects one of the dominant attitudes of the early Christians them-

selves toward the "pagan" culture. Consider Tertullian's famous
rhetorical question, "What has Athens to do with Jerusalem?" In
large part the attempts of modern scholars and thinkers to understand the relationship between these two cultures is still dominated
by this early Christian habit—for them, doubtless, a social necessity!—
of defining themselves as over against Hellenism. The interest of a
philosopher and historian, however, should be to understand the intellectual shifts of late antiquity. And for this it is necessary to see
what the ancients thought history was rather than, in effect, what
they thought about what history is by a definition worked out only by
a later tradition. I know of no clearer statement of the problem and
its correct solution than Werner Jaeger's, speaking of the history of
paideia:

> Some critics have laid down that a historian of paideia must begin by
> giving his own definition of it. That is rather as if they expected a
> historian of philosophy to start either from Plato's definition of philos-
> ophy, or from Epicurus', or from Kant's or Hume's—all four being
> widely different. A history of paideia should describe as accurately as
> possible all the different meanings of Greek paideia, the various forms
> which it took, and the various spiritual levels at which it appeared,
> and should explain both their individual peculiarities and their histor-
> ical connexions.[38]

We need, therefore, to change the question asked: not "What ideas
have people had about (the one stable referent of the term)
'history'?" but rather, "What different referents has the term 'history'
had for these different ages and cultures?" This question is more sat-
isfactory; for it does not presuppose a lack of development in the
content of ideas but, rather, begins from the quite real, if too little
appreciated, permanence of the terms making up the intellectual vocabulary of the Western tradition. As Kurt von Fritz pointed out
nearly forty years ago,[39] the history of Greek intellectual terms is of

---

[38] Jaeger, *Paideia*, trans. Gilbert Highet 3 vols. (New York: Oxford University
Press, 1939–45), 3:300, n. 3 (to Bk. 4, Chap. 2). His *Early Christianity and Greek Paideia*
(Cambridge Harvard University Press, 1961) outlines "the transformation of the tra-
dition of Greek paideia in the Christian centuries of late antiquity" (Pref.).

[39] Von Fritz, "ΝΟΟΣ and NOEIN in the Homeric Poems," *CP* 38 (1943):79. Bruno Snell
["Die Sprache Homers als Ausdruck seiner Gedankenwelt," *Neue Jahrbücher für
Antike und Deutsche Bildung* 2 (1939):393–410] had already defended analysis of the
language as a source for understanding the thought-world of antiquity. The view
perhaps has its source in Hegel: "Die Ausgedehnte consequente Grammatik ist das
Werk des Denkens, das seine Kategorien darin bemerklich macht." *Einleitung in die*

interest because these terms still comprise the heart of our intellectual vocabulary and because therefore a knowledge of their development will clarify persistent problems by disclosing where, when, and in what context the terms acquired such significations as made for confusions about them or as a result of their employment.

A word has, ordinarily, many significations—some very diverse—but there is reason to suppose that an examination of the attested uses of a word at a given time and place may be discriminated into a relatively few kinds from which may be determined a basic meaning or underlying idea. This should provide a starting point, a backdrop, against which the acquisition of new areas of signification or the loss or decline of older ones will appear either as further developments of older (original) facets of the idea or as the introduction of new ones.

An examination of the uses of the ancient Greek words ἱστορεῖν, ἱστορία, ἱστορικός, and their ancestor, ἵστωρ, and the ancient Latin words *historia* and *historicus* will reveal what the term "history" in its various linguistic forms was taken to mean. This, properly speaking, is what "history" was thought to be in antiquity, and this, therefore, should be the primary focus for explicating the idea of history in antiquity. Secondarily, an examination of such semantically related terms as τὰ προγεγόνατα and *res gestae* and of political, religious, and philosophical attitudes toward the past, would provide a more complete picture of the ancient idea of history, and, in particular, would enable us to see what, if anything, the ancients thought about the especially modern use of "history" as the whole temporal process. But these latter questions do not and need not form a part of the present study, because the weight of previous work, as I have argued, is, in fact, about ideas and attitudes toward the past; and while to some extent it examines uses of the Greek and Latin words based on ἵστωρ, it considers ἱστορία and *historia* to mean the same thing as τὰ προγεγόνατα or *res gestae*—which, of course, by a modern definition they do.

I have been arguing that a study of the development of the idea of history in antiquity must, in the first place, take a cultural-historical

---

Vorlesungen über die Philosophie der geschichte, Sämtliche Werke (Stuttgart: Fromman, 1928), 1:100. At least one student of von Fritz, Martin Ostwald, has [Νόμος *and the Beginnings of the Athenian Democracy* (Oxford: Clarendon Press, 1969)] employed this method in a book-length analysis of the terms Νόμος and Θεσμός, which attempts to explain and assess the significance of the replacement of the latter by the former as the ordinary word for "statute" at just about the time of Cleisthenes' reforms in the Athenian democracy.

standpoint, and must, in the second place, proceed from the meanings of the term "history." There have been a few philological studies of this term in the past century, and it will be well to review them. By the fifth and fourth centuries, ἱστορία, with a lengthy period of development already behind it, was one of a variety of words in use for designating knowledge or the acquisition of knowledge. This constellation of Greek words—σοφία, γνώμη, γνῶσις, σύνεσις, ἱστορία, μάθημα, ἐπιστήμη—was first studied collectively in the dissertation of Bruno Snell.[40] He follows and supplements Aly's[41] work on ἵστωρ, the ancestor of ἱστορεῖν and ἱστορία; but he is concerned with "history" insofar as it became one of the words for knowledge in the vocabulary of Greek philosophy and his concern ends with the period of early Greek achievement. Consequently, various other and later meanings are omitted. Moreover, Snell, like Dombart's study of *historia* somewhat earlier,[42] is circumscribed in its citations.

Soon after Snell's groundbreaking work F. Muller[43] undertook a somewhat more extensive study of the term, but still not extending to late antiquity or to non-Graeco-Roman sources. Büchsel, in the article "ἱστορέω (ἱστορία)" in Kittel's work,[44] like Snell, begins by considering ἵστωρ along with ἱστορεῖν and ἱστορία. However, Büchsel takes this broad view only until the family of words becomes associated with history writing; the substance of the article concentrates on Greek and Christian historiography. Two other studies, the dissertation of Karl Keuck and the shorter study of Rupp and Koehler[45]

[40] Bruno Snell, "Die Ausdrücke für dem Begriff des Wissens in der vorplatonischen Philosophie," *Philologische Untersuchungen* 29 (1924):100. Snell, however, omitted νοῦς and νοεῖν. These terms were examined partially by Joachim Boehme in *Die Seele und das Ich im Homerischen Epos* (Berlin: Teubner, 1929), by Julius Stenzel ["Zur Entwicklung des Geistesbegriffes in der griechischen Philosophie," *Die Antike* 1 (1925):244ff.], somewhat further by Snell in his view of Boehme [*Gnomon* 7 (1931):77ff.], and finally thoroughly in four articles by Kurt von Fritz: (1) op. cit. in n. 39., *supra*; (2) "Νοῦς, Νοεῖν and Their Derivatives in Pre-Socratic Philosophy (excluding Anaxagoras). Pt. 1. From the Beginnings to Parmenides," *CP* 40 (1945):223–42; (3) Pt. 2 of same article, "The Post-Parmenidean Period," *CP* 41 (1946):12–34; and (4) "Der Νοῦς des Anaxagoras," *Archiv für Bergiffsgeschichte* 9 (1964):87–102.

[41] Aly, *De Aeschyli copia verborum capita selecta* (Berlin: Pormetter, 1906).

[42] Dombart, "Historia," *Archiv für Lateinische Lexicographie und Grammatik* 3 (Leipzig: Teubner, 1886):230–34.

[43] Muller, "De 'Historiae' vocabulo atque notione," *Mnemosyne*, n.s 54 (1926):234–57.

[44] Gerhard Kittel, *Theologisches Wörterbuch zum Neues Testament* (Stuttgart: Kohlhammer, 1933); in English, trans. and ed. Geoffrey W. Bromiley (Grand Rapids: Wm. B. Eerdmans, 1966–71).

[45] Karl Keuck, *Historia. Geschichte des Wortes und seiner Bedeutungen in der Antike und der*

following him, deal with antiquity in a few pages and devote most of their attention to the diffusion and diversification of cognate words in the Romance languages during and after the Middle Ages. And both of them focus on ἱστορία and *historia* while paying little attention to the related verbs and adjectives that would further illuminate its meaning and thus contribute to understanding the basic idea involved in its use. A thorough understanding of the meanings of these words and the changes that occurred in them requires that attention not be restricted to one realm of discourse—history as a kind of knowledge or in connection with history writing—or to one part of antiquity, or to only some of the words involved.[46] In general, the philological studies have limited themselves to one language, one realm of discourse, or one period of time, and have not considered the words in the broader context of cultural history. My enterprise, then, is to integrate the aims of previous philosophical and theological studies with the methods of the philological studies and to avoid the shortcomings of both; thus (1) to study the term "history" as a member of the Greek, Latin, and thence of our own intellectual vocabulary; (2) to determine, through the study of the term, the content and development of the idea of history in antiquity; and (3) through the determination of the history of the idea of history, to learn something about the cultural transformation of the ancient world (*a*) as a detailed study of the specifically intellectual relationship between Graeco-Roman and Judaeo-Christian cultures and (*b*) as a reexamination of the popular linear-cyclic account of the idea of history in the two cultures. This is, therefore, a study in the history of ideas or the history of culture; for, rejecting customary limitations of language, realm of discourse, and period of time, it focuses on the impact of Judaeo-Christianity on Graeco-Roman ideas. It is also, I believe, a philosophical inquiry because its aims and consequences are properly philosophical—self-knowledge through a deeper under-

---

romanischen Sprachen (Lechte: Emsdetten, 1943). H. Rupp and O. Koehler, "Historia, Geschichte," *Saeculum* 2 (1951):249–72. See also G. Stadmueller, "Aion, Saeculum," *Saeculum* 2:315–20. I have been unable to find the article by A. Frenkian ["ἵστωρ, ἱστορέω, ἱστορία," *R. des Études Indo-Europeen* 1 (1938)] that is mentioned in a bibliography of the author. I am unable to read J. Wikarjak's short article on the history of *historia* in *Filomata* (1962–63), pp. 204–9.

[46] In his study of the ancient idea of philology, Heinrich Kuch sees a similar focus as proper, and similar problems with some of the previous literature [*Philologus* (Deutsche Akad. d. Wissensch. Berl., Sekt. für Altertumswissensch., 48. Berlin, 1965), p. 6].

standing of the history of our culture—even if its method and subject matter are unfamiliar under the rubric "philosophy."[47] It is not (merely) semantic history—though it may be an exercise in historical semantics—because this term "history" is, as I suggested earlier, a warp-thread in the fabric of the modern intellectual world and because the history of its meanings is, therefore, to be observed only in the broader context and to be understood as a development, at once determining and determined by other elements in this context, not as a mere succession. This is also not a study in the history of historiography; because the uses and meanings of the term are not restricted to history writing. The idea of history as a part of the intellectual vocabulary of culture is surely involved in what historians do; but it is also involved in other intellectual and practical pursuits, such as oratory, philosophy, and politics. And the origins of the term antedate history writing. Moreover, the history of historiography exceeds the limits of the idea of history; it is a significant but seldom observed fact that such "historians" as Thucydides and Livy do not call their works "history" and do not so characterize their research methods.[48] Finally, this is not a study in the speculative philosophy or theology of history; that is, I do not intend to examine the merits of claims that history has this or that pattern or meaning, or, for that matter, the claim that it has neither pattern nor meaning. Such claims will be of interest here only insofar as Greek, Roman, Jewish, or Christian

---

[47] Quentin Skinner's observation ["Meaning and Understanding in the History of Ideas," *H & TH* 8 (1969):53] on the value of the history of ideas is worth quoting at length: "The allegation that the history of ideas consists of nothing more than 'outworn metaphysical notions', which is frequently advanced at the moment, with terrifying parochialism, as a reason for ignoring such a history, would then come to be seen as the very reason for regarding such histories as indispensably 'relevant', not because crude 'lessons' can be picked out of them, but because the history itself provides a lesson in self-knowledge. To demand from the history of thought a solution to our own immediate practical problems is thus to commit not merely a methodological fallacy, but something like a moral error. But to learn from the past—and we cannot otherwise learn it at all—the distinction between what is necessary and what is the product merely of our own contingent arrangements, is to learn the key to self-awareness itself."

[48] An instructive comparison may be drawn between Herodotus and Thucydides. Herodotus uses ἱστορεῖν, ἱστορία and ἱστορικός relatively frequently [some nineteen times; see J. E. Powell, *Lexicon Herodoteum* (Cambridge: Cambridge University Press, 1938), p. 174], and uses them to describe what he is doing. Thucydides, by contrast, does not use the words a single time [see M. H. N. von Essen, *Index Thurcydideus* (Berlin: Weidmann, 1887)], but rather, uses the language of reason and logical inference; see Jacqueline de Romilly, *Histoire et Raison chez Thucydide* (Paris: Les Belles lettres, 1956).

writers might be found to make such claims about history. Indeed, the crucial question, in light of the prevailing linear-cyclic account, will be whether anyone in antiquity *did* think that history was linear or cyclic, meaningful or meaningless.

And, in fact, this study yields results quite different from what is widely believed. The idea of history that underlies the uses of the ancient words ἱστορία, *historia*, and the like throughout antiquity, and among Christians as well as non-Christian Greeks and Romans, was either an informational account (or the information itself) about persons, natural things, and human customs, or social and political events, or a written account about events either specifically or generically; that is, the literary genre called "history." By the end of the Hellenic Age both of these modes of usage existed. In the Hellenistic Age the latter was clearly dominant. Under the early Roman Empire the modes returned to a balance, while the limits of the subjects permitted in a history were relaxed and the previously required accuracy or factuality declined; history is understood as story both in the cultural mainstream and in the apologies of the early Christians. Under the later Roman Empire the growing estrangement between the Greek-speaking and Latin-speaking worlds appears in the divergence between the uses of history in Greek and Latin. In Greek, history continues to be used as story by the Christians both in the apologies and in the exegetical writings that showed the various meanings that a Bible story might have besides the literal one, the one which was "according to history." In Latin the same apologetical and exegetical uses are made of history by the Christians; but the implication of factuality is restored. So that the same account which is a history is taken to have some other meaning, to communicate or express something besides the facts. Finally, Augustine articulates in his *De civitate Dei* the distinction, adumbrated among his contemporaries, between the account of the past events of the Jews and Christians and that of the other nations, that is, between sacred and profane history.

It follows from this that the linear-cyclic account seems incorrect, using as it does a definition utterly alien to antiquity. Although there may be, in some transhistorical sense, a logical connection between the idea of time and the idea of history, the ancients, as a matter of historical fact, did not see them as connected; they occasionally reflect on the nature of time, never on the nature of history. While some writers of historical works say that events (τὰ προγεγόνατα, *res gestae*) repeat themselves and some philosophers speculate about cosmic cycles, there are also other views expressed and no one says that history is circular, repetitious, or meaningless. The Greeks and Romans were not pessimistic about history, nor did their view of history fail to satisfy their spiritual needs. On the other hand, the ancient Jews and Christians, whatever they may have thought about the creation and end of the world, did not think that history was rectilinear and unique. They were not especially optimistic about history, nor was their view of history spiritually satisfying. From their own point of view they were not engaging in speculation about the nature and meaning of history.

All of these denials are based on and may be reduced to two fundamental negative insights about the development of the idea of history in antiquity: first, the idea of history was *not* an influential and formative idea in antiquity as it has been since the Renaissance;[49] and second, in antiquity history was not thought to be a real entity, capable of exhibiting a pattern, having a meaning, inspiring hope, or possessing a nature.

It is often said that history comes to be seen as meaningful and goal-directed under the impact of Christianity. This is true, but not in the sense in which it is usually meant. History came to be seen as meaningful as a result not of reflection on the details of Christian belief, but of apologetical disputes with the non-Christian Greeks and Romans; the idea of history as goal-directed is not so much theological as rhetorical. If the original utility of this changed idea of history was rhetorical, however, it has come to be transferred to the realm of inquiry in modern social theories, philosophies, and theologies of history. And although the idea was (and is) adequate for polemical purposes, it has been a source of persistent problems when put to other uses, of which the quest for understanding is only one. To put the point somewhat more specifically, while the view that history is goal-directed may be adequate when it is used to win adherents, it poses problems when it is employed in social theories that prescribe actions or in philosophies that purport to offer understanding or knowledge.

---

[49] See M. I. Finley, "Myth, Memory and History," *H & Th* 4 (1965):281–302; cf. P. Munz, "History and Myth," *Philosophical Quarterly* 6 (1956):1–16.

II

History as Inquiry in the Hellenic Age

T HE ENGLISH WORD "history" is a transliteration of the Latin
word *historia*, itself a transliteration of the Greek ἱστορία. An
examination of the idea of history in antiquity must therefore begin
with the meanings of the term ἱστορια. But ἱστορία is just one member of a family of cognate words that includes the verb ἱστορεῖν and
the adjective ἱστορικός. All of these originate from the ancient word
ἵστωρ, and, since ἱστορεῖν, ἱστορία, and ἱστορικός are not attested
in the earliest surviving texts, the inquiry may begin with ἵστωρ.

The earliest occurrence of ἵστωρ is *Iliad* 18 at the beginning of the
description of the wonders Hephaistus wrought on the shield he made
for Thetis' "doomed son," Achilles. On this great shield he
fashioned the earth, heavens, sea, and stars, and on the earth two
cities; in the one, people are gathered in the agora because there is a
dispute in progress between two men over the blood-price of a slain
man. To resolve the dispute the men go ἐπὶ ἵστορι, which is ordinarily translated "to a judge, arbiter, umpire, or referee."[1] Similarly,
during the funeral games for Patroclus, Ajax and Idomeneus get into
a dispute over who is leading in the chariot race; and Idomeneus
challenges Ajax, saying:

> Come then,
> Let us put up a wager of a tripod or a cauldron,

---

[1] *Il.* 18.499–501. The proper interpretation of this whole passage has been debated;
cf. Leaf, *JHS* 8:122ff., and Murray in the Loeb edition of the *Iliad*, Vol. 1, p. 324, n.
1. Where not otherwise indicated the translations are my own.

And make Agamemnon, son of Atreus, witness [ἴστορα] between us
As to which horses lead. And when you pay, you will find out.[2]

In both passages the ἴστωρ is one who adjudicates a difference of
opinions between two parties at the request of the parties themselves.
More precisely, he decides a case in which conflicting accounts are
given by the disputants about something distinct from but of interest
to both of them. And the dispute, or the subject of it, is also of great
emotional impact upon its audience or the community in which it
occurs.[3] The dispute between Ajax and Idomeneus portends a split in
the ranks of the Hellenes at just the moment when their ten-year
stalemated siege of Troy is about to succeed. The dispute over the
blood-price, too, is emotionally charged, as can be inferred both from
the fact that the people are gathered about rooting for one man or the
other and from observation of the importance attached by other
primitive occidental civilizations to the payment of blood-price as an
institution for maintaining civic peace.[4] Evidently, then, the ἴστωρ is
one whose authority in deciding such disputes is well known; he is
good at such things. It is in this conventional sense, rather than in
any official sense, that the role of the ἴστωρ is one of arbitration. And
what he determines is whose account of the matter at issue is the
more accurate; so that the result of his adjudication in a matter of
law is justice and in a matter of perception accurate information. He
is perceptive or judicious. It is in this sense that Hesiod says of the
ἴστωρ, μάλα γάρ τε νόον πεπυκασμένος ἐστίν, that he is sound-
witted, matured in mind, or wise.[5] Similarly, the word is used adjec-
tivally in a Homeric Hymn (32) to describe the abilities of the Muses
as ἴστορες ᾠδῆς, knowledgeable or well skilled in song.[6] Here too the

---

[2] *Il.* 23.485–87. The translation is Lattimore's. Murray (Loeb) renders the concluding phrase, ἵνα γνώῃς ἀποτίνων, more literally: "that thou mayest learn by paying
the price."

[3] This is a point that is usually missed in accounts of ἴστωρ and the origin of
ἱστορεῖν and ἱστορία, as for example by Pohlenz [*Herodot, der erste Geschichtsschreiber
des Abendlandes* (Berlin: Teubner, 1937), p. 44]: "ἴστωρ ist ursprunglich der Zeuge,
der etwas gesehen hat, und noch nach dem attischen Rechte nur das bezeugen soll,
was er aus eigener Wahrnehmung weiss, mit eigenen Augen beobachtet hat, weiter
dann der Schiedsrichter, der durch Verhör der Augenzeugen sich ein Wissen aneignet
(*Il.* 18.501)."

[4] This is a repeated cause of litigation in the *Saga of Burnt Njal* and of battle in
Beowulf, to cite only two instances.

[5] Hes. *Op.* 793. Lattimore translates: "well-armed with brains."

[6] Trans. Evelyn-White (Loeb); cf. Bacchyl., *Epin.* 9.44: ἐγχέων ἴστορες κοῦραι.

word indicates being notedly good at giving or knowing how to give an account of a certain kind.

In all of what remains of those early Greek attempts to give accounts of the natural or human world, the "pre-Socratic philosophers" and the *logographoi*, ἴστωρ and its cognates are found but three times.[7] In the testimony of Clement of Alexandria, Heraclitus held the opinion that wisdom-loving men must be εὖ μάλα πολλῶν ἴστορας.[8] Freeman, following Diels, renders this phrase "inquirers into very many things,"[9] a translation that seems to derive less from the earlier meaning of ἴστωρ itself, which has already been examined, than from the lexicon definitions of cognate words of later coinage, namely ἱστορεῖν and ἱστορία.

But whether one reads "inquirer" or (merely) "perceptive," which would accord with the results so far, this occurrence would be most interesting. For it would suggest already a "philosophic" interest in that kind of knowledge which went by the name of history, were it not that another fragment of Heraclitus declares that "Pythagoras, son of Mnesarchus, practiced ἱστορίη most of all men, and making extracts from these treatises he compiled a wisdom of his own, a mere accumulation of learning (πολυμαθίη), and poor workmanship (κακοτεχνίη)."[10] Ἱστορίη here indicates the collecting of accounts or of information and deriving therefrom one's own account. The new word ἱστορίη is thus clearly related to ἴστωρ, which indicated knowing how to discriminate between competing accounts of something and in that sense being good at account-giving of a second-order sort. And importantly Heraclitus rejects this activity, equating it with polymathy, as not only wrongheaded, but also pernicious.[11]

---

[7] The other three citations listed in the Diels-Kranz "Register" use ἱστορία in neither direct nor indirect quotation, but rather, in the surrounding literary context, and therefore may not be specifically attributed, i.e., to Acusilaus or to Hecataeus.

[8] D–K[7], 1:159; Fr. (22) B35 = Clem. Al. *Strom.* 5.14.140 (Dindorf). Cf. Porph. *Abst.* 2.49: ἴστωρ γὰρ πολλῶν ὁ ὄντως φιλόσοφος. The wording *may* be Clement's; but Wilamowitz (*Phil. Unters.* 1:215) considers the phrase genuine, and it is thus used here.

[9] Freeman, *Ancilla to the Presocratic Philosophers* (Oxford: Blackwell, 1962), p. 27.

[10] D–K[7], 1:180; Fr. (22) B129 = D.L. 8.6. R. D. Hicks (Loeb ed. of D. L., 2:325), however, translates: ". . . and in this selection of his writings made himself a wisdom of his own, showing much learning, but poor workmanship."

[11] Heraclitus' dislike of πολυμαθίη is also attested by Fr. 40: "Polymathy does not teach understanding, otherwise it would have taught Hesiod, Pythagoras, Xenophanes, and Hecataeus" (trans. Wheelwright).

A similar idea seems to underlie another cognate that appears for the first time in the pre-Socratic literature, the verb ἱστοϱεῖν. Democritus says: "I have travelled most extensively of all men of my time, have pursued inquiries (ἱστοϱέων) in the most distant places, and have seen the most climes and lands, and have heard the greatest number of learned men; and no one has ever surpassed me in the composition of treatises with proofs."[12] Here too what is suggested is getting the account right, though as distinct from the earlier occurrences of ἵστωϱ and ἱστοϱίη, ἱστοϱεῖν, a verb, seems more to indicate the activity or process of getting the right account or getting the account right. It is in this sense that one should understand the usual translations of this passage and of ἱστοϱεῖν generally as "making inquiries" or "pursuing inquiries."[13] And interestingly, Democritus, unlike Heraclitus, seems to think highly of this kind of knowledge.

There is one remaining occurrence of ἱστοϱία in these writings. According to the later Epicurean, Philodemus, a *logographus* named Nausiphanes distinguishes between ἱστοϱία and "knowledge of the facts" (εἴδησις τῶν πϱαγμάτων), saying, "For he says that the cause of the power to persuade arises not from ἱστοϱία but from knowledge of the facts; so that just as he [sc. the natural scientist, φυσικός] persuades these men, so might he persuade any group of men."[14] This usage seems to be at variance with that of ἵστωϱ, ἱστοϱεῖν, and ἱστοϱία earlier on. But the expression εἴδησις τῶν πϱαγμάτων is so unlike anything in the pre-Socratic remains that it seems more likely a paraphrase or an example of the lamentable state of corruption in our text of Philodemus.[15]

In the literary remains of the fifth century, the time of the Athenian hegemony over the fortunes, both political and cultural, of the Hellenic world, the situation is rather different. The literary remains are more substantial than for the earlier period; and in these writings there are far more frequent occurrences than previously, so that one may now, with some confidence, delineate the meanings of the words based on ἵστωϱ.

[12] Clem. Al. *Strom.* 1.15.69; D–K[7], 2, 208, Fr. (68) B299.
[13] Philip Wheelwright, *The Presocratics* (New York: Odyssey, 1966), p. 186; Freeman, *Ancilla*, p. 119.
[14] Fr. (75) B2, D–K[7], 2, 249, 3–5 = Phld. *Rh.* 2, 19, 1–20, 7 (col. 25); cf. 1, 299, 1–7 (col. 25).
[15] Von Arnim, however, accepts the reading as genuine [*Leben und Werke des Dio von Prusa* (Berlin, 1898), p. 48].

In the earlier period ἴστωρ indicated the quality of skill in, perceptiveness at, or knowing how to choose between competing accounts of something, a second-order sort of knowing. In the fifth century ἴστωρ is used as "knowing" of a first-order, direct-acquaintance sort, although it is still a knowing of the facts. Euripides' King Thoas, for example, threatens to punish the women τὰς τῶνδ' ἴστορας βουλευμάτων, who knew about what was planned.[16] Likewise Electra says of the painfulness of life, κ'αγω τοῦδ' ἴστωρ, ὑπερίστωρ, I know it, know it overmuch.[17] The knowledge ascribed to someone by the use of ἴστωρ in these ways is still, as in the *Iliad*, emotionally charged. Similarly, among the fanciful etymologies in Plato's *Cratylus* Artemis is said to have got her name because she is ἀρετῆς ἴστορα, proficient in virtue;[18] and a few lines later Hephaistus is referred to as τὸν γενναῖον φάεος ἴστορα, the eminent knower of light. In the use of ἴστωρ in the dramatists, the word had given up its sense of knowing how to distinguish other people's possibly factual accounts in favor of knowing the facts oneself. In Plato's usage the term reverts to its older sense of skill or know-how; but where the object of the knowledge had been rather concrete, now the object has become more abstract.

As in the earlier period, so in the fifth century ἱστορεῖν has primarily to do with the activity of acquiring the kind of knowledge indicated by referring to someone as ἴστωρ, getting the correct account of the matter, inquiring. And as with ἴστωρ, so with ἱστορεῖν does the increased usage show a diversificaton of meanings. Ἱστορεῖν may mean inquiring. Oedipus describes himself to his daughters as a man who οὔθ' ὁρῶν οὔθ' ἱστορῶν, neither seeing nor inquiring became their father by his own mother.[19] More specifically, ἱστορεῖν indicates inquiring for a factual account. Thus Talthybius, pressed by Hecuba to relate what became of her children after the fall of Troy, asks her τίν ἱστορεῖς, of whom do you seek an account?[20] We find ἱστορεῖν used in like manner by Herodotus, who relates the ver-

---

[16] Eur. *IT* 1431.

[17] Soph. *El.* 850.

[18] *Cra.* 406B, 407C; cf. Nauck, *TGF²*, Fr. 2 of Apollonides (*apud* Stob. *Flor.* 67, 6; 4, 22ᵃ7 Hense):γυναικὸς ἀρετὰς ἀξίως ἐπαινέσαι

σοφοῦ τίνος γένοιτ' ἂν ἴστορες λόγων.

See now Bruno Snell, *TGF*, Vol. 1 (152), Fr. 2.

[19] Soph. *OT* 1484.

[20] Eur. *Tro.* 261. Similarly, Aesch. *PV* 632, the Chorus wants to inquire about Io's troubles.

sion of the story of Helen given by the Egyptian priests ἱστορέοντι, it being inquired of them.[21]

There is another use of the verb in Herodotus: to mean inquiring an account of the facts about natural phenomena. He says, in this sense, that he has told us everything that he could find out about the Nile's course ἐπ' ὅσον μακρότατον ἱστορεύντα, by inquiring as lengthily as possible.[22] Possibly a third kind of factual account for which one might inquire, again in Herodotus, seems to relate to one's thoughts or motives. Thus Darius' band is stopped on its way to assassinate the Magi usurpers and asked (ἱστόρεον) with what intentions they have come to the palace.[23]

There is another group of uses, peculiar to the dramatists, distinguished from the preceding by its quest for individual facts rather than connected accounts; interestingly all occurrences of this usage relate to individual facts about persons and, in the first place, to the facts about one's parentage. As the dénouement approaches, for example, Oedipus tells the old herdsman that his offense lies in not answering τὸν παῖδ' ὃν οὗτος ἱστορεῖ, what he asks about the child.[24] Similarly Euripides' Ion is going to inquire (ἱστορήσω) of Phoebus who his father is,[25] and Orestes considers it honorable of Athena that ἱστορεῖς, you inquire after his father.[26]

If one may inquire for individual facts about one's parentage, so too, still in the dramatists, one may inquire for someone, ask his whereabouts. So it is that Orestes says he is trying to determine (ἱστορῶ) where Aegisthus lives.[27] Likewise Orestes declares himself to Menelaus: "I am Orestes ὃν ἱστορεῖς, whom you seek, Menelaus."[28] And the verb may even be used to indicate asking a yes-or-no question about a matter of fact; thus Herodotus relates that the second wife of the tyrant Pisistratus told her mother that her new husband had held wrongful intercourse with her, although Herodotus comments that he does not know εἴτε ἱστορεύσῃ εἴτε καὶ οὐ, whether the wife was asked or not.[29]

[21] Hdt. 2.113.1; cf. 1.24.7 and 1.122.1.
[22] Hdt. 2.34.1; cf. 2.19.3; 2.29.1; and 4.192.3.
[23] Hdt. 3.77.2; and cf. 3.51.1.
[24] Soph. *OT* 1150; cf. 1156.
[25] Eur. *Ion.* 1547.
[26] Aesch. *Eum.* 455; cf. Soph. *Trach.* 415.
[27] Soph. *El.* 1101.
[28] Eur. *Or.* 380; cf. Eur. *Hel.* 1371.
[29] Hdt. 1.61.2.

Besides these uses of ἱστορεῖν to indicate inquiring about matters of fact, there are also two occurrences in the fifth-century materials that seem to indicate not the activity of inquiring but, rather, the upshot of it, finding out or discovering, or, as the lexicons suggest, "knowing by inquiry." The first of these is from Aeschylus' *Agamemnon*. The herald hopes for the return of Menelaus:

> At least if some beam of the sun ἱστορεῖ him
> Alive and well, by the design of Zeus,
> Who is not yet minded utterly to destroy the race,
> There is some hope that he will come home again.
> Hearing so much, be assured that the truth is as thou hearest.[30]

Similarly, according to Herodotus, Croesus ἐφρόντιζε ἱστορέων, bethought himself to discover who were the mightiest of the Hellenes.[31] The first passage is closely related to the use we earlier saw of inquiring for someone's whereabouts, the activity here transferred to a sunbeam; but in this occurrence the fact that the passage is a conditional requires a rendering more conclusive than just "seeking" or "looking for" Menelaus, if hope is to be a suitable response. Thus ἱστορεῖν in the fifth century may, in passive forms, indicate the facts for which one is inquiring, but primarily it means to inquire.

Likewise the primary meaning of the noun ἱστορία is an instance of this activity, that is, an inquiring. When Herodotus, in his discussion of geography, passes from what is based upon his own observation to what is based upon his study of the chronicles of the Egyptian priests, he states that so far what he has said arises from his own seeing (ὄψις), judgment (γνώμη), and ἱστορία.[32] The Liddell–Scott lexicon suggests "a learning or knowing by inquiry" as the primary meaning of the noun; and they offer two citations of Herodotus as paradigm cases of that meaning. In the first, Herodotus is trying to sort out the conflicting accounts of Helen given by Homer and by the Egyptians. He says:

> But when I asked the priests whether the Greek account (λόγος) of the
> Trojan business were vain or true, they gave me the following answer,

[30] Aesch. *Ag.* 676–80, trans. Smyth (Loeb). But Morshead (Random House), "descries."

[31] Hdt. 1.56.1–2.

[32] Hdt. 2.99.1

saying that they had inquired (ἱστορῄσι) and knew (εἰδέναι) what Menelaus himself had said.[33]

And having completed his retelling, he says:

> They [i.e., the priests] said that some of these things they knew by inquiring (ἱστορῄσι . . . ἐπίστασθαι), but that they spoke with exact knowledge (ἀτρεκέως ἐπιστάμενοι) about what happened in their own country.[34]

In both passages ἱστοριῄσι seems to be a dative of means, describing only the means by which the knowledge was acquired; the knowledge itself is indicated by εἰδέναι in the first passage and by ἐπίστασθαι in the second. In both of these contexts ἱστορία means only an inquiring, an instance of the activity indicated by the verb ἱστορεῖν.

There are some instances, however, in which ἱστορία may mean the results of inquiring or, more precisely, information or accurate information, since the verb has to do with getting the facts straight. Thus we find Plato's Socrates saying that observation of birds and other signs provides ἱστορία to human thought for investigating the future.[35] And it is in this secondary sense that one must read the famous opening line of Herodotus: Ἡροδότου Ἁλικαρνήσσεος ἱστορίης ἀπόδεξις ἥδε, the results of the inquiring of Herodotus of Halicarnassus are here set forth.[36]

It seems clear that the inquiring indicated by ἱστορία has to do with facts, and evidently by the end of the fifth century that usage was ordinary enough that it might indicate a discrete intellectual approach to the world. Thus the well-known passage of Plato's *Phaedo* (96A) in which Socrates narrates to the young Pythagoreans, Simmias and Cebes, how he came to seek wisdom in the peculiar way that he did begins, "When I was young, Cebes, I was tremendously eager for that kind of wisdom which they call περὶ φύσεως ἱστορία, history of nature." What Socrates is referring to here, as the re-

---

[33] Hdt. 2.118.1, trans. Godley (Loeb).
[34] Hdt. 2.119.3.
[35] Pl. *Phdr.* 244C–D.
[36] Hdt. 1.1.1. Thus I think that statements such as T. S. Brown's ["The Greek Sense of Time in History. . . ," *Historia* 11 (1962):269] about "the old Ionian ἱστορίη . . . factual reports on geography, customs, racial character and religious beliefs" mistake the secondary for the primary meaning. Pohlenz, *Herodot*, p. 44, is nearer the mark in defining the Ionian ἱστορίη, "als allgemeinen Ausdruck für 'Erkundung'."

mainder of the passage shows, is the ways of understanding the world of those who are today called pre-Socratic philosophers, but whom Aristotle called φυσικοί, evidently following Plato in considering that their concern was solely or largely to understand φύσις nature and natural phenomena. The use of ἱστορία here clearly accords with that of the verb as inquiring an account of the facts about natural phenomena: an inquiry into such facts, though here the scope is broader than any single phenomenon or class of phenomena. Socrates, however, was interested in inquiring into the causes (αἰτία) of natural things; and so he finds this "natural history," which merely obtains facts, unsatisfactory, and hence rejects it as philosophically insufficient.

It should be clear that the basic idea underlying all the uses of ἵστωρ, ἱστορεῖν, and ἱστορία is that of inquiring for the facts, with the ordinary implication that what the facts really are is unclear or disputed to begin with. It may be noted that the uses of the verb far outnumber those of the noun and that among verb uses there are more active than passive ones. These two observations jointly suggest that what "history" means at this time is primarily an activity, inquiring, and only secondarily an object or product, the results of inquiring, knowledge in some sense. It does not yet indicate a kind of writing, an art. Insofar as what Herodotus is doing is indicated by his referring to it (1.1.1) as ἱστορίη, one should understand the word in its ordinary acceptation: these are the results of Herodotus' factual inquirings, the accurate information, the right account, which he acquired about some matters of importance to himself and to his audience and about which conflicting accounts have been given.

To complete the account of the earliest uses of the progeny of ἵστωρ, the period of the decline of Athenian political hegemony may be considered, the great orators who presided over the decline and Aristotle, at once the first great "knower" in the Western intellectual tradition and the tutor of Alexander, the man whose conquests and foundations set the cultural tone for the Hellenistic Age.

There are almost no occurrences of ἱστορεῖν in this transitional period, although in its old and ordinary active sense of inquiring for the facts about natural phenomena, Aristotle wants to discuss the parts of plants "about which we inquired (ἱστορήσαμεν) before."[37]

Ἱστορία in this period seems to have settled down as the name for a particular kind of intellectual or literary product and, in a related

---

[37] Arist. *Pl.* 818b27–28.

sense, as a word indicating knowledge or the acquisition of knowledge of a certain kind. It could still be used in its older sense as the results of inquiring, an account of the correct information, the correct account. In his famous speech "On the Crown," for example, Demosthenes speaks of the great benefit that the Athenians will derive from ἱστορία of public affairs.[38] But Herodotus had described his writings, in accordance with the nature of their contents, as ἱστορίη.[39] And perhaps by mistake, or perhaps from some other cause, this descriptive use of the noun is transformed into a denominative one, ἱστορία as history writing.[40] Thus Aristotle points out that whereas books of travel (αἱ τῆς γῆς περίοδοι) are useful for law-making, "αἱ τῶν περὶ τὰς πράξεις γραφόντων ἱστορίαι, the histories of writers about (human) acts" are useful for political debates.[41] And Isocrates, who is elsewhere reported to have taught history writing as a distinct genre, says in his Panathenaic speech that it will be difficult for the audience to understand because it is jam-packed (γέμοντα) with ἱστορία and φιλοσοφία, philosophy.[42]

By this time, evidently, both philosophy and history are recognized and reasonably clearly defined departments of intellectual culture. And there is further evidence of this not only in Aristotle's distinctions between the kinds of plot (μῦθος) appropriate for an epic and a history, the former being concerned with a unity of action, the latter with a unity of time,[43] but also in his famous and much debated

[38] Dem. *Cor.* 144.

[39] While Herodotus was (perhaps partly for this reason) considered the father of history even in antiquity, he was also (a propos the example of Thucydides) considered a liar by critics until the sixteenth century; and, more recently, P. Treves, "Herodotus, Gelon, and Pericles," *CP* 36 (1941):321–45. See Momigliano, "The Place of Herodotus in the History of Historiography," *History* 13 (1958):1–13; reprinted in A. D. Momigliano, *Studies in Historiography* (London: Weidenfeld and Nicolson, 1966), pp. 127–42.

[40] That Herodotus did not use the word in this way is recognized by Pohlenz, *Herodot*, p. 44.

[41] Arist. *Rh.* 1360a33–37.

[42] Isoc. *Pan.* 246. The nature and value of Isocrates' φιλοσοφία have been discussed; see, for example, Cope in the *Journal of Classical and Sacred Philology* 5:150, Thompson's Appendix II, "On the Philosophy of Isocrates," to his edition of Plato's *Phaedrus*, and Jebb, *Attic Orators*, 2:34–50. But the fact that Isocrates' φιλοσοφία represents a more general understanding of the term and the magnitude of its influence on the history of ancient culture is seldom appreciated. For a slight appreciation, see Anne-Marie Malingrey, *Philosophia* (Paris: Klincksieck, 1961), pp. 42–46; for a more serious treatment, Jaeger, *Paideia* (New York: Oxford University Press, 1944), 3:46–155.

[43] Arist. *Po.* 1459a17–29.

distinction between historian and poet as concerned respectively with what *did* happen and what *might* have happened.[44]

On the one hand, then, ἱστορία in this transitional period means a particular kind of intellectual or literary product—a "history" in very much the same sense that we would today call something a history; on the other hand, at least for Aristotle, it indicated a particular kind of philosophic or scientific activity. Earlier on, the noun had been used to indicate an inquiring into the facts about persons, things, or events. Aristotle develops the sense of inquiry into natural phenomena into a typically philosophical mode of inquiry by expanding the scope of the inquiry to the limits of the various *classes* of natural phenomena. Thus there is for Aristotle, as there was at least for Plato's Socrates, a περὶ φύσεως ἱστορία, history of nature,[45] and besides this there is a τῆς ψυχῆς ἱστορία, history of the soul,[46] and ἱστορίαι περὶ τῶν ζώων, histories of animals.[47] Besides history as a mode of inquiry, Aristotle even seems to think of ἱστορία as one phase of other inquiries; for he says that it is according to nature (κατὰ φύσιν) to proceed to a discussion of causes when we have finished the ἱστορία of details.[48] Similarly, he describes a list of all the true attributes of an object as an ἱστορία.[49]

For Aristotle, then, ἱστορία has a special philosophic usage to indicate a particular mode or phase of inquiry into the natural world in its broader aspects. But while it is interesting to observe that the word was capable of being so employed in Aristotle's time, one must be wary of taking this as evidence of a great constriction of meaning. While Aristotle's usage clearly derives from the ordinary usage, it is specialized and philosophical, and thus to some extent idiosyncratic.

Before proceeding to the Hellenistic Age, mention may be made of the adjective ἱστορικός. In Plato's *Sophist*, a self-conscious neologism is committed in drawing a distinction between imitation based on opinion, which is called δοξομιμητική, and imitation based on

---

[44] Ibid. 1451a35–b6. For summary of the debate, see C. O. Brink, "Tragic History and Aristotle's School," *Proc. Cambr. Philol. Soc.*, N.S. 6 (1960):14–19.

[45] Arist. *Cael.* 298b2.

[46] Arist. *De An.* 402a4.

[47] Arist. *GA* 716b31, referring to his own work which, perhaps because of these references, has come to be called *History of Animals*. Similarly: *GA* 717a33–34, 728b13–14; *Resp.* 477a6–7, 478a27–28. Or he may refer simply to "the histories": *GA* 719a10, 740a23, 746a15, 750b31, 753b17, 761a10, 763b16; and *Resp.* 478b1.

[48] Arist. *HA* 491a11–13.

[49] Arist. *APr.* 46a24–27.

knowledge (ἐπιστήμη), which is called "ἱστορικήν τινα μίμησιν, a sort of historylike imitation."[50] And Aristotle says that in order to advise well about the economies of city-states, one needs not only to have some general views derived from one's own experience, but also to be ἱστορικόν, well versed, about what others have learned.[51] Both of these usages seem to derive from the notion of ἱστορία as factual inquiry or information-seeking, so that whatever is ἱστορικός is factual or informed. The second sort of imitation, then, would be "a sort of informed imitation" and Aristotle's advice is to be "informed" about what others have learned.

This attributive usage of the adjective derives from ἱστορία as inquiry or the results of inquiry. The adjective is also used once substantively by Aristotle in the famous passage of the *Poetics*[52] in which he distinguishes between the historian (ἱστορικός) and the poet, and which has already been discussed.

The idea of history in the fifth century was dominated by a sense of activity; but in the transitional period a reification appears to have begun that continues in the subsequent period. History shifts from an activity that one performs on certain kinds of objects with the aim of obtaining certain kinds of results—"I inquire"—to a subsistent entity, inquiry, understood as either a distinct and recognizable (investigative) process—I engage in (or, prosecute) an inquiry—or, perhaps, the written results of that process, that is, histories. By Aristotle's time the verb has come to take a secondary place to the noun, which now indicates not so much the inquiring itself as the results of that inquiring, a definable sort of literary product with its own specific uses, values, and traits.

[50] Pl. *Sph.* 267D–E.
[51] Arist. *Rh.* 1359b30–32.
[52] Arist. *Po.* 1459a17–29.

III

History as a Literary Genre:
The Hellenistic Age

J OHANN GUSTAV DROYSEN gave the name "Hellenism" to the period of Greek civilization following the death of Alexander the
Great because he thought that Ἑλληνισταί in the Acts of the
Apostles (6:1) referred to orientalized Greeks and that this blending
of Greek with Oriental was the defining characteristic of the age.[1]
Subsequent investigation has shown that this interpretation of the
text of Acts is indefensible and that the Greeks rather than the Orientals were the chief contributors to whatever cultural fusion occurred.
Nevertheless it was Droysen who instigated the study of the period as
a distinct period in the ancient world, and the name, however inappropriate, has become canonical.

---

[1] In 1836 Droysen called his work on the Diadochi and Epigoni *Geschichte des Hellenismus*. He did not, of course, invent the term. In the sixteenth century, J. Scaliger
interpreted Ἑβραίοι and Ἑλληνισταί in the same passage as a contrast between
Jews who used Hebrew and those who used Greek in the synagogue. D. Heinsius, on
the other hand, thought that the Jewish Ἑλληνισταί used a special dialect (*lingua
hellenistica*) which is identical with the language of the Septuagint. In the seventeenth
century, C. Salmasius denied that this was a special dialect, but retained the term
lingua hellenistica for Old Testament and New Testament Greek. In the eighteenth
century, J. G. Herder used "Hellenismus" to indicate the way of thinking of Jews and
other Greek-speaking Orientals. And in the nineteenth century, J. Matter connected
"Hellenisme" with the thought of Greek-speaking Egyptian Jews. The classic account
of the history of the term is R. Laquer, *Hellenismus* (Giessen, 1925). On Droysen's *own*
confusion about the meaning of the term, see A. Momigliano, "J. G. Droysen between
Greeks and Jews," *History and Theory* 9 (1970):139–53.

The Hellenistic Age, or Hellenism, was, from all accounts, an age of unprecedented cultural productivity. At Athens, still the home of philosophy, the schools of Plato, Aristotle, Epicurus, Diogenes the Cynic, and Zeno the Stoic flourished, perpetually engaged in quarrels with each other and steadily attracting numbers of students from all over the Greek-speaking world. But Athens was no longer the center of all Greek cultural life. With the conquests of Alexander, intellectual activity had become international.

Art and science in the Hellenistic Age were centered in Alexandria. Primarily this may be attributed to the rich endowments of the Ptolemies. Ptolemy I founded the Museum, a home for the Muses, as a workshop and training ground for scholarship in all fields—apart from the turmoil of mundane existence. It became the recognized institution for establishing definitive texts, preparing critical editions, and publishing authoritative commentaries on earlier writers. Ptolemy II Philadelphus founded the great Library of Alexandria, which ultimately came very near its founder's intention of collecting Greek literature in its entirety; for it contained perhaps 700,000 volumes when, in 47 B.C., it was burned during the general conflagration of the harbor district. In addition to Alexandria and Athens, however, Pergamum, Antioch, and Rhodes at various times and for varying periods were lesser centers of vigorous cultural life. All of these cities produced not only works of scholarship and philosophy, but also poetry, drama, and history, as well as studies of rhetoric, grammar, mathematics, astronomy, medicine, geography, and technology. Frequently a variety of these were produced by a single person.[2]

Yet of all of this cultural activity very little remains besides the testimonies that it occurred.[3] The philosophers are known by a few fragments and by notices in doxographies, themselves surviving only in fragments in many cases, which attribute numerous works to the philosophers. Of the many historians whose names we know, there

---

[2] The librarians of Alexandria are so reputed: Zenodotus, Apollonius of Rhodes, Eratosthenes, Aristophanes of Byzantium, Apollonius the Idographer, and Aristarchus. Callimachus, though never head of the Library, drew up the first catalogue of its holdings, which *Pinaces* alone ran up to 120 books. But besides this he is credited with works *On Contests, Customs of Foreign Peoples, Rivers of the World, Marvels,* and *On Nymphs,* to name only a few, and also volumes of *Hymns* and *Epigrams.* Similarly extensive intellectual attainments are attributed to the Stoic Posidonius of Apamea, the Epicurean Philodemus, the Peripatetic Theophrastus, and Eratosthenes.

[3] See, e.g., E. A. Barber's comments on the "fragmentary nature" of the Hellenistic literary remains in the *Cambridge Ancient History* 7:249.

are only fragments; the sole work that has survived in anything like its integrity is Polybius' account in Greek of the rise of Rome. And so it goes for the greater part of the literary output of the age.

In circumstances such as these it is not surprising to find that occurrences of ἱστορεῖν, ἱστορία, and ἱστορικός are not at all widely dispersed through the cultural remains; indeed, they occur mostly in the works of two writers, Polybius and Dionysius of Halicarnassus, a leading proponent of the first-century reaction against the degeneration of literary Greek that called itself Atticism. The confidence with which conclusions may be drawn on the basis of such evidence will have to be qualified accordingly. Generally speaking, however, the uses of these words in Hellenistic writings continue and solidify the tendencies operating during the decline of the Hellenic period. The idea of history undergoes little change.

Ἱστορία is still used in its older signification as the facts or a factual account about some person or some important event in the person's life. It is so used by Dionysius, praising the continuity of Herodotus's work, "even though he added a ἱστορία of Xerxes' flight."[4] Similarly, Polybius interrupts the main line of his *Histories* to give a description (ἐξήγησις) of the Italian Celts, but he says he thinks that "the ἱστορίαν of these people"[5] is worth remembering in order to understand the sort of people against whom Hannibal had to fight in northern Italy.

The noun seems to retain its reference to natural facts throughout the Hellenistic Age, and indeed throughout antiquity.[6] According to Theophrastus, successor to Aristotle as scholarch of the Lyceum, Thales was the first among the Hellenes to "set forth history about nature" (περὶ φύσεως ἱστορίαν);[7] Plato too concerned himself "about history of nature."[8] And at least within the circle of Peripatetic philosophers in the Hellenistic Age, factual inquiry about natural things seems to have been practiced and to have been called ἱστορία,[9] meaning the facts or a factual account about natural phenomena.

[4] D. H. *Pomp.* 3.14.
[5] Plb. 2.14.1–2.
[6] E.g., Plb. 2.14.7; 4.40.3; and Thphr., Fr. 12, in Diels, *DG* 486, 17–21.
[7] Thphr. Fr. 1 (*DG* 475, 10–13).
[8] Ibid. Fr. 9 (*DG* 484, 19–485, 4).
[9] To Theophrastus are attributed *Botanical Histories, Astrological History, Numerical Histories of Growth, Geometrical Histories, History of the Divine* (D. L. 5.46–50), and the doxographical *On Physical Opinions*, which may have been called *On Natural History* (Diels, *DG*, Prol., p. 102). Menon is said to have written a history of medicine and Eudemus of Rhodes a *Numerical History, Geometrical Histories*, and *Astrological Histories*.

There is a related and very important occurrence in the first surviving treatise on grammar, that of the second-century scholar Dionysius Thrax, a student of Aristarchus, who succeeded Aristophanes of Byzantium as chief librarian at Alexandria. According to Dionysius, the third of the six parts of grammar (γραμματική) is γλωσσῶν τε καὶ ἱστοριῶν προχείρος ἀπόδοσις, the ready exposition of languages and histories.[10] In antiquity, as in the Middle Ages, "grammar" referred to both the theoretical or scientific study of language (our "grammar") and the first stage in the literary education of a child (our "grammar school"). Of the "parts" into which Dionysius divided grammar, some are scientific and some pedagogical. But he is interested only in the scientific, so he does not explain what he means by an "exposition of languages and histories." What he is talking about, though, is familiar to anyone who has taken a course in a classical language; the pedagogical terrain has not changed much in twenty-five centuries.[11] Going over exercises or reading assignments, one comes across unfamiliar words or linguistic forms and unfamiliar names of persons, places, objects, or events. These the teacher identifies. Such identification of an unfamiliar word of linguistic form is still called, following the usage of the ancient grammarians, a "gloss"; and the identification of an unknown person, place, object, or event would consist in giving some facts or information about it. Ἱστορία is thus here being used, as in the preceding group of uses, to indicate facts or a factual account, but with a somewhat wider signification that includes, besides natural objects or phenomena, persons, places, and events.

Here, then, history makes its modest debut in the educational curriculum of Western civilization; not as a discipline, a science, or a body of knowledge, nor even as acquaintance with the writings of historians primarily, but as information about various matters mentioned in whatever literature one studied. The treatise of Dionysius Thrax was very brief, but it was extraordinarily popular. It immediately became the basic text on the subject; it was continually copied, edited, and provided with commentaries until the twelfth century; and it has provided the foundations for both Greek and Latin gram-

[10] Dion. Thr. *De Arte Grammatica*, para. 1.
[11] Henri Marrou (*History of Education in Antiquity*, pp. 165–72) distinguishes four different stages in the literary study over which the *grammatikos* presided: διόρθωσις (textual criticism), ἀνάγνωσις (reading), ἐξήγησις (glosses and "histories"), and κρίσις (evaluation).

mars until the present time. The scholia on the passage of Dionysius we have been discussing suggest that the ancient commentators understood ἱστορία more narrowly than Dionysius did. It is explained as "narratives (διηγήματα)," the "narrating of ancient doings (παλαιῶν πραξέων ἀφήγησις)," and "the narration of affairs in earlier times (τὴν διήγησιν τῶν πάλαι πραγμάτων)."[12] Although the scholiasts whose commentaries have survived are much later than Dionysius Thrax, their explanations mark a development in the usage of ἱστορία that had already begun in the Hellenistic Age.

In addition to the older and narrower use of the word as information about natural phenomena, and Dionysius' wider use as information more generally about whatever arises in a literary text, in the world of letters ἱστορία more often has to do with social and political events. Polybius says, for example, that "the history of past events (τὴν . . . ὑπὲρ τῶν προγεγονότων . . . ἱστορίαν) in Asia and Egypt has already been published many times and is well known."[13]

Thus far the contexts in which ἱστορία is used do not provide enough information to make it clear whether history is the information about certain objects—such as natural things, persons, and the like—or an account of the information, the facts or a factual account. However, the uses examined so far in the Hellenistic materials seem to emphasize the matter or content of the history, its factuality.

The second broad group of uses that may be discriminated in the period emphasizes the manner or form of the history, considering it precisely as an account. Where the first group concerns history as facts, a kind of knowledge, the second concerns history as an account, a kind of literature. The beginning of this modal distinction between history as facts and history as account was in Herodotus' calling his work ἱστορίαι.

Polybius regularly uses ἱστορία as a referential term when he is reflecting upon the account he is engaged in giving. He says, for example, that a résumé (ἐξήγησις) of Greek history to the 140th Olympiad is "appropriate to the arrangement of the history (πρὸς τὴν τῆς ἱστορίας σύνταξιν οἰκείαν)."[14] These are the concluding lines of

---

[12] *Scholia in Dionysii Thracis Artem Grammaticam.* The citations are respectively from Melampos (or Diomedes), p. 14.19; Stephen of Byzantium, p. 303.4; and Heliodorus. 470.4. On the influence of Dionysius Thrax, see John Edwin Sandys, *A History of Classical Scholarship* (New York: Hafner, 1958), 1:138–40.

[13] Plb. 2.37.6; see also 5.31.6.

[14] Ibid. 3.118.2.

Book 3 of the *Histories* and act as his justificatory transition to Book 4. The reference of ἱστορία to his account as such is clear from the use of ἐξήγησις to refer to the subordinate account of Greek history.[15] Similarly, Chares of Mytilene, who participated in Alexander's journey to the East and afterward wrote an account of it, tells about the romance of Odatis, daughter to the king of Marathon, "as it has been written (γέγραπται) in the histories (ἱστορίαις)."[16] The use of γέγραπται makes it clear that the histories referred to are written. Dionysius of Halicarnassus criticizes the prose style of Thucydides for its excessive use of parentheses, of which there are a great many "in the entire ἱστορίαν."[17] And he repeatedly refers to Thucydides' work as ἱστορία.[18]

Such uses tend to be more taken up with the mechanics of the account-giving, organization and style, the account as a piece of literature. The word is used straightforwardly to indicate a piece of literature as such. What ἱστορία evidently signifies in this large group of uses, then, is a species of literature, a branch of culture.

Like other branches of culture, history has its own special use and value. Aristotle suggested that histories were useful for political deliberation, unlike travel books, which were useful for legislating. Thucydides supposed that, since human events recur, his work would be an instructive possession for all time; Herodotus, rather differently, wrote in order that mighty deeds might not lack renown lest the reasons why the Greeks and the barbarians waged war against each other be unknown.

In the Hellenistic Age (and even down to the present day) there seems to have been little doubt that the study of accounts of actions performed in the past along with the consequences that followed from them—the study of historical works—provides the student with a kind of experience of affairs that may serve as a corrective in the

---

[15] Polybius marks the distinction between the overall narrative and some lesser part in the same way at 2.14.1–2 and at 3.57.4–5, using the infinitive ἐξηγήσασθαι. See also Plb. 1.3.8; 2.37.3; 3.4.8, 5.9, 58.1; 4.2.2, 28.4; and 6.2.2–3. But D. H. *Pomp*. 3.14 has διήγησις for the major, ἱστορία for the minor narrative.

[16] According to Athen. [13.35; 575B = Jacoby, *FHG* (125) Fr. 5].

[17] D. H. *Amm*. 2.15; see also *Th*. 5, ἀναγράφοντες ἱστορίας and Plb. 2.62.6; 5.33.2–3; and 8.9.2.

[18] D. H. *Th*. 7, 9, 16, and 41; see also *Ant. Rom*. 5.17.3. He also has a formulaic way of appealing for confirmation of his evidence to αἱ κοιναὶ ἱστορίαι, the commonly known (published?) histories; *Amm*. 1.3 and 11. Para. 3 refers to the compilers of biographies (οἱ τοὺς βίους ἀνδρῶν συνταξάμενοι) and 11 to *Atthis* of Philochorus.

assessment of alternative courses of action. In this connection Polybius moralizes about the foolishness of men who, taking no precautions, allow their enemies to trade in their very marketplace, although they might acquire "such experience from history (ἐκ τῆς ἱστορίας . . . τὴν τοιαύτην ἐμπειρίαν)."[19] But perhaps the *locus classicus* for this view of the value of history is a passage from the *Art of Rhetoric* of Dionysius of Halicarnassus: "And Plato says this too, that the poetic, by beautifying the many deeds of the ancients, educates those who are born later. For education (παιδεία) is the conjoining of oneself (ἔντευξις) with character. And Thucydides seems to say this, speaking about history (περὶ ἱστορίας): that history is *philosophy from examples* (ὅτι καὶ ἱστορία φιλοσοφία ἐστὶν ἐκ παραδειγμάτων)."[20]

If history as a species of literature has its specific cultural or practical values, it also has its specific standards. In Polybius' words, "if truth (ἀλήθεια) is taken away from history (ἐξ ἱστορίας) what is left of it is a useless tale."[21] In addition to this standard for the relationship between the account and its subject matter, there are also precepts of art that concern choice of subject, arrangement, style, and so forth,[22] matters that need not be discussed here. For the present purposes it is sufficient to observe that ἱστορία has come to be the name for a species of literature and a cultural phenomenon. Indeed the Epistle of Dionysius of Halicarnassus to Pompey, already mentioned, is largely a discussion of the art of history writing. And treatises "On History" (περὶ ἱστορίας), apparently about history writing, are attributed to Theophrastus and to Praxiphanes.[23]

The modal distinction between history as the facts and history as literature is also found in the occurrences of ἱστορεῖν in Hellenistic writings. It is still used occasionally in its original sense of inquiring for the facts about persons, things, or events. Polybius, concluding an account of the "tragic" accounts of Hannibal's crossing of the Alps, says that he can report confidently about these things "because of having inquired (ἱστορηκέναι) about the events from those who were

[19] Plb. 5.75.5–6; see also 1.1.1–2, 35.9–10, and 2.35.5–6.
[20] D. H. *Rh.* 11.2; see also Plb. 2.61.3–6.
[21] Plb. 1.14.5–6; see also 3.20.5.
[22] Choice of subject: D. H. *Pomp.* 3, 4, 6. Arrangement: Plb. 3.57.4–5, 58.1, 118.12. Conclusions: D. H. *Pomp.* 3.
[23] For Theophrastus, see D. L. 5.47. The claim of G. Avenarius (*Lukians Schrift zur Geschichtsschribung*) that Theophrastus' work cannot have been about history writing is rejected by Walbank [*Gnomon* 29 (1957):416–19].

there and having inspected the terrain" and having made the crossing himself.[24] The verb is also occasionally used in the closely related
sense of learning or knowing by inquiry, or, as we might call it,
"historical knowledge." Thus Philodemus says that those who are
ignorant of the proper medicine for curing a disease are conquered
"by their own lack of expert historical knowledge (ὑπὸ τῶν ἰδιωτῶν
... ἱστορηκότων)."[25] Literally translated, ἱστορηκότων means
"things that have been learned by inquiry."

Although the verb is sometimes used in these relatively older ways,
in its most common usage it means to "report" or to "relate" some
facts about persons, things, or events. Thus Dionysius of Halicarnassus undertakes to prove that Demosthenes published twelve speeches
before Aristotle began writing his *Rhetoric*, using evidence "from
things that have been reported (ἐκ τῶν ἱστορουμένων)."[26] And
Theophrastus says, "This was an abridged version of things related
(τῶν ἱστορημένων) about first principles, written down not according to time, but according to similarity of opinion."[27] Also, both Antigonus of Carystus, the third-century paradoxographer, and Polybius
use the verb in this way frequently.[28]

Finally, a word about the adjective ἱστορικός in the Hellenistic
Age. It is used primarily in the substantive way found earlier in Aristotle; it means "historian," one who engages in ἱστορία. Dionysius of
Halicarnassus, for example, discusses the "task of a historian (ἔργον
ἱστορικοῦ)."[29] And there is also the word ἱστοριογράφος, "historical
writer," to indicate the historian in his more distinctly literary
aspect.[30] In fact, this aspect wholly dominates the uses of the adjective in this period. Dionysius has a pet phrase, ἡ ἱστορικὴ πραγ-
ματεία, in which the attributive usage derives from the substantive,
so that the phrase indicates "the historical business" or "craft."[31]
And this craft is literary, not scientific or philosophic.

[24] Plb. 3.48.12; see also 1.63.7; 2.17.2; 3.38.2–3; 9.19.3–4; and Phld. *Rh.* 1.44,
16–21.
[25] Phld. *Rh.* 1.345, 1–8; see also 2.105 (Fr. 12), 5ff., and Plb. 2.62.6 and 3.61.2–3.
[26] D. H. *Amm.* 1.4; see also *Ant. Rom.* 5.17.4, 56.1, etc.
[27] Thphr. *Physical Opinions*, Fr. 8 (Diels, *DG* 484, 17–18). This passage suggests that
at least for the Peripatetics, a "history" did not require chronological arrangement.
[28] Antig. pp. 6, 27, 80, 169, 179–80, 192, 194, 197, 199, 202, 205, 207. Plb. 1.37.3;
2.16.13–14, 71.2; 4.8.4, 47.2; 6.49.2, 54.6.
[29] D. H. *Pomp.* 3.13; also Phld. *Rh.* 1.28, 34–29, 14, 1.200, 18–30 and Caecil. 124.3.
[30] Plb. 2.62.2; 8.11.2; Antig. p. 180.
[31] D. H. *Pomp.* 3.8; *Amm.* 2.2; *Th.* 2 and 24.

Perhaps the basic feature of Roman culture is the pervasive and sustained influence of the Greek culture. Andronicus, the first Latin poet, was Greek; he made a translation of the *Odyssey* that remained a school text well into the Augustan Age, and he also translated certain Greek tragedies into Latin meters. Likewise his successor, Naevius, produced plays of Greek origin in Latin meters, while Ennius, the third of the early poets, wrote his *Annales* of Rome in the characteristically Greek hexameters also used later by Lucretius and Vergil. The comic poets of this period, Plautus, Caecilius, and Terence, all produced translations of the Greek New Comedy of Philemon, Diphilus, and Menander; and the earliest historians of Rome—Quintus Fabius Pictor, Lucius Cincius Alimentus, and Postumius Albinus —all wrote in Greek.

Scholarship in both Greek and Latin literature was begun at Rome at the instance of Crates of Mallos, the Greek Stoic grammarian from Pergamum, who, detained at Rome in 159 B.C. with a broken leg, awakened the admiration of many Romans for the sophistication of Greek study. And what interest there was in philosophy at Rome was inspired by the embassy from Athens in 155 B.C., consisting of Critolaus the Peripatetic, Diogenes the Stoic, and Carneades the Academic, whose auditors may have included the earliest of the "Scipionic Circle," which included C. Laelius, who appears in several of Cicero's dialogues, Lucilius the satirist, Terence the comic poet, Polybius, and the Stoic Panaetius, who was the first to attempt philosophy at Rome.

In sum, the Romans borrowed their intellectual culture whole cloth from the Greeks; not only the forms but also the models and styles of those forms as well as the conceptual terminology. Indeed we owe mostly to Cicero the translation (and, not infrequently, the mistranslation) of the technical vocabulary of philosophy, which through the Middle Ages and especially through Scholasticism, passed into modern philosophy and which still lies at the heart of our discussions of sensation, perception and cognition, action, passion, and evaluation. More often, however, the Romans borrowed by simple transliteration; as, for example, *philosophia*. In the same way they borrowed by transliteration the words *historia* and *historicus*; but they did not borrow either the ancient word ἴστωρ or the verb ἱστορεῖν.[32]

---

[32] A medieval Latin verb, *historiare,* is attested; see Du Cange, *Glossarium Mediae et Infimae Latinitatis* (Paris, 1883–87) 4:210.

This is of considerable importance. For, as has been seen, ἱστορία derived originally from ἱστορεῖν and had the meanings (1) an inquiring or inquiry and (2) the results of inquiry either as the facts or information so obtained or a factual account, or as the written account per se. Now what these various meanings have in common is inquiry of a certain kind. Even in the Hellenistic remains, which show a dominance of history as a species of literature, there is still the recognition, at least implicitly, that the content of this sort of literature is related as product to a particular kind of intellectual activity, inquiring. Insofar as one explicates a basic meaning of *historia–historicus* it will not have this core of original active meaning because there was not such a Latin verb.

Uses of *historia* and *historicus* in Latin writings of republican times are infrequent. The only exception is Cicero, who uses *historia* a great deal relative to what is found in the scanty remains of the works of other writers. Both for this reason and because of the magnitude of his influence upon subsequent Western thought,[33] it seems worthwhile to consider Cicero's usage separately after examining those of other republican writers.

The earliest occurrences of *historia* are in the comedies of Plautus. In the *Trinummus* (381), Lysiteles begs the permission of his father, Philto, to wed an undowered wife. Philto replies that he could argue against it, for "this my old age holds old and ancient history." Similarly in the *Bacchides* (158), Lydus, the tutor of Pistocles, objects that if the young man takes a mistress as he wishes, then he, Lydus, like Phoenix, the tutor of Achilles, will have to bear sad tidings to his father. Pistocles replies, "Satis historiarumst! That's enough of histories!" The history in both of these passages seems to be an account of important events in the lives of persons. Philto evidently knows what happened to others who did what Lysiteles proposes; and the latter passage alludes to the story of Phoenix's sad mission to Peleus. We are reminded of the regular signification of ἱστορεῖν in Attic drama as inquiring for the facts about a person's life.

If *historia* has this rather antique meaning in reference to personal events, there is another occurrence in Plautus reminiscent of a different

---

[33] For a résumé of Cicero's influence, see Richard McKeon, "Introduction to the Philosophy of Cicero," pp. 1–9 of the *Chicago Edition of Cicero* (Chicago, 1950). More diffuse is John C. Rolfe, *Cicero and His Influence* (New York, 1963); and for an interesting application, see Stephen Botein, "Cicero as a Role Model for Early American Lawyers: A Case Study in Classical Influence," *CJ* 73 (1977–78):313–21.

Greek usage. Menaechmus Sosicles, with his servant Messenio, has been looking for his twin brother all over the Mediterranean for six years without success. Messenio complains that they have wandered among Istrians, Spaniards, Massilians, Illyrians, all around the Adriatic, up the whole coast of Italy and into Greater Greece: "You're hunting for a knot in a bulrush. Why don't we go back home—that is, unless we're going to write a history?"[34] What is suggested by the use of *historia* here is an account of firsthand observations of geography, peoples, and customs, which is very like the older usage of ἱστορία to indicate the facts or a factual account about natural things.

There are, however, only these few attestations of *historia* in older, more Hellenic ways. More frequently, *historia* and *historicus* have to do not with things or persons, but with social and political events. The biographer Cornelius Nepos relates that Cato "was already an old man when he began to write a *historia* of which he left seven books. The first contains the accomplishments of the kings of the Roman people; the second and third the origin of all the states of Italy—and it seems to be for that reason that he called the entire work *The Origins*."[35] Nepos evidently understands *historia* in a broad sense here as including political events, the actions of kings, and the origins of cities; but the *historia*, whatever its subject, is a written account.

Historia as a written account of events is distinguished from annals in the famous fragments of the historian Sempronius Asellio (ca. 140–90) preserved by Aulus Gellius.[36] The first fragment distinguishes *annales*, which state only what happened year by year, from "writing of the things done by the Romans, *res gestae a Romanis perscribere*," which shows "the purpose and the reason for which a thing was done, *quo consilio quaque ratione gesta essent*."[37] The second fragment says: "To write, however, by which consul a war was begun and by which completed and who came into the city from it in a triumph, and not to state in that book what was done in the war or what the senate decreed meanwhile or what law or bill was carried, not to go into the motives for which these things were done: that is to tell stories to children, not to write history, *id fabulas pueris est narrare, non*

---

[34] *Men.* 247–48.
[35] Nep. *Cato* 3.3; see also *Att.* 16.3.
[36] Gell. *NA* 5.18.8–9.
[37] Fr. 1 in H. Peter, *Historicorum Romanorum Fragmenta* (Leipzig, 1883).

historias scribere."[38] If Asellio distinguishes *historia* from *annales* by its inclusion of the motives of the actors, Nepos distinguishes *historia* from biography (*vitam . . . narrare*) as being concerned with public and private deeds (*res*) respectively.[39] It would be imprudent to suppose that these distinctions reflect distinctions ordinarily made among accounts of past events or among narrative genera. But the fact that these writers draw the distinction indicates that *historia* was the name for an ordinarily recognized species of literature. So it is that Nepos describes Thucydides as one of the writers who have left a history, *historiam reliquerunt.*[40] And similarly Nepos uses the adjective *historicus*, like ἱστορικός in Greek, substantively to indicate a writer of history, a historian, saying that Alcibiades has been praised by three very serious historians, *tres gravissimi historici.*[41]

Historicus is used in a slightly different way in a passage from Varro's treatise *On Rural Things:* "'Well,' said I, 'I shall speak about what is historical (*quod est historicon*), about the two things which I mentioned first, the origin and the dignity. Concerning the third part, where it is a matter of art, Scrofa will take it up.' "[42] The subject of the historical here has been referred to before, the origins. Yet it is not in relationship to written accounts called history that something is called "historical"; but rather, in relation to the complete knowledge of the subject under discussion, which in this passage is understood to include a part concerned with "history" and a part concerned with "art" or science. The two parts of knowledge here seem to be knowing about something and knowing how to do it; and the "historical" knowing is knowing about something. Similarly, the use of *historia* in Plautus' *Trinummus*, already considered in terms of its subject, a personal occurrence, indicates more the knowledge possessed than the account of it. Although there are not enough attested uses upon which to base a confident assertion, we seem to find in these early Republican materials both a distinction among the subjects of history and a modal distinction between the account of what one knows about these things and the knowledge itself.

Cicero's uses of *historia* and *historicus*, while more frequent, are substantially the same as those of his contemporaries. He sometimes uses

[38] Fr. 2 (Peter).
[39] Nep. *Pelop.* 1.1.
[40] Nep. *Them.* 9.1; also Lucil. 612.
[41] Nep. *Alc.* 11.1.
[42] Varro *Rust.* 2.1.2.

historia as a factual account; the subject of it may be a personal occurrence,[43] or natural phenomena.[44] More often, however, his uses of *historia* have to do with social and political events. He points out, for example, that his side of the argument against the Epicureans *On Ends*[45] can cite numerous examples of noble action from the past, while "in your discourses history is silent (*historia muta est*). In the school of Epicurus I have never heard mention of Lycurgus, Solon, etc." Similarly, he considers the preservation of certain laudatory speeches of the great orators by the families who commissioned them a mixed blessing; for they include many things that never happened, and in this way "the history of our affairs (*historia rerum nostrarum*) has been made more faulty."[46]

In all of Cicero's uses so far examined, *historia* is understood as the facts or information about the particular subject, and it might be translated as "the facts" or "account of the facts." But in just this respect, all of these differ from what is by far the largest group of Cicero's uses of *historia*, in which it refers to a written account about social and political events.

Such an account may be referred to specifically as a written work. "But a *historia*," he says, "cannot be completed unless a period of leisure has been arranged, nor can it be completed in a short time."[47] And in the same way he mentions the various *historiae* written in Greek and Latin.[48] He reports what "the histories say, *historiae loquantur*" about Publius Africanus, and he worries about "what the histories might be saying about us, *quid vero historiae de nobis . . . praedicarint.*"[49]

Although we have no historical composition as such from his pen, we know that Atticus urged him to write history[50] and that he was taken with the suggestion; for he asks Atticus to send him certain dates and details about the consulship of C. Fannius, saying, "I am

---

[43] Cic. *Att.* 1.16.18.

[44] Cic. *Nat. D.* 1.31.88; see also *Fin.* 1.7.25; 2.33.107; and *Tusc.* 1.45.108.

[45] Cic. *Fin.* 2.21.67; also 5.2.5; and *Div.* 1.19.38 and 24.50.

[46] Cic. *Bru.* 16.62; also *Rep.* 2.18.33. For a philosophical interpretation of Cicero's view of history in *Rep.*, see Ronald Hathaway, "Cicero's Socratic View of History," *JHI* 29 (1968):3–12.

[47] Cic. *Leg.* 1.3.9.

[48] E.g., *Bru.* 83.283; *Nat. D.* 2.27.69; *Off.* 3.32.115; *Div.* 1.24.49; *Att.* 1.19.10, 12.3.1; *QFr.* 1.1.10; *Fam.* 5.12.2.

[49] Cic. *Ac.* 2.2.5; also *Div.* 2.32.69; *Att.* 2.5.1 and 2.20.1.

[50] Cic. *Att.* 14.14.5.

enflamed with zeal for history, *Ardeo studio historiae.*"[51] Again, Antonius in the dialogue *On Oratory*[52] defends the subordination of history to oratory: "And as history, *historia* is the witness of the times, the light of truth, the life of memory, the tutor of life, the messenger of antiquity, by what other voice than the orator's can she be commended to immortality?"

Where *historia* in the first group of uses meant a written work about political events, in this second group it seems to indicate a branch of literature or literary culture, the species of which the "histories" in the first group are individuals. This is perfectly clear in the *Brutus* when he discusses the *historia* of Licius Sisenna, observing that "this type of writing, *genus hoc scriptionum*" has yet to be cultivated in Latin literature.[53]

In another cluster of occurrences, *historia* is defined or distinguished from other species of literature. In his youthful *De inventione*,[54] *historia* is defined as one of the subspecies of the genus "narrative"; for narrative "is divided into two parts: one is concerned with events (*negotiis*), the other mainly with persons. That which consists of an exposition of events has three parts: *fabula, historia,* and *argumentum. Fabula* is the term applied to a narrative in which the events are not true and have no likeness to truth. . . . *Historia* is an account of things done, remote from the memory of our own age, *historia est gesta res ab aetatis nostrae remota.* . . . *Argumentum* is a fictitious narrative which nevertheless could have occurred." On the other hand, in *The Orator*[55] Cicero attributes to the Greeks the view that *historias*, along with eulogies, descriptions, and exhortations, comprise the class of epideictic speech. Likewise, in his discussion of the ideal orator, Cicero has occasion to distinguish *historia* from the oratorical style of the Sophists. For "history is nearly related to this class, *huic generi historia finitima est*" in that it too narrates, describes countries and battles, and includes speeches; but they differ in that history seeks a smooth, flowing style, unlike the terse, vigorous style of an oration.[56]

However, Antonius, in the dialogue *On Oratory*,[57] reportedly gives a

---

[51] Cic. *Att.* 16.13.c.2; also *Att.* 2.8.1.16.
[52] Cic. *De Or.* 2.9.36.
[53] Cic *Bru.* 64.228; also *Leg.* 1.2.5–7.
[54] Cic. *Inv.* 1.19.27.
[55] Cic. *Orat.* 11.37.
[56] Cic. *Orat.* 20.66; also 12.39; *Bru.* 75.262 and 83.286.
[57] Cic. *De Or.* 2.15.62–64.

short account of the development of *historia* from a collection of annals (*annalium confectio*) as part of his argument that history, like the other branches of literature, receives no special stylistic rules from oratory, since the rules of history are common knowledge:

> For who does not know that history's first law (*primam . . . historiae legem*) is that one dare not say what is false? Next that he must say only what is true? That there be no suggestion of favor in his writing? Nor of malice? These foundations, that is, are known to all; the finished work, however, rests on the things and the words (*rebus et verbis*). The order of things (*rerum ratio*) requires temporal arrangement and geographical description; . . . the plans of campaign, the executive actions and results, also what the writer holds to be important, and that it be declared among the things done not only what was done and said, but also in what manner; and while speaking of consequences, that all the causes be explained, either accident, or wisdom, or foolhardiness, and of the people themselves not only the things done (*res gestae*), but also the life and character of those who excel in renown and in dignity. However, the order of words and the type of speech (*verborum ratio et genus orationis*) to be sought are the easy and flowing.

In *De legibus* he also invokes truth as the criterion of history where he distinguishes the laws to be followed in history from those to be followed in poetry, even though Herodotus and Theopompus include numerous stories (*fabulae*).[58] And in *De finibus*[59] he opposes *historia* to *fabula*, saying that examples of noble conduct "have been recorded not in false *fabula* only, but also in *historia*."

Cicero also occasionally uses the adjective *historicus*, and usually in ways that reflect his uses of *historia*. On the one hand, he remarks that Demochares wrote a history of Athens "not so much in the historical as in the oratorical manner, *non tam historica quam oratorio genere*."[60] Here *historicus* suggests "in the style proper to a historical composition." Then again he observes that public opinion is naïve not only about politicians, "but also about orators, philosophers, poets, and historians, *historicos*,"[61] using the adjective substantively, as it had been used in Greek. There is, however, another occurrence of the

---

[58] Cic. *Leg.* 1.1.5; also *Fam.* 5.12.3.
[59] Cic. *Fin.* 5.22.64.
[60] Cic. *Bru.* 83.286.
[61] Cic. *Top.* 20.78.

word in this sense that is somewhat odd. In *De natura Deorum* he says: "There are also several Vulcans; the first, the son of the sky, was reputed the father by Minerva of the Apollo said by the ancient historians (*antiqui historici*) to be the tutelary deity of Athens."[62] It is, unfortunately, not clear to whom he is referring in this passage; whether to someone who collected the various accounts of the lineages of the gods and attempted to rationalize them, which would have been ἱστορία of an ancient type, or to some historian who, as Cicero says of Timaeus,[63] include various supposed acts of the gods amid their properly historical accounts. As has already been seen, Cicero does not seem to accept such matters as proper to *historia*.

For both the Greeks and the Romans, history has come to be understood primarily as a species of literature, aiming to give an accurate and well-written account of social and political events. When *historia* is defined or discussed, it is in treatises of rhetoric or grammar, never in philosophical works; it is the art of history writing that is under discussion in these places, never any such thing as "the nature and meaning of history."[64]

Both ἱστορία and *historia* have, as a secondary meaning, "the facts" or "accurate information," in which sense history is a kind of knowledge: namely, the facts. This kind of knowledge was evidently nót problematic for them. In some contexts this sense of history is nearly akin to what we mean by "scientific" pursuits; but "history of nature" (περὶ φύσεως ἱστορία, *historia naturalis*) was descriptive, relating the facts about natural phenomena, not explanatory. Indeed it was for precisely this reason that Plato's Socrates gave it up, and not only Cicero but also other Latin writers oppose *historia* to *ratio*.[65] Everyone seemed to know what it was to have or to recount history

---

[62] Cic. *Nat. D.* 3.22.55.

[63] Cic. *Nat. D.* 2.27.69.

[64] On history as a species of literature and its inclusion in rhetoric, see *inter alia* E. R. Bevan, "Rhetoric in the Ancient World," in *Essays in Honour of Gilbert Murray*, ed. H. A. L. Fisher (London, 1936), pp. 189–213; F. H. Colson, "Some Considerations as to the Influence of Rhetoric on History," *Proc. of the Cl. Assn.* 14 (1917):149–73, M. L. Clarke, *Rhetoric at Rome* (London, 1966), pp. 57–58, 76–77, 96, 122–23; and, on Cicero in particular, B. L. Hallward, "Cicero Historicus," *Cambr. Hist. Journal* 3 (1931):221–37. Paul Scheller's *De Hellenistica Historiae Conscribendae Arte* (Leipzig, 1911) concludes that the art of history developed within the rhetorical tradition. H. J. Rose observes [*A Handbook of Latin Literature*, 3rd ed. (New York: E. P. Dutton, 1966), p. 111] that in the age that followed Isocrates, the historian was "a rhetorician in the first place, a researcher in the second only."

[65] E.g., Varro *Ling.* 8.2.6; Cic. *Nat. D.* 1.31.88; and *Fin.* 1.7.25.

in this sense. In fact, one problem with rendering the term by our word "facts" is that for us the notion of facts might require explication; for the ancients *historia* did not. The questions that they felt compelled to ask and answer about "history" were questions of art.[66]

It is only in its primary meanings as a species of literature that history is a branch of intellectual culture; it is not a science. In its secondary meaning as "accurate information" it might indicate a kind of knowledge; but this is not taken to be a branch of intellectual culture as it has been since the Renaissance.[67] History in this latter sense is not a subject of discourse; one might relate the facts, but not discuss them. History is not a subject for philosophical inquiry; one is either acquainted with the facts or one is not.

In neither of the modes of its usage, then, did history raise scientific or metaphysical questions of the sort that so exercise modern philosophers and historiographers. On the other hand, the subjects for history seem to have remained the same for quite a long time; history has to do with persons, things, or events. It does not have to do with the origin and descent of the gods, the origin of mankind or of the world, or the acts of the gods among mortals. Cicero was slightly scandalized by the fact that the Hellenistic historian Timaeus had included certain accounts of the wishes of the gods in his work.[68] History and poetry are different genres; in the latter it is perfectly proper and customary to deal with mythological subjects, but in the former it is improper and grounds for criticism. The employment of ἱστορεῖν, ἱστορία, *historia*, and so forth implies that the thing being talked about is matter of public and observable fact; the accounts of the gods are not.

It is against this backdrop of regular usage in Greek and Latin that one must examine the usage of these words by Jews and Christians in the ancient world. In this way one may compare the Graeco-Roman with the Judaeo-Christian idea of history.

Of the many national groups who inhabited Alexander's cosmopolis not the least was the Jews, who, according to Philo,[69] numbered

---

[66] Ulrich von Wilamowitz-Moellendorff has noted [*Greek Historical Writing*, trans. Gilbert Murray (Oxford: Clarendon Press, 1908), especially pp. 21–26] that the Greeks had only an art, but not a science of history.

[67] E.g., Benoît LaCroix, *L'Histoire dans l'Antiquité* (Montreal, 1951), p. 211: "The emancipation of history as an autonomous discipline is a relatively modern fact."

[68] Cic. *Nat. D.* 2.27.69.

[69] Philo *In Flacc.* 43.

one million in his time and comprised the predominant population in two of the five sectors of Alexandria. As with the Romans, so for the Jews in Egypt: prolonged contact with Greek civilization exercised a great influence on their social and intellectual life.

It remains a disputed question to what extent Alexandrian Jews were educated in the Greek manner, in the *gymnasia* and *ephebia*.[70] As a matter of course they learned to speak Greek—even to the extent that the knowledge of Hebrew became rare. Indeed it seems to have been for fear that this situation would result in the restriction of knowledge of the Scriptures to a small elite that there came into being a Greek version of the Old Testament, which acquired the name Septuagint through the apocryphal account of its origins in the *Letter to Aristeas*. The translation was used in synagogues increasingly until a reaction set in after the destruction of the Jerusalem temple in A.D. 70. This translation, which seems to be the result of a movement lasting several centuries rather than a single project, is both the first and the greatest document of Jewish Hellenistic literature.

Besides the Septuagint, the influence of Greek literary culture is evidenced by other works of Jews writing in Greek and in Greek literary forms. Eusebius has saved for us some verse from a tragedy called *Exodus (Exagoge)* by the second-century writer Ezechiel as well as some hexameters of Jewish historical epics by Philo the Elder and Theodotus. Eusebius also saved most of the surviving fragments of Demetrius, who wrote *On the Kings in Judaea* based on the Septuagint. Of more historical writers, the first-century compiler Alexander Poly-histor excerpted passages from works by Artapanus and by Cleode-mus (called Malchus), each of whom attempted to demonstrate the superiority of the Jews to the Greeks both in age and in greatness of achievements. In addition, Second Maccabees, like Philo's *Embassy to Gaius* and Josephus' *Jewish Wars*, shows a strong stylistic influence of Thucydides and Polybius.

Of more philosophical writings, the Wisdom of Ben Sira, known as Ecclesiasticus, uses Platonic and Stoic technical terms and, like

---

[70] Harry Austryn Wolfson [*Philo* (Cambridge: Harvard University Press, 1947), 1:78ff.) denies extensive cultural (including educational) interpenetration. However, L. H. Feldman (*Encyclopedia Judaica*, article on "Hellenism") points out that there was no special Jewish educational system in Egypt and that what there was taught the four Greek cardinal virtues. Part of the dispute involves contrary interpretations of the decree of the emperor Claudius discouraging Jews from sending their children to the *gymnasia* and *ephebia*.

Fourth Maccabees, is reminiscent of Cynic and Stoic diatribes.[71] The second-century writer Aristobulus presents a more philosophical version of the theory of Jewish superiority to the Greeks. He evidently held that the Hebrew Scriptures were available in a Greek version long before the Septuagint, and argued from this that Pythagoras, Socrates, and Plato, acquainted with this version, derived the basis of their own philosophies from it, a view customarily attributed to Philo.

For present purposes, the most important representative of Jewish Hellenistic thought is Philo of Alexandria (ca. 20 B.C.–ca. A.D. 40). Schooled in the Old Testament and in the Hellenistic literary culture of which Alexandria was the center, Philo undertook to reconcile Judaism with Greek (particularly Platonic) philosophy. His works are the first in which may be observed the ferment of modes of thought characteristic of the Graeco-Roman world and those characteristic of the Judaeo-Christian, not so much because of the particulars of any philosophical or theological project in which he was engaged, but just because he is trying to write about things Jewish in a language in which those things had not previously been much discussed. He is constrained, therefore, to apply Greek words to new things; in particular, the constellation of Greek intellectual terms must be so applied.

This shift to a new set of objects is evident as soon as one considers Philo's use of the passive voice of the verb ἱστορεῖν. He concludes his account of the origin of the Passover Feast saying, "these things are recorded (ἱστορεῖται) according to the ancient account of the origin."[72] Again, he states that the priests of the Hebrews were in-

---

[71] Cynic influence has also been demonstrated in first-century Jewish thought by tracing the transformation of a *chria* from Xenophon into a first-century version about Hillel; Henry A. Fischel, "Studies in Cynicism and the Ancient Near East: The Transformation of a *Chria*," in *Religions in Antiquity: Essays in Memory of Erwin Ramsdell Goodenough*, ed. Jacob Neusner (Leiden: Brill, 1968), pp. 372–411. On the diatribe, see the article "Diatribe" by W. Capelle and H.-I. Marrou, *Reallexikon für Antike und Christentum* 3:990–1009. Naturally Jewish borrowings became early Christian borrowings; and Rudolf Bultmann showed [*Der Stil der paulinischen Predigt und die kynischstoische Diatribe* (Göttingen: Vandenhoek and Ruprecht, 1910) = *Forschungen zur Religion und Literatur des Alten und Neuen Testaments*, 13] the extent to which Paul's style coincides with that of the Cynic and Stoic popular philosophers. And elements of diatribe have been seen in the Epistle of St. James [J. H. Ropes, *A Critical and Exegetical Commentary on the Epistle of St. James* (Edinburgh, 1916; 1961), pp. 10–18] and in Hippolytus' *Contra Noetum* [Robert J. Butterworth, *Hippolytus: Contra Noetum*. (London, 1977), pp.118–141].

[72] Philo *Spec. Leg.* 2.146.

stalled "in a way very new and worth being recorded (ἄξιον ἱστο-
ϱηθῆναι)."[73] He uses the same phrase in another place, saying, "The
manner of his [i.e., Noah's] preservation, as the sacred books contain
it, is worth being recorded both as a marvel and for the improvement
of character."[74] The verb is thus used only in the passive, which, as
already noted, is typically Hellenistic; and the meaning suggested,
also typically Hellenistic, is "being recorded" rather than the older
sense of "inquire." The usage is standard, but the objects involved
are certainly not; for the information recorded has to do with the
origin of the Passover Feast, the installation of the Jewish priests, and
the escape of Noah from the belly of the whale. The first two,
concerned with the rites performed by a certain people, easily compare with history understood as ethnographical information; and the
account of Noah's escape is very like history understood as an emotionally charged event in a person's life.

This sameness and difference also appears in Philo's uses of ἱστοϱία as facts or information. There is a first group of uses concerning natural phenomena. In a general sense he says that of those who
go abroad for long periods of time "some acquire ἱστοϱίαν of what
they did not know previously."[75] More specifically, he points out that
his inquiry into the reason why Moses speaks of the "lips" of a river
"is not about the history of rivers (πεϱὶ ποταμῶν ἱστοϱίας)";[76] and
he mentions the ἱστοϱία about the Sicilian straits and the ἱστοϱίαν
about the geography of Delos and Rhodes.[77]

The last two passages are found in Philo's statement and criticism
of four arguments for the creation and future destruction of the
world. The fourth argument runs as follows:

If the world was everlasting, the animals in it would be everlasting
also, and most especially the human race inasmuch as it is superior to
the rest. But man also is seen to be of late origin by those who wish to
search into the facts of nature. For it is probable or rather necessary
that the existence of the arts should coincide with that of man, that
they are in fact coeval, not only because system and method are natu-

[73] Philo *V. Mos.* 2.143.
[74] Ibid. 2.59.
[75] Philo *Abr.* 65.
[76] Philo *Somn.* 2.302.
[77] Philo *Aet. Mundi* 120 and 139.

ral to a rational animal, but also because it is impossible to live without them, disregarding the myths palmed off on the gods by the playwrights. . . . But if man is not from everlasting, so neither is any other living creature, therefore neither the regions which have given them a habitat, earth and water and air. This clearly shows that the world is destructible.

But Philo objects that it is folly to measure man by the standard of the arts:

And if indeed people must say that the arts are coeval with the race of men, then they must speak with natural history (μεθ' ἱστορίας φυσικῆς), not unquestioningly and carelessly. And what is the history? (ἡ δ' ἱστορία τίς;).[78]

What follows (146–49), that is, the "natural history," is a very general account of the cyclic destruction of things on earth by fire and water, which seems to be largely derived from Plato's *Laws* and *Timaeus*.[79] In all of these cases, ἱστορία is concerned with natural phenomena and indicates the facts or information or a factual account about them, that is, a piece of knowledge of a certain kind, rather than the account in itself, a piece of literature of a certain kind.

There is a second group of uses of ἱστορία as facts or information, which reminds us of Dionysius Thrax because of the repeated mention of "history" as a part of grammar and hence of education. "Knowledge of the encycylical studies," he says, "adorns the whole spiritual house; grammar on the one hand, searching into the poetic and investigating the ἱστορίαν of ancient happenings."[80] I have translated the genitive plural ἐγκυκλίων, in the first line of this passage, "of the encyclical studies," as an ellipsis for ἐγκύκλιος παιδεία. This phrase, recurrent in ancient writings,[81] suggests the same sort of

---

[78] Ibid. 130–46, trans. Colson (Loeb).

[79] As Colson notes in his Appendix to this passage (Loeb 9:530), Philo is similarly dependent upon these passages in the *Laws* and *Timaeus* for his accounts of terrestrial disasters at *Abr.* 1 and *V. Mos.* 2.53. and 2.263.

[80] Philo *Cher.* 105.

[81] For a fuller discussion of the ἐγκύκλιος παιδεία and citation of the sources, see Henri Marrou, *A History of Education in Antiquity*, trans. George Lamb (London: Sheed and Ward, 1956), pp. 176–77, and H. Fuchs, "Enkyklios paideia," *Reallexikon für Antike and Christentum* 5:365–98. Philo (*De Congressu quaerendae Eruditionis gratia*) uses the rather more complicated phrases τὴν τῶν μέσων καὶ ἐγκυκλίων ἐπιστημῶν μέσην παιδείαν (14) and ἡ ἐγκύκλιος μουσική (23).

thing we mean by "general education" as distinguished from specialized or professional education. It refers to a regular set of subjects, a "cycle of studies," acquaintance with which was thought to constitute the necessary foundation for any socially significant career.[82] The encyclical studies mentioned in the present passage are, besides grammar (which seems to include poetry and "history"), geometry, music, and rhetoric. However, in his treatise on preliminary education, Philo has Wisdom advise us to hold intercourse with this encyclical education because of the various offspring that our association with each of these studies will beget. "For (the study of) Grammar will produce ἱστορίαν, the thought brought forth by the poets and prose writers, and wealth of information (πολυμαθείαν)." And he also mentions the effects produced by music, geometry, rhetoric, and dialectic. Later in the same work he says that his own association with grammar taught him "writing, reading and ἱστορίαν of the works of the poets."[83]

In all of these passages, history is considered a part or product of the study of grammar, as it was by Dionysius Thrax. Where the grammarian's usage left open the range of subjects of history, Philo tends to limit it to events. So also the commentators of the work of Dionysius. But in either case, history indicates the facts or information rather than the account of them, a kind of knowledge rather than a kind of literature. One investigates (μεταδιώκουσα) it,[84] or receives learning (ἀναλήψιν) of it,[85] rather than writing or composing it. Likewise, insofar as it is treated in conjunction with poetry, as the two parts of grammar, it is a kind of knowledge rather than a species of literature.

---

[82] Werner Jaeger's influential interpretation of ancient educational thought, *Paideia*, should perhaps be supplemented by Marrou (*Education in Antiquity*), especially P. 2, Chap. 11 and Conclusion. This encyclical education was taken over by the Romans, who gave to the subjects the collective name *liberales artes*. The "liberal arts," at first nine and later seven, and divided into the Trivium and the Quadrivium, were the substance of medieval education. See M. L. W. Laistner, "Pagan Schools and Christian Teachers," in *Liber Floridus: Mittellateinische Studien, P. Lehmann zum 65. Geburtstag gewidmet*, ed. B. Bischoff and S. Brechter, pp. 47–61. The *liberales artes* may have fallen into some disrepute among the Scholastics, but still formed the basis for the remaking of the curriculum of Western civilization during the Renaissance. See L. Abelson, *The Seven Liberal Arts* (New York, 1906); and, for a sketch of the development of the ἐγκύκλιος παιδεία from antiquity to modernity, see H. J. Mette, "Ἐγκύκλιος παιδεία," *Gymnasium* 67 (1960):300–307.

[83] Philo *Congr.* 15 and 74; cf. *Somn.* 1.205.

[84] Philo *Cher.* 105.

[85] Philo *Somn.* 1.205.

Philo thinks of the encyclical education as a cycle of bodies of knowledge or sciences (ἐπιστῆμαι).[86]

For the most part, then, Philo uses ἱστορία to indicate facts or information; but there is one instance in which he seems to mean not the information, but the account of it. Hearing is a wonderful thing, he says, since by its means we are acquainted with music and with "the many kinds of speeches according to their delivery in court trials, in deliberations, or in laudations, and even those in ἱστορίαις and dialogues."[87] The objects of history in Philo's usage are not extraordinary for Hellenistic times, though they are different; but he differs markedly from the others in emphasizing history as knowledge to the detriment of history as literature.

Let us turn, finally, to the adjective ἱστορικός. Philo uses it substantively to mean "historian,"[88] but more often attributively. One such occurrence is very similar to the substantive. While explicating the dream of Jacob (Gen. 28:10) he says: "The information that Terah left the land of Chaldaea and migrated to Haran, taking with him his son Abraham and his family, is given us not in order that we might learn, as from a historical writer, that certain people became emigrants . . . but lest a lesson (μάθημα) about this thing most useful for life and well-suited to man be neglected."[89] The "historical writer," on Philo's view, relates the facts for their own sake, or at least has nothing further in mind; and this accords with the then standard views of what "history" and "history writing" were about, as we have seen. Similarly, he points out that Moses' account of Abraham's family "is not an historical genealogy (οὐχ ἱστορικὴ γενεαλογία) . . . but a bringing to light through signs of matters capable of profiting the soul (πραγμάτων ψυχὴν ὠφελῆσαι δυναμένων διὰ συμβόλων ἀναπτύξις)."[90] Again the historical as mere facts is contrasted with some other matter, which the facts symbolize.

What is here implicitly denied, however, that the Pentateuch is to be understood in some sense historically, is elsewhere explicitly maintained. Philo distinguishes the oracles delivered by Moses into three kinds: "The one is about the creation of the world (κοσμοποιίας), the next is historical (ἱστορικήν), the third is about legislation. . . .

---

[86] Philo *Congr.* 14 and 23.
[87] Philo *Spec. Leg.* 1.342.
[88] Philo *Sacr. Ab.* 78.
[89] Philo *Somn.* 1.52.
[90] Philo *Congr.* 44.

the historical part (ἱστορικὸν μέρος) is a record of worthy and unworthy lives and the rewards and punishments settled on both in
each generation."[91] Philo makes a similar distinction with respect to
the Pentateuch as a whole.

> Now of these books the one part is historical (ἱστορικόν), the other
> concerns commandments and prohibitions, about which we will speak
> later, examining thoroughly first what is first in order. Of the histor-
> ical (ἱστορικοῦ), then, one part is about the genesis of the world (τοῦ
> κοσμοῦ γενέσεως), the other is genealogical; of the genealogical, one
> part is about the punishments of the impious, the other is about the
> honors of the just. Now we must state why he [i.e., Moses] began his
> law books with that part and put the part about commands and pun-
> ishments second. For he did not, like a prose writer (συγγραφέως)
> make it his business to leave behind for posterity records of ancient
> deeds for the sake of their useless pleasantness; rather . . . in order that
> he might show two very necessary things: . . .[92]

Thus although he maintains that certain passages are not to be
understood simply *historically*, that is, following standard Hellenistic
usage, as simply factual, still he holds that these books do have a
"historical part."

A conjunction occurs here that is decisive for the development of
the term "history" not only in antiquity, but throughout the Middle
Ages and well into modern times. Philo's method of explaining the
text of the Pentateuch is allegorical. In a very broad sense this means
that the text is to be understood not according to the words themselves, not literally but, rather, according to the "lessons" of which
the actual words are merely "symbols." We need not digress upon
the intricacies of allegorical exegesis as Philo practiced and taught
it.[93] Long before Philo, Greek scholars had interpreted Homer alle-

---

[91] Philo *Praem. et Poen.* 1–2.

[92] Philo *V. Mos.* 2.46–48.

[93] For the purpose of this study, the details of particular allegorical systems are not
important. It is sufficient to show the connection between the idea of history and the
literal level of exegesis. For a brief history of allegorical exegesis, see Johannes
Geffcken's article "Allegory" in the *Encyclopedia of Religion and Ethics*, ed. James Hast-
ings (New York, 1925), 1 : 328–31. For a more detailed treatment of Philo's allegorism
within the Jewish tradition, see E. Stein, "Die allegorische Exeges des Philo aus Alexandria," *Ztschr. f. d. alttestamentliche Wissenschaften*, 51 (1929); and on the relation
between Jewish and Christian biblical exegesis, see R. Lowe, "The Jewish Midrashim
and Patristic and Scholastic Exegesis of the Bible," *Studia Patristica*, 1 [= *Texte und
Untersuchungen zur Gesch. d. altchr. Literatur* 63 (1957)]:492–514.

gorically. The stories involved, like those of the Pentateuch, played a role in the religious life of the community; but unlike the Pentateuch, these stories were not thought of as histories, that is, factual accounts. This is a crucial point. The Greeks and Romans repeatedly held, as has been seen, that the difference between history and poetry is precisely that a history must be *true* to fact, must contain accurate information. Philo does not disagree; the historical is the factual for him. But besides its factuality, the account evidently has another meaning; besides communicating the correct information, it also (and on Philo's view this is much more important) communicates a *lesson*. What is thus suggested, and for the first time, is that the facts stand for or signify something beyond or behind the facts. Philo does not actually say this; at most he only suggests that what is historical may be understood allegorically, that is, as containing a lesson with a message.

Philo was speaking about things of Jewish culture in the language of a different culture. He had no choice but to use words laden with associations acquired over a period of almost a thousand years of cultural development, associations which he, as an outsider relative to that culture, could scarcely have fully appreciated. And the Greek language itself, moreover, had formed in a way suitable for use in the Greek world. To speak Greek about things Jewish required the application of old words to new things.[94] One has little difficulty in understanding why Philo should have used ἱστορεῖν, ἱστορία, and ἱστορικός in the contexts in which he did. The origin of the Passover Feast and the manner of installing the priests as well as information about rivers, islands, and straits are all subjects of "natural history" in a very old sense. In the same way, it was not too strange to suggest that the account of the world's genesis was a kind of "natural history." Nor was it particularly inappropriate to describe the sacred writings of the Jews as "historylike" since they include accounts of great leaders, notable speeches, and events of great emotional impact upon the relevant community. These are the furniture of an ἱστορία in the ordinary sense.

In addition to the characteristics that fit this new object for being called ἱστορικός, however, there are certain other characteristics that

---

[94] H.-I. Marrou has noted [" *'Doctrina'* et *'disciplina'* dans la langue des pères de l'église," *Archivum Latinitatis Medii Aevi* 9 (1934):12] how words acquire new meanings by being applied "to things of the Christian religion."

run counter to the associations which, as previous discussion has revealed, those words carried in Greek and Roman thought. One instance
of this partial (but only partial) fit in the language has just been examined, concerning the allegorical interpretation of history. Similarly,
accounts of the origin of the world or of mankind were not considered
history. Plato himself, in the very dialogue from which Philo derives his
"natural history" of terrestrial disasters, has Timaeus argue that since
we are only human we must be satisfied with a "likely story" (μῦθος)
about such matters. Moreover, history in the Graeco-Roman tradition
suggests a publicity of the "information"; it suggests that these "facts"
could be known firsthand by anyone who took the pains that the historian himself had taken. This is, perhaps, why Greek and Roman
historians often include in their narratives some account of the sources
of their information and even some criticism of these sources. But there
is no such account in the Pentateuch of the writer's sources or of his
criticism of them; in fact, there is no sign of who wrote the work. And
besides all of these difficulties, there is simply no sense in which Moses
or any other mortal might have acquired (firsthand) information about
the creation of the world or of man. The guarantor for any such account
would have to be a god. But, again, Philo does not actually say that the
Pentateuch is a history. His uses of ἱστορεῖν, ἱστορία, and ἱστορικός as
applied to certain matters in Jewish culture result in the implications
that the facts that history indicates might themselves be signs of some
other thing, and that the reliability of the facts might be guaranteed
not by their publicity but by their divine origin. It would, however, be
far overstepping the evidence to suppose that these are any more than
suggestions at this period; but the ways in which Philo's usage differs
from the ordinary is to be observed.

IV

The Early Roman Empire: History as Story and the Rhetorical Use of History by the Early Christians

THE "fall" of Egypt under Roman domination in 30 B.C. is a landmark in the political and cultural fortunes of the ancient world. It marks the end of the Hellenistic Age, for the Egypt of the Ptolemies was the last of the great Hellenistic kingdoms established by the successors of Alexander and its assimilation thus completes the unification of the Graeco-Roman world under the sole governance of Rome. The fall of Egypt also marks the passing of the Roman Republic, the establishment of what we call the Roman Empire. At long last the civil wars are ended. Caesar, who sought to save the Republic by unrepublican means, is assassinated by a band of republican nobles in 44. After thirteen years of armed struggle among his colleagues and opponents, thirteen years of anarchy and bloodshed, Octavius defeats Antony at Actium in 31, thus suppressing the last challenge to his own power and consolidating authority in a single government.

The next two centuries saw the completion and perfection of the imperial system; the age of the *Pax Romana*. If these were two centuries of comparative peace and prosperity throughout the empire, it was a peace without freedom, in the sense that government service ceased to be widely available and that private opinion ceased to be one's own business only. On the one hand, political power was no longer the reward of persuasive speech and, on the other, expression

of an opinion disliked by an emperor could easily bring ruin and
death. These two new features of social life had a marked effect on
the culture generally. First, an environment of imperial danger, in-
trigue, caprice, jealousy, and spying does not encourage creativity.
Second, the disappearance of the great incentive for rhetorical study
placed a strain on the predominantly rhetorical educational system,
which distorted such works as were nonetheless produced. There remained for persons so trained the options of practice in the law
courts, rhetoric for its own sake, or literature. As the new political
influences were more strongly (or, at least, more steadily) felt, literary taste tended toward artificiality and ornateness of style exercised
on themes that varied only in the degree of their artificiality. Gradually the distinction between poetry and prose was effaced as both
were affected by the influence of rhetoric.

The uses of the term "history" in these texts retain, for the most part,
the lineaments of the earlier period; but there are shifts of
meaning and relaxations of boundaries previously respected. Let us
look first at Roman thought.

The use of *historia* as facts or information is carried on in the Latin
writings of the Imperial Age, and the kinds of subjects of *historia* re-
main the same: the facts or information about natural things,[1] information generally (following Dionysius Thrax and the grammatical
tradition),[2] and information about persons.[3] But far more often *historia* is understood to be about social and political events.[4]

What these four uses of *historia* have in common is one modal use
understood as facts or information, which emphasizes the matter of
the account. What is related by these uses of *historia* is that the account in question is factual, it is the (presumably correct) information. As in the earlier period, however, so too in the remains of imperial times, *historia* is used not only to refer to the matter of the
account, but to the manner of the account-giving and, in particular,

---

[1] E.g., Apul. *Flor.* 16; *Plat.* 1.4.7; Festus *Gloss. Lat. s.v.* Mamertini, p. 150, 35–36;
Gell. *NA* 5.14.1–2; Hyg. *Astr.* p. 77, 1; Pliny *Ep.* 3.5.6; [Soranus], *Q. Med.*, in Karl
Deichgräber, *Die Griechische Empirikerschule* (Berlin, 1931), pp. 90, 24–91, 2.
[2] E.g., Hyg. *Astr.* p. 19, 1–7; Quint. *Inst.* 1.4.4, 8.18, 8.20.
[3] E.g., Gell. *NA* 2.16.6–7; Hor. *Carm.* 3.7.20; Ov. *Am.* 2.4.44; *Tr.* 2.416; Phdr. *Fab.*
4.6.2; Pliny *HN* 35.139; Prop. 2.1.16, 4.7.64.
[4] E.g., Fronto, p. 198, 8; Suet. *Rhet.* 1.3.

as a written account. There is a variety of uses within this second or literary mode.

In the most general sense, *historia* is used to refer to a written work either by its kind or by its title,[5] and it is also frequently used to name this literary genre as opposed to other genres.[6] As in the earlier period, however, attempts are made to define the genre and distinguish it systematically from other genres.[7] History, then, is a genre at least generally distinguished from other literary genres and, at least generally, is expected to relate the truth about the events narrated; as we saw in the earlier period, it is a genre useful as a source of examples.[8]

There is another use of *historia* in the second mode, which invokes the standards of the genre, standards of style and language rather than standards of accuracy, critical thought, or thoroughness of research.[9] In this second mode history refers to a literary genre, more or less definite, with its own characteristics and styles. It is something written or read, rather than something known or understood. This is reflected in the verbs and substantives regularly conjoined with *historia: componere, scribere* and *legere, auctor* and *scriptor* are the most common. As something known, *historia* is known by acquaintance; the verb used is *noscere*. It is in this sense that Vitruvius recommends that an architect "be acquainted with many histories (*historiae . . . plures novisse*)."[10] There is a single instance in which *historia* is said to be known in some other way. In the Sixth *Satire*, Juvenal advises us, "Let not the wife of your bosom possess a special style of her own; let her not hurl at you in whirling speech the crooked enthymeme! Let her not know all the histories (*nec historias sciat omnes*); let there be something in her reading which she does not understand."[11] But this is the only such occurrence, and otherwise *historia* is something known only insofar as it is known by acquaintance.

---

[5] E.g., Columella *Rust.* 1.4.3; Festus *Gloss. Lat. s.v.* Obsidium, p. 210, 5–9; Gell. *NA* 1.11.7; Ov. *Tr.* 2.443–44; Sen. *Contr.* 1.praef. 18, 3.praef. 8, 10.5; *Suas.* 6.15; Sen. *Ep.* 95.2, 114.17; Suet. *Claud.* 41.1, 41.2, 42.2; *Dom.* 20; *Gal.* 3.3; Vell. Pat. 2.9.5.

[6] Apul. *Apol.* 30; *Flor.* 9, 20; Hor. *Carm.* 2.12.10; Mart. *Epig.* 2.7.1–2; Pliny *HN* 7.205; Pliny *Ep.* 2.5.5; Quint. *Inst.* 2.8.7; Sen. *Suas.* 5.8; Sen. *Dial.* 9.9.7; Suet. *Calig.* 34.2.

[7] E.g., Gell. *NA* 2.16.8, 5.18.4–5; Pliny *Ep.* 7.33.10; Quint. *Inst.* 2.4.2–3, 2.4.18–19.

[8] Fronto, p. 122, 7; Quint. *Inst.* 3.8.67; Sen. *Ep.* 24.11.

[9] Fronto, p. 100, 2–4; Gell. *NA* 13.29.2; Pliny *Ep.* 5.8.5, 7.9.8; Quint. *Inst.* 9.4.129.

[10] *Arch.* 1.1.5; see also 1.1.3, 1.1.6; Juv. *Sat.* 7.231.

[11] Juv. *Sat.* 6.450.

The second mode also includes the usage of *historicus* in early imperial times; it is used substantively to indicate writers of histories, that is, historians. Sometimes particular historians are mentioned,[12] but more often it is historians as a group.[13] Seneca uses *historicus* to indicate those who write descriptions of natural things, "natural histories";[14] but otherwise *historici* are those who write about social and political events. And it is as *writers* that they are referred to. They are distinguished from other kinds of writers[15] by giving a straightforward account of events[16] and because of the use of language that is characteristic of them;[17] and they provide us with examples.[18]

The uses of *historia* and *historicus* in early imperial times seem very much the same as those of the republican period, but it is worth noting that the second mode, literary genre, is predominant in the Hellenistic period, while both are of equal frequency in the Roman.

In addition to the shift in balance, the usage of *historia* is expanded in two ways. The first is a development of an earlier use, originally observed in the Attic drama and still found in early imperial times, to indicate an account of the life or a crucial event in the life of a person. In that use the persons (or characters) whose "histories" were referred to were semilegendary. They had, perhaps, at one time been real human beings. But their lives had been continually reexamined and reinterpreted by the poets and playwrights, the rhetoricians and philosophers, and thus became in time archetypal lives, stories the common belief in which provided the affective basis for the unity of the Greek people. If they were "persons," they were not ordinary persons, not ordinary individuals, but what might be called generic persons, that is, capable of signifying the whole nation or race. For example, whatever particular mistake Oedipus made, still it was archetypal. Oedipus is Everyman in the sense that his mistake and his fate are possibilities for each of us. And the matter was so understood even in antiquity.

---

[12] E.g., Gell. *NA* 15.23.cap.; Sen. *Con. Ex.* 9.1; *Suas.* 6.21; Suet. *Gramm.* 15, 20; Vell. Pat. 1.17.2.

[13] E.g., Festus *Gloss. Lat. s.v.* salutaris porta, p. 436, 27–28; Quint. *Inst.* 1.10.40, 2.1.4; Sen. *Contr.* 7.2.8; *Suas.* 6.14; Suet. *Rhet.* 1.5; *Tib.* 61.3.

[14] Sen. *Q.Nat.* 1.11.2; 4.3.1; cf. *historica lingua, Q.Nat.* 1.13.3.

[15] Gell. *NA* 13.7.6; Gran. Lic., p. 33, 10; Quint. *Inst.* 10.2.21–22; Sen. *Con. Ex.* 9.1.

[16] Petr. *Satyr.* 118.6; Sen. *Apocol.* 1.

[17] Pliny *Ep.* 9.16.1; Quint. *Inst.* 1.6.2, 6.11; 8.6.65.

[18] Quint. *Inst.* 12.2.22, 11.17.

In imperial times, however, the persons whose "histories" are mentioned have begun to lose that stature. The younger Pliny, for example, encouraged to write history by his friend Capito, says that he wants to do so, "Not that I have any confidence of success . . . but because I hold it a noble task to rescue from oblivion those who deserve to be eternally remembered, and extend the fame of others, at the same time as our own."[19] Pliny wants to rescue the deeds of certain individuals, not necessarily of heroic proportions. Similarly, Suetonius tells us that L. Voltacilius Plotus "set forth the exploits (*res gestas*) of Pompey's father, as well as those of the son, in several books. He was the first of all freed men to write history (*scribere historiam*), in the opinion of Cornelius Nepos, which had been written only by men of the highest position before that time."[20] Fronto, too, was encouraged by Marcus Aurelius to write a "history" of his brother's deeds,[21] and history about an ordinary mortal is a common use by Aulus Gellius.[22]

Gellius seems almost aware of the lesser intrinsic importance attaching to a *historia* as he uses the term. He tells us "the entertaining history (*iocunda historia*)" of how Papirius Praetextatus got his surname.[23] Although the text of Book 8 of his *Noctes Atticae* has disappeared, the titles of the various chapters survive; that of Chapter 16 is "A pleasant and remarkable history (*historia . . . iocunda et miranda*) from the books of Heracleides Ponticus." And Chapter 5 of Book 6 contains "A noteworthy history (*historia . . . memoratu digna*) about the actor Polus." Earlier, to call something a "history" at least implied that it was an accurate account, and that there was some importance attaching to it. For Gellius, however, what seems to be important is not so much that the account be true or important but that it be entertaining or that it point a moral.[24]

Aristotle had already distinguished poetry or fables from history on the grounds that poetry aims at pleasure, while history aims at truth or

[19] Pliny *Ep*. 5.8.1, trans. Melmoth (Loeb).

[20] Suet. *Rhet*. 3; cf. Pliny *Ep*. 6.16.21f. The account to Tacitus of his uncle's death in the eruption of Vesuvius is *historia*, though he is aware that "there is a great difference between a letter and a *historia*."

[21] Fronto, p. 191, 4–5.

[22] E.g., Gell. *NA* 1.8.1, 23.1; 3.7.cap.; 4.5.cap.; 4.5.6; 14.cap.; 6.19.cap.; 7.9.cap.; 13.2.1.

[23] Gell. *NA* 1.23.cap.

[24] Gell. *NA* 4.20.10; and cf. Apul. *Met*. 2.12, 6.29, 7.16, 8.1. That Gellius had less than scholarly intentions in writing his work is indicated by his saying that it was his endeavor (*negotium*) only "to strew these *Nights* of mine lightly here and there with a few of these flowers of history (*historiae flosculis*)" [17.21.1, trans. Rolfe (Loeb)].

accuracy. This ancient distinction between poetry and history is now beginning to fade. Seneca advises the hot-tempered man to train his mind. "Let the reading of poems soothe it and let history hold it by its fables (*fabulis*); let it be led softly and delicately."[25] Suetonius informs us about Tiberius that "his special aim was a knowledge of fabulous history (*notitiam historiae fabularis*), which he carried to a silly and laughable extent."[26] And just as Gellius equivocated in the distinction between *historia* and *annales*, so too he equivocates about *historia* and *fabula*. The title of Book 16, Chapter 11 is: "*Historia* taken from the books of Herodotus about the destruction of the Psylli"; but then he says that it was in the fourth book of Herodotus that he found "this fable (*hanc fabulam*) about the Psylli."[27]

This first expansion of the idea of history suggests a relaxation of the earlier standards. The persons involved are still, for the most part, famous, but they are simply not of the social and cultural stature of the earlier usage. And as the distinction between history and poetry is blurred, truth or accuracy as the distinctive characteristic of the kind of account called *historia* gives way somewhat to entertainment or pleasure. Here *historia* seems to have more nearly the meaning of our word "story" than of our word "history"; indeed, this would seem to be the beginning of the development of "story."[28] If a history is an account of the facts about real things the point of which is to inform, and a fable is an account of unreal things the point of which is to entertain or to please, then a story is an account of the facts about real things the point of which is to entertain, please, or point a moral.

The second expanded use of *historia* is history as the past. Most uses of *historia* about events have to do with the literary genre. When it means the facts or information, however, the limits of it are vague. *History* about persons is usually limited to a particular episode in the person's life; perhaps this is because of the exigencies of dramatic literature in which this use is most often found, and perhaps because

---

[25] Sen. *Dial.* 5.9.1.

[26] Suet. *Tib.* 70.3; and cf. Juv. *Sat.* 10.175.

[27] Gell. *NA* 16.11.3. Similarly *historiae* in Hyg. *Astr.* regularly refers to accounts of the gods after whom the constellations are named; e.g., pp. 31, 18; 38, 7; 66, 6; 71, 25; 73, 21–22. Also Gell. *NA* 3.3.8. Hyginus himself, Suetonius tells us, "was called Polyhistor on account of his knowledge of antiquity, a sort of *historia*" (*Gramm.* 20).

[28] This late use of *historia* = *mythus* has been noted by Dombart ["Historia," *Archiv für Lateinische Lexicographie und Grammatik* (Leipzig: Teubner, 1886), 3:230–34. Cf. Hor. *Serm.* 1.3; Prop. 3.20.25–28.

βίος, or what we should call "biography," was a literary genre distinct from history.[29] The limits of a history about natural things are those of the kind of thing that is the subject-genus. The limits of a history about events as literature are those of a particular written history. *Historia* as facts about events should derive its limits, like history of natural things, from the limits of the subject-genus. But whereas the limits of a genus of material things is, at least broadly speaking, clear, the limits of a genus of immaterial things—for example, the events of a nation or people—are not clear without further specification. Thus history as facts about events of a nation could be taken, analogously with history of natural things, to indicate *all* the facts, the aggregate of information, the past as it were—though it is not in general clear whether it is the whole past or some portion of the past.

When Cicero complains that through the preservation of laudatory speeches "the history of our affairs (*historia rerum nostrarum*) has been made more faulty,"[30] it is not clear what "affairs" he means, though by "our" he presumably means "of Rome." He says this explicitly in another place, observing that "Roman history is obscure (*obscura est historia Romana*)," since we do not know the name of the father of King Ancus Martius.[31] Elsewhere, however, *historia* seems to indicate a more extended past. He criticizes the Epicureans because "in your discourses history is silent (*historia muta est*). In the school of Epicurus I have never heard mention of Lycurgus, Solon, Miltiades. Themistocles, Epaminondas."[32] And he sometimes even seems to be thinking of the past altogether; for it is objected that, although the oracle at Delphi has declined, still "you must admit what cannot be denied, unless we pervert all history (*nisi omnem historiam perverterimus*), that for many centuries the oracle was true."[33]

History as the past is a somewhat more frequent use in imperial times. Propertius says, "Fame, Rome, is not ashamed of your history (*Fama, Roma, tuae non pudet historiae*)."[34] Aulus Gellius relates a discourse of the philosopher Taurus about the courtesies that fathers

---

[29] On ancient biography, see A. Momigliano, "Problems of Ancient Biography," *Quarto Contributo alla Storia degli Studi Classici* (Rome, 1969), pp. 77–94, and *The Development of Greek Biography* (Cambridge: Harvard University Press, 1971).

[30] Cic. *Bru.* 16.62.

[31] Cic. *Rep.* 2.18.33; cf. *Div.* 1.18.37.

[32] Cic. *Fin.* 2.21.67; cf. *Div.* 1.24.50.

[33] Cic. *Div.* 1.19.38.

[34] Prop. 3.22.20; also 3.4.10, and cf. Juv. *Sat.* 2.103.

and sons ought to show each other along with "an example from
Roman history (*ex historia Romana*)." And he tells us "what errors
Julius Hyginus observed in the Sixth Book of Vergil, errors in Roman
history (*in Romana historia erratos*)."[35] The elder Pliny insists that
horns, properly so called, are found only on quadrupeds, and hence
reckons as fabulous both Acteon "and also Cipus in the Latin history
(*in Latia historia*)," who are alleged to have grown horns.[36] In these
passages *historia* seems to indicate the aggregate of information about
events, that is, the past.

From a modern point of view the two expanded meanings just discussed, history as story and history as the past, might seem to move
in opposite directions from the older center of meaning. For we tend
to associate the notion of "story" with fiction and falsehood but "the
past" with the "science" of history, which, we suppose, tells us the
facts and the truth. From the ancient point of view, however, the two
expansions were congruent, as is illustrated by an epigram on the too
little appreciated fact that Vergil's *Aeneid* survived the author's death
only in violation of the explicit provisions of his will. I quote the
entire passage from Probus' *Life of Virgil* (22–28):

> The *Aeneid* was saved by Augustus, although [Vergil] himself had
> provided in his will that the parts of it that he had not published
> should not survive; which Servius Varus attests in the following epi-
> gram:

> > Virgil had ordered destroyed in devouring flames
> > These songs which sing the Phrygian leader.
> > Tucca and Varius together oppose; you, greatest Caesar,
> > Do not allow it and are looking after Latian history.

To preserve the written poems is to preserve the *historia*, the aggregate of information about the past.

There are some other occurrences, however, in which it is less clear
whether what is meant is the information per se or a written account.
Vergil laments the loss of Octavius' Roman "history."[37] Gellius men-

---

[35] Gell. *NA* 2.2.cap.; cf. 10.16.cap.; Mart. *Epig.* 14.191.
[36] Pliny *HN* 11.123. The story of Cipus is related both in Ov. *Met.* 15.565 and in
Val. Max. 5.6.3. Gellius can even distinguish between knowing about Praxiteles *ex
libris et ex historia* (13.17.4).
[37] Verg. *Catal.* 11 (14), 6.

tions Asellio "and several other writers of Roman history," and tells us things that are "written in Greek history."[38] Similarly, Pompeius Festus tells us how Rome got her name according to "Antigonus, the writer of Italian history" and mentions a "writer of Cuman history."[39] "History" in these passages may refer to an unspecified written account—that is, the proper reading may be "writer of *an* Italian history" or "written in *a* Greek history"—or it may refer to the subject of the writing, the Greek, Roman, or Italian past. Perhaps there is some of each involved.

The unity of a history as the facts about events was previously episodic, similarly a history about persons. In a larger or smaller compass, it was the facts about *some* past events. In this second expansion, history as the past, these facts are being drawn together into a conceived whole. There are not very many such uses in early imperial times, and they are often equivocal. However, for the first time *historia* is being used to indicate the whole past of a nation or a people; for the first time "history" resembles what we mean when we say that something "has a history."

After the Battle of Actium the political dependence of the Greek world on the Roman was complete. Mainland Greece, along with Macedonia and Thessaly, had already been united as the province of Achaea. And now Egypt was being exploited for Rome. A hotbed of anti-Roman sentiment and hence kept securely under Roman domination, Alexandria ceased to be the greatest center of literature and science; the Greek cities of Asia Minor, to whom Rome granted a measure of municipal freedom, came to have a vigorous cultural life in the first centuries of the Roman Empire. This is reflected in the unfamiliar names of the towns from which many writers of this period came.

The remains of Greek intellectual life under the early empire are far more extensive than those of the Hellenistic Age; but they show little creativity, little originality. If this later age sees the first flowering of the prose romance, it also sees the increased production of catalogues, compendia, anthologies, and compilations. There is a marked decline in poetry; the living movements of the age were in prose, but a prose which, like the Latin prose of the same time, is

[38] Gell. *NA* 1.13.10; 6.1.1.
[39] *S.v.* Roman, p. 328, 2–7.

strongly marked by the influence of rhetoric—and for the same reason: in the Greek-speaking world as in the Latin-speaking, education was a predominantly rhetorical enterprise and, consequently, rhetoric influenced every branch of intellectual culture. Nor was this influence, on the whole, beneficial. The oratorical style of the Hellenistic Age tended to be flowery and bombastic. Toward the end of the period a reaction set in, an attempt to return to an idealized purity of the ancient Attic.[40] This "Atticism," however, no less than the "Asianism" it opposed, was carried to extremes, in this case to an excessive and ludicrous archaism which, in turn, provoked a counter-reaction. Under the empire, from our point of view at least, the worst characteristics of both styles were combined in a renewed burst of rhetorical activity called the Second Sophistic.

The shifts of meaning and relaxations of semantic boundaries observed in the uses of *historia* during the early empire may also be found in the uses of ἱστορεῖν-ἱστορία, though there is little change by and large. The verb is still used occasionally in its oldest sense of "inquiring,"[41] and a few times it indicates learning by inquiry or discovering.[42] Usually, as in the Hellenistic Age, it means "report," "relate," or "record." What is "reported" may still be facts about natural things and customs,[43] and in the empirical medical tradition "reported" case histories are very important.[44] Episodes in the lives of semilegendary persons are also "reported,"[45] but most often social and political events.[46] These uses of the verb are familiar; but the usage is relaxed in several ways. First, the persons are of decreased

---

[40] However, A. E. Douglas ["Introduction" to *M. Tulli Ciceronis Brutus*, ed. Douglas (Oxford, 1966), pp. xii–xiv] argues that the Atticist controversy was real but that "its significance has been greatly exaggerated by modern scholars" (p. xiii). See also E. S. Gruen, "Cicero and Calvus," *Harvard St. in Cl. Philol.* 71 (1966): 232–33.

[41] Arr. *Epict.* 2.14.28, Lucian *Syr. D.* 11, Plu. *Curios.* 516C, S.E. *Math.* 8.291.

[42] Arr. *Epict.* 3.7.1, S.E. *Math* 11.191.

[43] Aet. *Plac.* 5.7 (Diels, *DG* 419, 12–18), Heracl. *Q. Hom.* p. 69, 9–17, Plu. *Mus.* 1135F, *QConv.* 7.701C, 8.733B, S.E. *Pyr.* 3.225, 232.

[44] See the Galenic treatise περὶ τῆς ἀρίστης αἱρήσεως in Karl Deichgräber, *Die Griechische Empirikerschule* (Berlin, 1930), p. 127, 11, 21, 25, and 128, 1. It is arguable that ἱστορεῖν means "to inquire" at 127, 28, 31, 35, and especially 128, 20. But ἱστορία is defined as "the narration (διήγησις) of what has often been experienced in the same way" (127, 9–10; and cp. [Gal.] εἰσαγώγη ἤ ἰατρὸς 100, 17–20), so that each of the arguable citations above can be read as relating to those who have handed down, i.e. "related" or "recorded" case histories.

[45] E.g. Lucian *Alex.* 1, *Scyth.* 8, S.E. *Math.* 11.191.

[46] E.g. D.C. 7.25.6 (Zonaras), 7.25.1, Hdn. *Hist.* 3.7.3, 7.6, Lucian *Hist. conscr.* 7, Plu. *Glo. Ath.* 347D–E, Athen. 6.235C–D, 7.277F, 8.277A, 13.605D–E, 14.615B, 648E.

stature. Sextus Empiricus sets down things that are "recorded" about Pyrrho,[47] the founder of Skepticism, and about Pythagoras.[48] Then again, what "is related" may have to do with people famous in political affairs. Dio Cassius speaks of a certain Quadratus whose mistress, Marcia, became the mistress of the emperor Commodus, elder son of Marcus Aurelius: "It is related (ἱστορεῖται) that she greatly favored the Christians and did them many good turns, insofar as she could do anything with Commodus."[49] The persons are also sometimes just ordinary people, though notable for some particular. Sextus Empiricus, for example, cites Aristotle's *Meteorologica* (3.4): "Aristotle tells (ἱστορεῖ) of a Thasian who fancied that the image of a man was always going in front of him."[50]

There is a second relaxed sense of ἱστορεῖν in which the stature of the persons involved is greatly enhanced; for it is also used to "relate" episodes in the lives of the gods outside the dramatic context. Dio Cassius remarks that Commodus strangled two Cilician brothers, "just as Heracles, when an infant, is reported (ἱστόρηται) to have strangled the serpents sent against him by Juno."[51] Similarly, in his *Homeric Questions*, the literary critic Heraclitus says, "It is recorded (ἱστοροῦσι, lit., they say) that Mnemosyne is the mother of the Muses" and several times observes what is, or ought to be, recorded about the gods.[52] Plutarch, too, frequently tells us what is "reported" about the gods.[53] These relaxed uses also suggest that the earlier presumption, that what was being related was facts of some importance, no longer holds so strongly. Among those whose "reports" are cited in these texts are not only historians, in the broad sense of anyone who writes a prose account of past events, but also philosophers, antiquarians and scholars, poets and rhetoricians. For Plutarch, at least, the factuality of what is reported seems to have little to do with the instances in which he uses the verb; he even tells us[54] what "the mythographers relate (οἱ μυθολογοῦντες ἱστοροῦσι)."

---

[47] *Math.* 1.272.
[48] *Math.* 9.366; cf. Plu. *QConv.* 7.715E, 733C, 8.728E, etc.
[49] 72.4.7; cf. Plu. *Alex. Fort.* 330A, 331F, *QRom.* 272D, etc.
[50] *Pyr.* 1.84; cf. Plu. *Mus.* 1136C, *QRom.* 267B–C, 272F.
[51] 72.7.2; cf. Hdn. *Hist.* 1.11.5.
[52] pp. 39, 15–40, 9; 63, 5–13; 77, 9–19; 80, 20–81, 9; 84, 11–16; and 89, 2–15.
[53] E.g., Plu. *Fort. Rom.* 320B; *Mus.* 1136B; *QConv.* 9.738F, 741A; *QGr.* 293B; *QRom.* 269A, 278F, 285E.
[54] Plu. *QRom.* 268D.

Similarly with ἱστορία in the Greek of the early empire. It still means, as in the Hellenistic period, a factual account in terms of the account-giving, that is, a literary genre, either as a genre[55] or as a work of that genre, a history.[56] And Lucian wrote an entire work on *How to Write History*.[57] He distinguishes history from poetry (as well as from panegyric) and insists that it be kept separate.[58] Invoking the ancient distinction, he says that poetry aims at pleasure but history must aim at usefulness and at "setting forth the truth (τὴν τῆς ἀ-ληθείας δήλωσιν)."[59] "For this one thing [i.e., to relate the event as it happened, ὡς ἐπράχθη ἐιπεῖν], as I have said, is the peculiarity of history (ἴδιον ἱστορίας). One must sacrifice only to truth (τῇ ἀληθείᾳ), if one is going to write history; and one must subordinate all other aims to this one."[60] Herodian agrees with this.[61] So does Plutarch,[62] though he is so keenly aware of the pleasure that history gives as to suggest that the pleasure of fiction and poetry derive from their similarity to history in point of truth.[63] And the subject matter of history must have a certain dignity, at least according to Dio Cassius, who often characterizes incidents as worthy or unworthy of the dignity of history (ὁ τῆς ἱστορίας ὄγκος), or worthy of a place in history.[64]

The noun is also used in its other mode, as an account the factuality of which is emphasized rather than the account-giving; and this, as in the earlier period, about social and political events[65] and also about human customs or natural things.[66] Thus in Galen and the empirical tradition the use of a factual account (ἱστορία) of previous cases, remedies used, and their results is the repository of the πεῖρα or ἐμπειρία[67] that is their starting point[68] and their difference from

[55] E.g., D.C. 72.23.2; Max. Tyr. *Diss.* p. 28, 5; S.E. *Math.* 1.43.
[56] E.g., D.C. 37.17.4; 40.63.4; Did. *In D.* 12, 47; Hdn. *Hist.* 1.11.1; 2.1.1; 15. 11–13; Lucian *Hist. conscr.* 55; Plu. *Curios.* 517F.
[57] The expression ἱστορίαν συγγραφεῖν occurs frequently; *Hist. conscr.* 2, 4, 5, 6, 16, 17.
[58] Lucian *Hist. conscr.* 7, 8, and 10; cf. Hdn. *Hist.* 2.15.7 fin.
[59] Ibid. 9; cf. 42 and 63.
[60] Ibid. 39; Max. Tyr. also appreciates the educational value of *history* [*Diss.* p. 28, 5–6).
[61] Hdn. *Hist.* 1.1.1, 1.4.
[62] Plu. *Malign.* 855B–F.
[63] Plu. *Non Poss.* 1092F–1095A; cf. Max. Tyr. *Diss.* p. 28, 5.
[64] D.C. 54.23.1; 57.24.6; 59.22.5; 66.9.4; 67.8.1; 72.18.3.
[65] D.C. 56.18.1; Plu. *Gen.* 575B–C.
[66] E.g., App. *Hist.* 12.103; Gal. Ἱππ. Ἐπιδ., p. 237, 16–18; Plu. *QConv.* 8.724D.
[67] ἀρίστ. (127, 9–10 D.); αἱρήσ. 3.2.12 (95, 15–20D.); εἰσαγ. (91, 29–33 D.).
[68] εἰσαγ. (100, 17–20 D.); cf. *op. cit.* (91, 29–33D.)

the competing dogmatic and methodological medical schools,[69] as well as an important educational tool.[70] Two further points are worth noting about this use of the case history: first, because other schools also employ such case histories[71] and because not all such accounts are necessarily true, "some criterion of the history (ἱστορία) must be found, by which we shall distinguish the true one from the false ones."[72] And second, the criterion turns out to be πεῖρα, experiment or experience, not λόγος;[73] so that once again we see the old opposition between history and reason.

However, the usage of ἱστορία as information or facts has been expanded in several ways. As in Latin writings of this time, "history" may mean "story" as the result of a blurring of the old distinction between myth or poetry and history in terms both of the truth of the account and of the importance of its subject. Pseudo-Lucian recounts his walk through the temple of Dionysius on the walls of which are painted the heroic myths (ἡρωικοὺς μύθους); "and immediately two or three fellows rushed up to me, offering for a small fee to explain every story (πᾶσαν ἱστορίαν)."[74] And he also repeats to us a "strange, incredible story" told him by an attendant in the temple, about a youth who, having fallen in love with a statue by Praxiteles, left a stain from his passion on the marble thigh and committed suicide from remorse.[75]

Similarly, Sextus Empiricus attacks the need for grammatical study, saying, "It is certainly plain that all the sayings in the poets which are found useful for life and necessary . . . are expressed by them clearly and have no need of grammar; while those which have need of it—e.g., those which consist of foreign stories (ἐν ξέναις ἱσ-

---

[69] συνθ. φαρμ. (147, 27–31 D.)."The empirics use prior ἱστορία as much as possible" [ἀρίστ. (127, 8–9 D.)].

[70] ἀρίστ. (126, 23–127, 1 D.); ". . . it is impossible for one who is learning to happen upon all symptoms and to make his own observation of everything. So, lest he spend his whole life learning, but rather sometime make use of the art, for this reason they say that history is useful for practicing medicine (χρήσιμον πρὸς τὸ ἰατρεύειν τὴν ἱστορίαν)."

[71] Ibid. (97, 9–11 D.).

[72] Ibid. (127, 11–14 D.).

[73] Ibid. (127, 20–30, 128, 3 D.) and Ἱππ. φύσ.᾽ανθ. (128, 12–20 D.).

[74] Pseudo-Lucian *Erot.* 8.406, trans. Macleod (Loeb); cf. Philostr. *Im.* 2.9.7 (p. 355, 15); Callistr. *Stat.* 5.4 (p. 427, 22).

[75] Ibid. 15.414, trans. Macleod (Loeb). The same story is mentioned by the real Lucian (*Im.* 4) as a μῦθος.

τορίαις) or are enigmatically expressed—are useless."[76] And he relates that the Argo was the first ship to sail the seas, as "it has been handed down by history (διὰ τῆς ἱστορίας)."[77] Plutarch advises busybodies to mind their own business: "Shift your curiosity from things without and turn it inwards; if you enjoy dealing with a history of troubles (ἱστορία κακῶν), you have much to do at home."[78]

There are also a few instances in which, parallel to the Latin, ἱστορία seems to indicate the aggregate of past facts. Lucian says, "A few points from ancient history (τῆς ἀρχαῖς ἱστορίας) I remember are to the point, and I may as well add them."[79] And Appian, speaking of the rise of Rome, says, "These things many Greeks and many Romans have already written down, and the history (ἡ ἱστορία) is even longer than that of Macedon, which was the longest before then."[80]

It is not entirely clear in these passages to what extent "the past" is meant and to what extent written "histories." It seems prudent to suppose that both are meant; or, rather, that "the past" is a meaning that has not yet become separated from the older meanings.

There is another use of the noun as factual account, found only in the Greek: history of opinions or ideas. Beginning his inquiry into moral virtue, Plutarch says: "It is better, however, to run quickly through the opinions of others, not so much for the sake of history (οὐχ ἱστορίας ἕνεκα) as of making the proper ones clearer and more firmly established, when these have been presented."[81]

Sextus Empiricus uses "history" in the same way to refer to an account of previous opinions. Concluding a review of the opinions of Democritus and others, he says, "The history of the ancients, then, about the criterion of truth (ἡ τῶν παλαίων περὶ τοῦ κριτηρίου τῆς ἀληθείας ἱστορία) was such."[82] And the Stoic Epictetus observes that the Master Argument has three incompatible premises: "If, then, somebody asks me, 'But which pair of these do you maintain?' I shall give the answer to him that I do not know (οὐκ οἶδα) but

---

[76] S.E. *Math.* 1.278, trans. Bury (Loeb). Also 2.96; 9.57.
[77] S.E. *Math.* 9.32; cf. Lucian *Hipp.* 2.67.
[78] Plu. *Curios.* 515D; also 518C, and cf. 516D.
[79] Lucian *Laps.* 7; cf. Max. Tyr. *Diss.*, p. 28, 6.
[80] App. *Praef.* 12, but he proceeds to talk about the proper arrangement of his work; cf. *BCiv.* 9.67.284.
[81] Plu. *Prof. Virt.* 440E.
[82] S.E. *Math.* 7.140; 8.14; also 7.190.

that I have been given the following history (ἱστορίαν τοιαύτην)."[83] He goes on to list pairs of premises that various philosophers have accepted. In giving his own reply, Epictetus compares himself with the grammarian who uses a similar formula when asked for his own view about a literary matter; but while that is of no great consequence in a literary matter, according to Epictetus, philosophers are not entitled to give that reply.[84] So while we seem to have a distinctly philosophical use of "history" here, history so understood is still considered philosophically insufficient.

Certainly this third new use of "history" in Greek to indicate a factual account of opinions is not entirely new. Aristotle often used[85] an account of the opinions of his predecessors to clarify the issues on a given subject. The same practice seems to have been followed by his successors.[86] And in their desire for catalogues, compilations, and anthologies the Hellenistic and Roman ages, the Greek and the Latin, produced a whole literature of the recording of opinions and ideas, doxography.[87] What is new under the empire is calling such an account in Greek a "history."

---

[83] Arr. *Epict.* 2.19.5.

[84] Ibid. 2.19.7–11; also 2.21.10.

[85] Aristotle's use of his predecessors is extensively discussed by Harold Cherniss [*Aristotle's Criticism of Presocratic Philosophy* (Baltimore, 1935) and *Aristotle's Criticism of Plato and the Academy* (Baltimore, 1944)]. This attack on Aristotle's credibility as a historian was so thorough and persuasive that by 1957 Guthrie felt compelled to argue ["Aristotle as a Historian of Philosophy," *JHS* 77 (1957): 35–41] that Cherniss and those who accepted his views had gone too far. To be critical was one thing; to reject him whole cloth was too much. The problem is important, because to a very great extent our traditional picture of the history of philosophy up to Aristotle depends upon Aristotle; either directly, through his comments on his predecessors, or indirectly, through the doxographical tradition [see John B. McDiarmid, "Theophrastus on the Presocratic Causes," *Harvard St. in Cl. Philol.* 61 (1953): 85–156]. Kerferd ["Recent Work on Presocratic Philosophy;" *Amer. Philos. Q.* 2 (1965)] estimated the significance of this correctly: "If this view were to be correct it would be nearly fatal to the traditional picture of the Presocratics built up by scholars over a hundred years" (p. 130). And he sides with Guthrie, as do many. But the fact that the problem has ceased to be discussed does not make it go away, and as recently as 1975 Malcolm Scholfield ["Doxographica Anaxagorea," *Hermes* 103 (1975): 1–24] doubted Aristotle's (and Theophrastus') reliability as sources on Anaxagoras. For a moderate evaluation of Aristotle, see Kurt von Fritz, "Aristotle's Contribution to the Practice and Theory of Historiography," *Univ. of Calif. Publ. in Philosophy*, Vol. 28, No. 3, p. 118.

[86] Von Fritz, "Aristotle's Contribution," pp. 118–19.

[87] The remains of all the Greek doxographers are collected in Hermann Diels, *Doxographie Graeci.* He includes Aetius, Arius Didymus, Theophrastus, Cicero, Philodemus, Hippolytus, Plutarch, Epiphanius, Galen, and Hermeius. His "Prolegomena" (pp. 1–265) remains the basic discussion of the subject.

The range of possible subjects for history has grown, and now includes ordinary or famous persons, and the gods—history understood as story. Two characteristics of history from its earliest beginnings—discerned already in the uses of ἵστωρ in the *Iliad*—are accuracy of account and social importance of subject. When history is understood as story, however, the social importance of subject is somewhat diluted. Accounts of ordinary or famous people may be noteworthy or interesting, but they have not the impact of the account of Oedipus, Io, or Hecuba. If importance of subject is diluted, accuracy of account is virtually lost. What is important to a story is not that it be accurate, but that it be entertaining or edifying. Then too, at least in Greek, past ideas or opinions about a topic are now a subject for history. Galen's doxographical *History of Philosophy* (περὶ φιλοσόφου ἱστορίας)[88] represents probably the earliest occurrence of the expression "history of philosophy." It should be clear, however, that by "history" here is meant simply the facts, or accurate information. Galen's slender book is a sort of field guide to philosophy. He begins with a brief account of the origins of philosophy, the succession of philosophers, and the parts, problems, and terms of philosophy. The remainder of the work is largely taken up with various problems of physics and the opinions that had been held about them by previous philosophers. This is history of philosophy, then, not in the sense that previous philosophies are taken to be integrated wholes in which conclusions are advanced on the basis of arguments adduced, but in the sense that these are the facts as to what previous philosophers said about a given problem or topic. And finally, there is the incipient use of "history" to indicate the aggregate of facts about the past of something.

Christianity began as a religious and political reform movement among a small national and religious group, the Jews, and in Palestine or Judaea, a province of the Roman Empire. It attracted little notice in the Graeco-Roman world during the early stages of its development. To his contemporaries, Jesus seems to have fitted the tradition of prophecy common to all Jews and that of popular opposition to the Pharisees, who had retained a position of political and economic dominance by cooperation with the Romans. The earliest

---

[88] Galen, *Opera omnia*, ed. Kuhn (Leipzig, 1830), 19: 222–345.

followers of Jesus were Jews. Their intensely spiritual faith, diverse practice, and messianic expectations produced little in the way of literature besides the Gospels, and even these were written toward the end of the century. At any rate, the Gospels were written for the members of the new community; earliest Christianity was a culturally narrow phenomenon.[89] However, after the Romans destroyed the Jerusalem temple in A.D. 70, which led to the dispersion of many Jews, and after Paul's preaching to the non-Jews, the membership of the *ecclesia* came to be increasingly gentile.[90] Since the Roman conquest had continued in power the Greek dynasty that had ruled Judaea for over three centuries, the gentiles converted tended to be Greeks in language and culture, if not in place of national origin.

With the influx of Greeks came, of course, the influence of Greek education and culture; and within the new community new kinds of questions came to be raised. The most important questions of the first century had been whether Jews were still obligated by the Law of Moses; but in the second century the most important questions, to witness the Greek influence, were the Gnostic theory of creation, the philosophic implications of belief in the divinity of Jesus, and the (social) acceptability of the Christian cult.[91] The attempt to answer these new questions constitutes the beginnings of Christian literature. The second century also saw the beginning of the first distinctively Christian school, the Catechetical School of Alexandria,[92] which was

[89] William R. Arnold, "The Relation of Primitive Christianity to Jewish Thought and Teaching," *Harvard Theological Review* 23 (1930): 161–79. Jean Daniélou's *Théologie du Judéo-Christianisme* (Paris, 1958) reconstructs a pre-apologetical Christian theology. Since it is before the influence of Hellenistic philosophical ideas was felt, it is, he argues, a Semitic, a "Judaeo-Christian" theology.

[90] Since Paul's role in the creation of Christianity both socially and spiritually is so great, the question of his relation—and that of first century Jews in general—to the surrounding society is important. Edwin A. Judge ["St. Paul and Classical Society," *Jahrbuch für Antike und Christentum* 15 (1972): 19–36] observes that the older fashion of seeing "a sharp distinction between hebraic and hellenistic forms of expression" (p. 29) has been undermined recently. Rather than a pre-existing opposition, he argues, "it was the New Testament writers and Paul in particular who (in contrast with the hellenising spirit of other first century Jews writing in Greek) brought the two into a radical confrontation that was eventually to have great cultural consequences" (p. 30). And he thinks that "If we knew more about the antecedents of the sophistic movement that flourished in the second century, we might come closer to the social setting of Paul's mission" (p. 32).

[91] Massy Hamilton Shepherd ["The Early Apologists and Christian Worship," *Journal of Religion* 18 (1938): 60–79] contends that the social threat posed by Christianity had to do with cult rather than with belief.

[92] Cf. Gustave Bardy, "Pour l'histoire de l'école d'Alexandrie," *Vivre et Penser* 2

to play a decisive role in Christian thought for the next fifteen hundred years. By the second century, therefore, Christianity had set forth into the wider world of Graeco-Roman civilization; and the story of Christianity's influence on Western civilization must begin here. If the first century was one of variety and experiment in Christian belief and cult, the second was one of consolidation and defense against both the destructive influence of pagan (or Jewish) attacks from without and the disintegrative influence of heresies from within. The defense against attacks produced the apologetical literature, which, together with the antiheretical literature, provide us our first opportunity to observe the ferment of Graeco-Roman and Christian ideas.[93]

This raises a historiographical problem: How is one to differentiate between Judaeo-Christian and Graeco-Roman communities, whose uses of Greek and Latin are to be compared? It is misleading to speak of "Greeks," "Romans," and "Christians," because the Christians were quite as much Greeks or Romans as were the Syrians, Egyptians, Spaniards, or Gauls who are usually considered "Greeks" or "Romans" in contrast with the "Christians." Nor should one speak of "Christians" and "pagans" or "Gentiles," since both of the latter terms are wholly Christian characterizations and represent dichotomies foreign to the non-Christian Greeks and Romans. The terminological problem has the same origin in both cases: the concepts (categories) employed in thinking and writing about the cultural history of late antiquity, ultimately derived from the Christian apologists themselves, serve to set Christianity over against and in opposition to everything Greek and Roman. While this was all very well for apologetical—that is to say, polemical—purposes, it is unsatisfactory for purposes of historiography. "Greek," "Roman," or "Graeco-Roman" and "Christian" or "Judaeo-Christian" are not strictly comparable or, strictly speaking, alternatives. The former refer to something (or someone) primarily in terms of national, political, geographical, or linguistic considerations; the latter primarily in terms of

---

(1942): 80–109. On Clement's conception of παιδεία, see J. Wytzes, "Paideia and Pronoia in the Works of Clemens Alexandrinus," *Vigiliae Christianae* 9 (1955): 148–58; on his attitude to the pagan παιδεία, see Pierre Camelot, "Les idées de Clément d'Alexandrie sur l'utilisation des sciences et de la littérature profane," *Recherches de science religieuse* 21 (1931): 38–60.

[93] For a sketch of early Christianity as a culture, see M. Pellegrino, "La cultura cristiana nei primi secoli," *Convivium*, N.S. 1 (1954): 257–70.

religious considerations. Moreover, when "Graeco-Roman" is contrasted with "Judaeo-Christian" culture, the problem is compounded; for while the leading motive of the latter is unquestionably religious, that of the former is not. The entire history of Greek and Roman culture evinces an interest in religious matters, but it will not support the claim, or even the implication, that these were matters of special or dominant interest. The Christians were not a group separate or distinct from the group called "Greek," "Roman," or "Graeco-Roman." As a historical phenomenon, Christianity arises *within* Graeco-Roman civilization. Christian uses of Greek and Latin are not—indeed, *could* not be—in opposition to the ordinary uses but, rather, are based on them and developments of them. If Christianity comes to dominate the religious and political institutions of Western civilization and if the Christian world-view comes to supplant that of the Greeks and Romans, it is a conquest not from without but from within.

From the outset there is a difference between the Christians' relationship to Greek and their relationship to Latin. The language of Christianity in the first century, even in Rome, was Greek; for outside of Palestine, where Greek was the second language of the native population, the Christians were mainly Greek-speaking immigrants. By 150, however, Latin began to come into use although Christians at Rome, such as Justin Martyr, Gaius, and Hippolytus, were still writing in Greek throughout the second and early third centuries. By 250 Latin was in the ascendancy. The Christian literature of the first two centuries, which is not extensive, is therefore mostly in Greek.

The Christian use of Greek does not differ radically from that of the mainstream of Greek literature of the time. Ἱστορία is used by the early Christian writers to refer to the literary genre and, a first use of this mode, "history" as distinguished from other genres. Athenagoras of Athens, trying to show that the pagan gods were only men, says, "But even those of the Greeks who are eminent in poetry and history (οἱ περὶ ποίησιν καὶ ἱστορίαν σοφοί) say the same thing about Heracles."[94] Similarly, Clement of Alexandria, the second head of the Catechetical School, sets out to demonstrate the lack of originality of Greek writers by piling up examples of plagiarism, the unattributed borrowing of lines or passages from earlier writers by later. After giving examples from numerous poets, he proceeds:

[94] Athenag. *Chr.* 29 (*PG* 6, 957A).

"And in order that we may see that not only philosophy and history, but even rhetoric are not free of the like failing, it is well to set forth a few instances from them."[95] In the same vein Tatian the Assyrian, educated in philosophy, rhetoric, and Sophistic, denies that the Greeks invented the arts, for "the writers of annals of the Egyptians taught you to compose history (ἱστορίας συντάττειν αἱ παρ' Αἰγυπτίοις τῶν χρόνων ἀναγραφαί)."[96]

"History" is also used to refer to particular historical works. In the course of Clement's argument that Jewish institutions and laws are older (and hence more reliable) than Greek philosophy, he cites the "histories" of Apion, Berosus, and Josephus, and he elsewhere cites those of Thucydides and Antiochus.[97] Tatian also mentions the history of Berosus, and, like Clement, cites the histories of the Phoenicians, Theodotus, Hypsicrates and Mochus, to the effect that Moses is much older than Homer, for "in the histories of the aforesaid writers it is shown that the abduction of Europa occurred under one of the kings,"[98] but we know that the kings are all more recent than Moses.

"History" is also used in its other mode as the facts or a factual account; and, first, about persons, Tatian argues for the greater antiquity of Moses simply on the grounds that no one agrees when Homer lived. He says: "For it is possible to show that the opinions held about the matter are also false. For where the recorded dates do not agree together, it is impossible that the history be true (οὐδὲ τὰ τῆς ἱστορίας ἀληθεύειν δύνατον). For what is the cause of error in writing if it is not the setting down of things that are not true?"[99] Tatian also cites the testimony of Berosus as to the antiquity of Moses, establishing the writer's reliability by reference to Juba, saying: "Berosus is a very reliable man, and a witness to this is Juba, who, writing about the Assyrians, says that he learned the history (μεμαθηκέναι τὴν ἱστορίαν) from Berosus."[100] And Clement uses "history" as the facts about natural things while listing the subjects that it will be useful for the catechumen to know. He writes: "The same account also applies to astronomy. For treating of the history of

---

[95] Clem. Al. *Strom.* 6.2.16.
[96] Tatian *Ad Gr.* 1.1 (*PG* 6, 804A); also 39.1 (*PG* 6, 881B).
[97] Clem. Al. *Strom.* 1.21.101, 122, 147; 6.2.8; *Protr.* 3.45.1.
[98] Tatian *Ad Gr.* 36.2 (*PG* 6, 880B); 37.1 (880B–C).
[99] Ibid. 31.4 (872A).
[100] Ibid. 36.2 (880B).

celestial bodies (τὴν τῶν μεταρσίων ἱστορίαν) . . . it teaches quickness in perceiving the seasons of the year, changes of the air, and the appearance of the stars."[101] Clement also uses history as facts in the new way, already discussed, as an account of opinions or doctrines. The second book of his *Stromata* concerns the opinions about various matters that the Greek philosophers seem to have "borrowed" from Sacred Scripture. The last chapter concerns marriage; in evaluating it and trying to determine when people should marry, Clement says, "Let us consider the history in brief,"[102] and proceeds to recount the opinions of Plato, Democritus, Epicurus, the Stoics, and the Peripatetics.

The early Christian writers also use "history" as factual or informational accounts about the gods in the diluted sense of history as story. Arguing that the pagan gods were mere mortals, Clement describes how the Muses were actually people hired by Megaclo, daughter to King Macar of Lesbos, who was so pleased with their performance that she caused a temple to be built in their honor. He concludes: "Such then were the Muses; and the story (ἡ ἱστορία) is in Myrsilus of Lesbos."[103] We are also informed that among the Egyptians a ship sometimes symbolizes time, though time "is symbolized by a crocodile in some other priestly story (ἱερατικὴν ἱστορίαν)."[104] Athenagoras also uses "history" in this way in his attack on the belief in the gods. He ridicules the gods on account of the absurdities attributed to them, saying, "If such things be said, one must ask: What is the propriety or utility of such a story (ἱστορίας), that we should believe Kronos, Zeus, Kore and the rest to be gods?"[105] And again, he claims that the gods were mere men, "as can be known from the story (ἱστορία) about them."[106] Clement and Athenagoras are willing to follow the current usage and speak about stories of the gods in this diluted sense of history; but they also take the histories, that is, stories, seriously and employ them as weapons in their own attacks against such beliefs.

There is one final and very interesting occurrence of "history" in Clement. Having quoted Hebrews 11:3, 4, and 25 on the efficacy of

[101] Clem. Al. *Strom.* 6.11.90.
[102] Ibid. 2.23.138.
[103] Clem. Al. *Protr.* 2.31.4.
[104] Clem. Al. *Strom.* 5.7.41.
[105] Athenag. *Chr.* 20 (*PG* 6, 932B).
[106] Ibid. 26 (952A).

faith, he says: "Faith, therefore, having justified these before the law, made them heirs of the divine promise. Why, then, should I review and adduce any further testimonies of faith from the history in our hands (ἐκ τῆς παρ' ἡμῖν ἱστορίας)?"[107] And quoting Hebrews 11 again, he proceeds to argue that faith is the foundation of all knowledge and superior to knowledge. It is not clear whether Clement means by history here the Epistle to the Hebrews, from which he has just been citing examples of faith, or the Pentateuch, from which all of those examples ultimately come. Whichever is correct, it is interesting that a written work that occupies an exalted place in the community is said to be a history in some sense. Since, however, it is the only instance in these early materials, there is little to infer from it.

The verb ἱστορεῖν is used by the early Christian writers in senses that are ordinary for the time, although, as the uses of the noun form suggest, the objects of these uses are most often concerned solely with matters of religious interest. Thus Clement twice uses the verb in its oldest sense as "inquire" or "investigate," but in both cases he has in mind inquiry into divine things. He encourages us to work toward salvation by spreading the good news, but warns against doing so out of vainglory. He writes: "And according to this view [1 Thess. 2:5–7] those who take part in the divine words must be on their guard, lest they engage in this as they would in the building of cities, inquiring (ἱστορήσαντες) only for the sake of curiosity."[108] Similarly, he describes the spiritual improvement of education: "And by astronomy, again, raised from the earth in his mind, he is elevated along with heaven, and will revolve with its revolution, studying (ἱστορῶν) always divine things and their harmony with each other."[109]

Most often, however, the verb means "relate" or "record." One of the ways in which Clement pursues his attack on the pagan gods is by holding up to ridicule the religious customs of a particular place or people: "And among you the Thessalians pay divine homage to storks according to the ancient custom; the Thebans to weasels on account of (their assistance at) the birth of Heracles. And again, what about the Thessalians? They are reported (ἱστοροῦνται) to worship ants since they learned that Zeus, putting on the likeness of an ant, had intercourse with Eurymedusa, the daughter of Cletor,

---

[107] Clem. Al. *Strom.* 2.4.12–13, trans. Wilson (*ANF*).
[108] Ibid. 1.1.6.
[109] Ibid. 6.10.80.

and begot Myrmidon. And Polemo relates (ἱστορεῖ) that the people who inhabit the Troad worship field-mice."[110] Also indicative of this use are similar accounts given about Sparta, Sicily, Thuria, Phocaea, and Persia.[111] Clement tells us what is "related" about famous persons in his argument that Greek philosophy is derived from non-Greeks. "Pythagoras is reported (ἱστορεῖται) to have been a disciple of Soches, the Egyptian archprophet, and Plato of Sechnuphis of Heliopolis."[112]

What is related about the gods is used in the *First Apology* of Justin Martyr to rebut the claim that the Christian accounts about Jesus are silly. The immaculate conception, for example, is no sillier than what is believed about Zeus, Mercury, Asclepius, and Bacchus. He says: "And what kind of deeds are recorded (ἱστοροῦνται) of each of the sons of Zeus, it is not necessary to tell those who already know." And, he proceeds, even in death Jesus was like the sons of Zeus: "For their sufferings at death are recorded (ἱστορεῖται) to have been not alike, but diverse; so that the peculiarity of (His) suffering does not seem to make Him inferior to them."[113]

Thus what is believed about Jesus is no worse than what is believed about the gods; and, indeed, Justin argues that it is much better. For whereas the accounts of the pagan gods are the products of myth-making (μυθοποιηθείσι) and have no proof, what is said about Jesus is proved by the fulfillment of prophecy.[114] In the *Dialogue with Trypho*, a literary product of the Jewish controversies of the second century, he goes further and claims that the accounts about the sons of Zeus are originally borrowed from the Old Testament prophecies, saying, ". . . and when they relate (ἱστορῶσι) that being torn in pieces, and having died, he rose again and ascended to heaven . . . do I not perceive that (sc., the Devil) has imitated the prophecy announced by the patriarch Jacob and written down by Moses?"[115] Clement too tells us what Panyasis relates (ἱστορεῖ) about the gods.[116]

The Christian attack on polytheism naturally extended to idol worship, since one of the recurrent causes of persecution was that the Christians refused to pay their respects to the images of the gods or to

[110] Clem. Al. *Protr.* 2.39.6–7, trans. Wilson (*ANF*).
[111] Ibid. 2.30.3–4, 38.2; 3.42.4, 6, 8; 5.65.1.
[112] Clem. Al. *Strom.* 1.15.69; also 1.15.70, 72.
[113] J. Mart. *Apol.* 1.21 (*PG* 6, 360B); also 1.22 (361B).
[114] Ibid. 1.53 (405sqq.).
[115] J. Mart. *Dial.* 69 (*PG* 6, 637A), trans. (*ANF*).
[116] Clem. Al. *Protr.* 2.35.3, 36.2.

the Roman emperor's statue. The fourth chapter of Clement's *Exhortation to the Greeks* to become Christians exposes the absurdity and shamefulness of idol worship by repeatedly tracing the origins of idols or cults to particular times and places; and ἱστορεῖν is used to indicate what is "related" about these matters. He tells us what is "related" by Polemon about the statues at Athens and by Dionysius about the Palladion.[117] He illustrates the detrimental influence of such statues by the story of Pygmalion, as "related" by Philostephanus and Posidippus.[118]

There is a final group of uses of the verb by these early Christians which concerns their own religion rather than that of their opponents. Properly to understand God saying, "Let us make. . . ," says Justin, "I shall again relate (ἱστορήσω) the words spoken by Moses himself."[119] Similarly, Clement, discussing the mystic meanings of the tabernacle and its furniture, contends that there is certainly a hidden meaning in the reference to "the seven circuits around the Temple recorded among the Hebrews (παρ' Ἑβραίοις ἱστορουμένη)."[120] He also mentions, as an example of the benefits of endurance and patience, "the things recorded (ἱστορούμενα) about Ananias"[121] and devotes the second book of the *Stromata* to showing that the Greeks filched their philosophy from the Jews, part of the argument for which consists in showing that "they have imitated and copied the marvels recorded (ἱστορουμένων) among us."[122] Finally, Justin tells us that "Sodom and Gomorrah are recorded by Moses (ἱστοροῦνται ὑπὸ Μωσέως) to have been cities of impious men."[123]

There are only a few occurrences of the adjective ἱστορικός in these materials. Clement refers to the "historians" several times.[124] Tatian begins his argument that "our philosophy" is older than that of the Greeks by saying, "Moses and Homer shall be our limits since they are very ancient; the one is the oldest of the poets and historians (ἱστορικῶν), and the other the founder of all barbarian wisdom."[125] Moses, the writer of the Old Testament, is thus both poet and his-

[117] Ibid. 4.36.5–6, 47.6; cf. 4.47.2, 48.2, 54.3; and 3.45.3.
[118] Ibid. 4.57.3, trans. Wilson (*ANF*).
[119] J. Mart. *Dial.* 62 (*PG* 6, 617B).
[120] Clem. Al. *Strom.* 5.6.32.
[121] Ibid. 2.20.103.
[122] Ibid. 2.1.1.
[123] J. Mart. *Apol.* 1.53 (*PG* 6, 408B).
[124] Clem. Al. *Strom.* 1.21.142; 6.2.24, and 26 (ἱστοριογράφος).
[125] Tatian *Ad Gr.* 31 (*PG* 6, 869A).

torian, and is set up as having the same cultural stature in the Jewish and Christian world as Homer has in the Greek and Roman world. Furthermore, according to Clement, his philosophy is in part "historical" or "historylike." For he writes: "The Mosaic philosophy is accordingly divided into four parts—into the historic (τὸ ἱστορι-κόν) and that which is specially called the legislative, which two properly belong to an ethical treatise; and the third, that which relates to sacrifice, which belongs to the physical science; and fourth, above all, theology."[126]

The earliest Christian use of Latin parallels the use of the Greek terms both in meanings and in contexts of use. Sometimes "history" indicates a written work, as when Tertullian recounts the visit of Pompey to the Jerusalem temple, on the authority of Tacitus "in the fifth book of his *Histories* (*in quinta Historiarum suarum*)."[127] More often, however, at least for Tertullian, "history" refers to an informational account as such rather than as a literary product. The subjects of such an account vary. In the old sense of natural history, he mentions a history of dreams (*historia somnium*) in five volumes by Hermippus of Berytus,[128] and, rejecting someone's evidence of a transmigration of souls, he suggests that the account may have been found "in some very obscure histories (*in historiis aliquibus occultioribus*)."[129] Tertullian uses "history" in reference to social events when he replies to the charge that the Christians are the cause of certain public disasters by pointing out that there were plenty of such disasters before Christianity began. "Where were the Christians, then, when the Roman state furnished so many histories of its disasters (*tot historias laborum suorum*)?"[130] And he seems to use "history" as the past in his demonstration that Moses is of greater antiquity than Homer: "we must look into the history and literature of the world (*in historias et litteras orbis*)."[131]

We also find Tertullian using "history" as story. Against the attacks on Christianity, he argues that what is said about the gods by those who accept them vilifies them: "Is not their majesty violated,

---

[126] Clem. Al. *Strom.* 1.28.176.
[127] Tert. *Apol.* 16.3 (*PL* 1, 364); also *Apol.* 19.2 (383); *Ad Nat.* 1.11 (*CSEL* 20.80, 25–26); and Min. Fel. *Oct.* 21.
[128] Tert. *De An.* 46 (*CSEL* 20.377, 13–16).
[129] Ibid. 28 (348, 4–5).
[130] Tert. *Ad Nat.* 1.9 (*CSEL* 20.73, 15–16).
[131] Tert. *Apol.* 19.7 (*PL* 1, 388).

their deity defiled by your plaudits? But you really are still more religious in the amphitheatre, where over human blood, over the dirt of pollution or capital punishment, your gods dance, supplying themes and stories (*argumenta et historias*) for the guilty—unless it is that often the guilty play the parts of the gods."[132] Again, in attacking the Roman spectacles, he contends that the arts and art works are products of the daemons: "For none but themselves would have made provision and preparation for the objects they had in view; nor would they have given the arts to the world by any but those in whose names and images and stories (*historiis*) they set up for their own ends the artifice of consecration."[133] Similarly, the heresy of Valentinus is said to be concerned with "the stories (*historias*) and Milesian fables of their own Aeons."[134] Finally, both Tertullian and Minucius Felix use *historicus* substantively as "historian."[135]

These Greek and Latin uses of "history" by the Christian writers of the first two centuries are, aside from the predominance of religious subjects, not extraordinary. In some instances they invoke the distinctions among literary genres that were current in the Greek and Roman thought of the time. While they use the distinction, they do not make it, that is, they do not state nor do they evince any interest in the grounds or details of the distinction. This feature of their uses

---

[132] Ibid. 15.4 (360–61), trans. Glover (Loeb). *Ad Nat.* 1.10 (*CSEL* 20.80, 5–9), is almost *verbatim* identical with the passage cited in the text. Although the pair, *argumentum/historia*, have a prior history of use as (1) a distinction between two species of the genus *narrativa* or *narratio* and as (2) distinct parts in the construction of a legal case, those more formal and rigorous uses are here transferred to the domain of poetry. Thus Holmes (*ANF*) translates "proof and plot."

[133] Tert. *Spec.* 10 (*CSEL* 20.13, 14–17). At *Ad Nat.* 2.1 (95, 5–8) he asks, as a rhetorical question, whether we ought to believe in a god whom "history has thrown (*historia iactavit*) at us." In the preceding paragraph he has listed and described briefly the three sorts of gods Varro distinguished, "the physical class, of which the philosophers treat, the mythic class, which is the constant burden of the poets, and the gentile class, which the nations have adopted each one for itself." Parallelisms of construction suggest that *historia* refers to the second class, that of the poets, and should therefore accordingly be translated "story." Robert Dick Sider ["Tertullian, *On the Shows*: An Analysis," *Journal of Theological Studies* n.s. 29 (1978):339–65] argues that the classical rhetorical principles of composition are the keys not only to the language, but also to the theology of Tertullian. See also his "Structure and Design in the 'De resurrectione mortuorum' of Tertullian," *Vigiliae Christianae* 23 (1969):177–96 and *Ancient Rhetoric and the Art of Tertullian* (New York: Oxford University Press, 1971).

[134] Tert. *De An.* 23 (*CSEL* 20.336, 14–16).

[135] Tert. *Apol.* 19.4 (*PL* 1,387); Min. Fel.*Oct.* 21.1. Against the claim that the *Apologeticum* is an epideictic speech, Louis J. Swift argues ["Forensic Rhetoric in Tertullian's *Apologeticum*," *Latomus* 27 (1958):864–77] that it is a forensic speech which aims both to defend the Christians and turn the accusations against their accusers.

of the Greek and Latin words is merely an instance of the general character of the relationship between Christian and Graeco-Roman thought as it is revealed in these early materials: the Christians are using, but not participating in, Graeco-Roman culture. They use the languages, adopt certain of the literary forms, and borrow scientific or philosophic terms and distinctions; but their aim is not to understand or teach the language, to produce literary works that will provide pleasure to their readers, or to criticize in order to offer a more comprehensive or conclusive science or philosophy. Their purposes are apologetic, polemical, and persuasive. This reveals perhaps the most distinctive feature of the early Christian usage: their context is apologetic, polemical, and persuasive. These words occur in the midst of defenses against attack, counter-attacks, and exhortations to conversion. Nearly all of the occurrences that have been examined fall under one of four commonplaces of early Christian literature: (1) that Jewish (and hence Christian) culture is more ancient than Graeco-Roman; (2) that Jewish (and hence Christian) culture is better (i.e., more original, more rational, more moral) than Graeco-Roman; (3) that the pagan gods were mere mortals, and not divine; and (4) that the beliefs about the gods and the forms of worship of them are absurd and/or immoral.

What is distinctive about the early Christian idea of history, then, is not any special or new significance attributed to it but, rather, the persuasive context of its use. Considering the social circumstances in which this earliest Christian literature is produced and the educational and cultural circumstances of the writers, this does not seem odd; for this literature was occasioned by attacks from without and within. It should be recalled that of the six writers with whose works we have been concerned so far, five—Clement, Justin Martyr, Tatian, Minucius Felix, and Tertullian—were brought up in the non-Christian society and given the predominantly rhetorical education that was characteristic of that age. Of these five, only Clement, before he became Christian, seems not to have practiced the vocation of rhetor, preferring the life of scholarship and teaching.[136] Both Minucius Felix and Tertullian were practicing lawyers, and the latter seems to have obtained some eminence in Roman law.

---

[136] Even Clement, in contrast with Origen, is a polemicist, according to Jaeger, *Early Christianity and Greek Paideia* (Cambridge: Harvard University Press, 1961), Chap. 5.

V

The Distinction between Sacred and Profane History in Late Antiquity

I T HAS LONG BEEN THE CONSENSUS of Western scholars that a profound transformation of the ancient world began in the third century. Since Gibbon it has been customary to refer to this as the "crisis of the third century" and to the complete transformation as "the decline and fall of the Roman Empire," although, far from disappearing, the empire survived another thousand years, albeit centered in Byzantium and although the social and economic problems of the third century had a marked effect on the very formation of the Byzantine state.[1]

The second century saw the highest development of the imperial system; it was a time, relatively, of peace and prosperity, and the age of the "good emperors"—Hadrian, Trajan, Antonius Pius, Marcus Aurelius. However, the reign of Commodus (180–93), the son of Marcus Aurelius, was followed by a hundred years of wars, civil disorder, soldier-emperors, and disintegration of the empire into provincial army-factions. War, plague, and famine thinned the population and laid waste the land; as cities and towns decayed, commerce declined and tax revenues dwindled. The uneasy toleration that had

---

[1] For some recent discussions of the question, see Mortimer Chambers, "The Crisis of the Third Century," in *The Transformation of the Roman World*, ed. Lynn White (Berkeley: University of California Press, 1966); *The Fall of Rome: Can It Be Explained?* ed. Mortimer Chambers (New York: Holt, Rinehart and Winston, 1967); Andreas Alföldi, *Studien zur Geschichte der Weltkrise des 3. Jahrhunderts* (Darmstadt: Wissenschaftliche Buchgesellschaft, 1967).

been accorded all foreign cults gave way, with internal stress, to persecution of the Christians *inter alia* for civil disobedience. The decline of the central authority reached its peak under Gallienus (260–68); Aurelian (270–75) restored order and began a fortification of the empire against barbarian encroachments, which was completed by Diocletian (284–305). Diocletian also attempted to stabilize the government and to make the imperial administration more efficient. All traces of republicanism finally vanished; the emperor was the absolute ruler. In addition, there was a strong tendency to leveling of older local and national distinctions, privileges, and liberties; Italy and Rome officially became *provinces* among provinces. Diocletian's abdication was followed by nineteen years of struggles among his "colleagues." From these struggles Constantine emerged as sole ruler, Christianity as the state religion, and Byzantium, now called Constantine's *polis*—Constantinople—as the new capital of the empire. The latter paved the way for the separation of East and West, which was consummated in 364 with the making of Valentinian emperor of the West, Valens emperor of the East. Thus what had always been thought of as the heartland of the Roman Empire—Spain, Gaul, and Italy—could fall to the barbarians in the fifth century, while yet "the empire" survived.

The decline in the cultural tradition of Greece and Rome was already noted by Tacitus in the second century. The imitativeness and triviality of much of later imperial literature may be attributed in part to the decline in the importance of community life that characterizes the period, and in part to the universal influence of rhetoric in education and letters, already noted in connection with the early empire. What literature there was, was rhetorical, and intellectual energy produced its most creative results in commentaries on the ancient masters. Like the literary tradition, the tradition of mathematics and natural science also declined through lack of creative force and loss of all confidence in the efficacy of reason. Similarly, philosophy expended its energies on exhortations to moral conduct, commentaries on earlier philosophers, or working out the details of a Platonic theology. By the fourth century the Christians already held the leadership of the intellectual world. For these reasons, and because of the actual paucity of the literary remains, only a brief examination of non-Christian Greek and Roman usage seems in order before proceeding to the Christian ascendancy.

In the Latin writings of the later empire the shifts in usage already noted are continued: from history as a literary genre to history as an account per se and the decline of the accuracy or factuality implied in the use of the word.

Historia is still used to indicate the literary genre;[2] it is distinguished from other literary genres,[3] certain rules are laid down,[4] and the word is also used to indicate particular works, instances of the genre "history."[5] But *historia* is more often used in its other mode as the facts or a factual account about something, emphasizing the content rather than the literary form. The subjects of history in this sense may be natural things,[6] social and political events,[7] and, in the grammatical tradition, following Dionysius Thrax, information in general.[8] More often, however, the subjects of history are gods and heroes; thus history as story. Servius, the commentator on Vergil, for example, noting the disagreement among Cato, Varro, and Diomedes about the arrival of Anchises in Italy, remarks, "such is the variety and confusion of stories (*historiarum*) among them."[9] Pomponius Porphyrio, a commentator on Horace, often explains obscure points by invoking the known story (*nota historia*) of a god or hero, and he applauds Pindar as a singer of new stories (*novas historias*) in dithyrambs.[10] That the use of *historia* no longer implies the accuracy, factuality, or truth of the matter is further suggested by Servius' use of *vera historia*, a true story,[11] reminder of a similar use by Aulus Gellius.

If the uses of *historia* indicate the persistence of change from the earlier to the later empire, the adjective *historicus* does not exhibit a similar continuity of development. For the most part it is now used substantively to indicate a historian, thus retaining its intimate con-

[2] Serv. *Aen.* 1.443; Porphyrio *Carm.* 2.1.17; Mart. Cap. 5.526.

[3] Auson. 5.20.7–8; 21.25–26; 26.1–4; 18.10.21–22; Mart. Cap. 5.550; Serv. *Aen.* 1.373, 382.

[4] E.g., Amm. Marc. 27.2.11; 26.1.1; Fortun. *Rhet.* pp. 83, 10–13; 84, 14–20; Mart. Cap. 5.551–52; Serv. *Aen.* 9.742.

[5] E.g., Amm. Marc. 24.2.16; Dar. Phryg. *Tro.* pp. 1, 14; Diom. *Gramm.* 1 (1.341, 4); Porphyrio *Carm.* 2.1.1; *Serm.* 1.1.101–2; Veget. *Mil.* 1.8; 4.28.

[6] Serv. *Aen.* 2.15; 3.76.

[7] Auson. 20.15.69; Porphyrio *Carm.* 2.1.10, 12.1; *Serm.* 2.1.14.

[8] Diom. *Gramm.* 2 (1.426, 18–26); 3 (1.482, 11); Donat. *V. Verg.* 191–99.

[9] Serv. *Aen.* 4.427; cf. 1.168, 487; Auson. 12.10; Macrob. *Sat.* 1.8.4; Porphyrio *Carm.* 3.19.

[10] Porphyrio *Carm.* 1.6.8; 3.7.16; 19.1–3; 4.2.10; 7.27–28; *Ep.* 3.9–10, 17.8.

[11] Serv. *Auct. Aen.* 1.651; cf. Serv. *Aen.* 1.526 and Auson. 19.76.1–4.

nection with history as a literary genre.[12] It is also used attributively, on occasion, as "factual."[13]

In the Greek writings of late antiquity the occurrences of ἱστορεῖν and ἱστορία are found mostly in the literature of commentary and doxography. They reflect the peculiar concern of that literature, and perhaps of that age generally, to hand down and explicate the thought of the old masters.

The verb is still occasionally used in its oldest sense, "to inquire,"[14] but more frequently in its latest sense, as what is "related." This may be events,[15] natural phenomena,[16] well-known persons,[17] or the gods;[18] but usually it has to do with opinions,[19] carrying on a use first found in the writings of Plutarch, Sextus Empiricus, and Epictetus. The noun is occasionally used as a literary work,[20] but for the most part a "history" is an informational account or information. It is so used by Alexander of Aphrodisias, known as *Exegetes,* one of the most voluminous of the ancient commentators on Aristotle and certainly the most important for the subsequent tradition. He observes that, on Aristotle's view, "both facts and histories (αἱ μαθήσεις τε καὶ ἱστορίαι)" are derived especially from hearing, whereas knowledge (ἐπιστήμη) comes especially from vision.[21] And here again, the old opposition between history and rational or contemplative knowledge is seen. On the other hand, Iamblichus, the Neoplatonist, contrasts ἱστορίαι with δόγματα, informing us that cases of life after death are known from both kinds of

[12] E.g., Amm. Marc. 21.10.6; 23.4.10; Auson. 18.5.41–42; Macrob. *Sat.* 5.14.11; Serv. *Aen.* 7.678; 8.190; *Auct. Aen.* 1.41; 3.334; Veget. *Mil.* 1.praef.

[13] E.g., Auson. 12.2.4; Diom. *Gramm.* 2 (1.440, 2), 3 (1.482, 31 sqq.); Serv. *Auct. Aen.* 9.144.

[14] Aet. *Plac.* (Diels, *DG* 307a4–8); Alex. Aph. *In Mete.,* pp. 40, 23–24; 31, 7–8; *In Sens.,* p. 4, 13–17.

[15] Olymp. *In Alc.,* pp. 167, 23–24; 155, 16–17; 154, 9–10 citing Xen. on the Persian παιδεία.

[16] Alex. Aph. *In Mete.,* pp. 31, 21–22; 37, 5–9; *In Sens.,* p. 72, 3–4; Olymp. *In Alc.,* p. 218, 14–15; Procl. *In Crat.,* p. 34, 24.

[17] Iamb. *VP,* pp. 11, 3; 22, 4; 23, 9; 25, 11; 41, 12; 68, 13; 99, 7; 105, 12; 106, 11; 136, 13; Porph. *V. Pyth.* 61 (p. 52, 7–9), 55 (p. 47, 20–22).

[18] Porph. *V. Pyth.* 2 (18, 10–12).

[19] E.g., Alex. Aph. *In Metaph.,* pp. 51, 12; 52, 10; 120, 1, 6, 15–17; Olymp. *In Alc.,* pp. 43, 12; 50, 8; Porph. *V. Pyth.* 44 (40, 20–23); Simp. *In Cael.* 510a41; *In Phy.* f. 25ʳ 16 (Diels, *DG* 483, 8–10).

[20] E.g., Porph. *Antr.* 2 (p. 55, 14–18); *V. Pyth.* 5 (p. 19, 15–17).

[21] *In Sens.,* p. 12, 6–10.

source.[22] Ἱστορία may also indicate an informational account about natural phenomena[23] or the gods.[24]

Often, however, ἱστορία means an informational account about opinions. Themistius, the fourth-century philosopher and rhetorician, intimate of the emperors Constantius and Theodosius, was also an expositor of Plato and Aristotle. His paraphrase of Aristotle's *De Anima* (1.2) begins, "Now it is clear from the history that two things to understand (θεωρεῖν) about the soul have been put forward, change and knowledge (κίνησιν καὶ γνῶσιν)." After discussing the views of Anaxagoras, Empedocles, Heraclitus, and Hippo, he concludes the discussion by saying, "Let us, then, end the history given out to us about the soul (τὴν παρὰ δοθεῖσαν ἡμῖν ἱστορίαν περὶ ψυχῆς)."[25] The change in the meaning of "history" from the fifth century B.C. to the fourth century A.D., even within the Peripatetic School, is clearly illustrated by this passage. Aristotle referred to his inquiry as τῆς ψυχῆς ἱστορία, that is, the facts or a factual account about the soul (*De An.* 1.1); and he began it by a review of the opinions of his predecessors (τὰς τῶν προτέρων δόξας). As Themistius understands it, however—and he is writing a paraphrase, not a commentary or an exposition—what is sought is knowledge or understanding (θεωρεῖν) about the soul, and one is to begin by examining the "history" of previous opinions. For Aristotle, the history was a first-order sort of knowledge, the facts about the subject matter; for Themistius, the history is a second-order sort of knowledge, the facts about previous opinions about the subject matter.

Similarly Aetius tells us the opinions of the Pythagoreans and of Philip of Opus about the earth and the counter-earth "according to the Aristotelian history (Ἀριστοτέλειον ἱστορίαν).[26] And Alexander of Aphrodisias repeatedly uses ἱστορία to indicate Aristotle's accounts of the opinions of his predecessors.[27]

The third century of Christianity within the Roman Empire was one of intermittent persecution except for the official suppression

---

[22] *VP*, p. 30, 15–16.
[23] E.g., Alex. Aph. *In Mete.*, pp. 32, 11–18; 57, 2–3, 25–28; *In Sens.*, p. 4, 13–17; Iamb. *VP*, p. 66, 9–12; Simp. in Diels, *DG*, pp. 480, 7; 483, 9.
[24] E.g., Iamb. *VP*, p. 169, 5; Porph. *Abst.* 1.25 (p. 102, 7–10).
[25] *In de An.*, p. 14, 4–6.
[26] Diels, *DG* 360b1–5.
[27] E.g., *In Metaph.*, pp. 9, 6; 16, 18; 23, 12; 41, 17; 42, 25; 60, 8.

under Decius (250–51). The empire was having its difficulties, and it was easy enough to blame both natural and social disasters on the growing movement, which neither believed in nor paid homage to the ancient gods. In 303, under Diocletian, though evidently at the insistence of Galerius, the Great Persecution began. It continued after Diocletian's abdication until 311 when Galerius, from his deathbed, granted toleration. The power struggles that dominated the beginning of the fourth century ended with Constantine's victory over Maxentius at the Milvian Bridge in 312. The victory was won under the sign of the cross, which Constantine adopted, according to Eusebius, after the appearance of a flaming cross in the noonday sky with the legend ἐν τούτῳ νικά, in this you shall conquer. It is a controverted question whether Constantine himself actually converted to Christianity,[28] but in 313 he issued an edict at Milan decreeing toleration for Christianity throughout the empire, and he later established Christianity as the official religion of the empire and moved the imperial capital from Rome to Byzantium, now christened Constantinople. Although pagan symbols continued to appear on imperial monuments and coins, Christianity was henceforth the dominant cultural and religious force. The pagan revival under the apostate Julian did not survive him.[29]

The problems confronting the *ecclesia* in late antiquity were both old and new. Responding to attempts to blame the Christians for social problems, the apologetical literature of the third, fourth, and fifth centuries is extensive, and makes substantially the same attacks on the popular cults as had the earlier apologies. In the continuing discussion about the proper way to interpret the Sacred Scriptures, the allegorical method of the Alexandrian School was opposed by the literal (or historical) exegesis of the Antiochene School in the works of its greatest representatives, Diodorus of Tarsus, Theodore of Mopsuestia, John Chrysostom, and Theodoretus of Cyrus.[30] And finally,

---

[28] In *The Conversion of Constantine*, ed. John W. Edie (New York: Holt, Rinehart and Winston, 1971) three distinct possible interpretations are offered—(1) that he was merely a political pragmatist, (2) that he was a pagan syncretist, and (3) that he was a genuine Christian convert—as well as a synthesis of all three.

[29] On Julian's use of education to promote this revival, see Glanville Downey, "The Emperor Julian and the Schools," *CJ* 53 (1957): 97–103.

[30] On Antioch itself and its role in the cultural history of the ancient world, see Glanville Downey, *The History of Antioch* (Princeton: Princeton University Press, 1961) and *Antioch in the Age of Theodosius* (Norman, Okla.: University of Oklahoma Press,

with the establishment of Christianity as the official religion of the empire, doctrinal and liturgical regularity, always ecclesiastically desirable, became politically imperative. Constantine himself presided over the first ecumenical convention of the Christian church, the Council of Nicaea, in 325. And the antiheretical literature of the fourth and fifth centuries especially is immense.

It has already been observed that the language of Christianity in the first and second centuries was Greek, even in the West, and that Latin came into its own in the third century. The Christian domain then began to mirror what was happening politically and culturally in the wider domain of the Roman Empire, namely, the growing estrangement of East and West. The Christian linguistic area divided into Western (Latin-speaking) and Eastern (Greek-speaking) blocs, which developed rather differently.[31] Since the Greek tradition is beginning to be separated from the Latin, and since it is this Latin

---

1962). On the School of Antioch, besides the general remarks in the discussions of particular figures in the Patrologies of Altaner and Quasten, see the historical, descriptive, and doctrinal profile (and basic bibliography) in the *Dictionnaire de Théologie Catholique* (Paris: Letouzey, 1899–1950), 1: 1435–39, article "Antioche (École Théologique d')." It is generally conceded that there was a substantial opposition between Alexandrian and Antiochene exegesis; e.g., A. Palmieri, "Alexandrian Mysticism and the Mystics of Christian Virginity," *Am. Cath. Qtrly. Rev.* 41 (1916): 390–405. But, to the contrary, Jacques Guillet, "Les éxègeses d'Alexandrie et d'Antioche. Conflit ou malentendu?" *Recherches de science religieuse* 34 (1947): 257–302, and Henri de Lubac, " 'Typologie' et 'Allegorisme'," ibid. 34 (1947): 180–226. On the later fortunes of the Antiochene method, see M. L. W. Laistner, "Antiochene Exegesis in Western Europe during the Middle Ages," *Harv. Theol. Rev.* 40 (1947): 19–31, and Beryl Smalley, *The Study of the Bible in the Middle Ages*, 2nd ed. (Oxford, 1952).

[31] See Gustave Bardy, *La question des langues dans l'église ancienne* (Paris, 1946). It has been shown, at least about Latin, that the language of the Christians differed sufficiently from the contemporaneous non-Christian language to justify speaking of a "Christian Latin language." The early contention was Schrijnen's. Einar Löfstedt [*Syntactica* (Lund, 1933), pp. 458ff.] noted the gradualness of the transition to a Christian Latin and argued that it was a matter more often of transformations than of neologisms. The thesis was most thoroughly explored and documented in the numerous studies of Christine Mohrmann. The state of the discussion as well as its prior history was well summarized by J. de Ghellinck ["Latin chrétien ou langue latine des chrétiens," *Les Études Classiques* 8 (1939): 449–78], who remained unconvinced. By 1946 Mohrmann ["Quelques traits caractéristiques du Latin des Chrétiens," *Miscellanea Giovanni Mercati* (Vatican City, 1946), p. 437] considered that the existence of the special language was already established, and proceeded to outline and document some of the traits of that special language. Numerous short studies will be found in her *Études sur le latin des chrétiens*, 2nd ed. (Rome, 1961). Also see the bibliography in Jean Cousin, *Bibliographie de la langue latine, 1880–1948* (Paris: Belles Lettres, 1951), "Latine 'chrétien,' " pp. 31–32.

tradition that constitutes the substance of the Christian intellectual inheritance of the Middle Ages, the Greek Christian writers might be the first to consider.

The use of ἱστορεῖν by the Christian writers of late antiquity is not extensive. While it is distributed, broadly speaking, into the same major groups as previously (i.e., to inquire and to record) Christian usage follows non-Christian in making the former virtually obsolete. Not surprisingly, nearly all of the uses of the verb either directly or indirectly relate to things Christian.

Ἱστορεῖν sometimes means to inquire into natural things. Theodoretus of Cyrus, the last representative of the Antiochene School during its most creative period, demonstrates the existence of Divine Providence from, among other things, the construction of the human body; and in particular the process of respiration, "as those who have inquired (ἱστορήσαντες) into such things closely say," leads us to see this.[32] Ἱστορεῖν as learning by inquiry into natural things is found in Basil the Great, the first of the three eminent Cappadocian Fathers. He shows us various ways in which, as God saw, water is good, among which is that "often it springs even from mines that it has crossed, deriving warmth from them, and rises boiling, and bursts forth of a burning heat, as may be learned by inquiry (ἔξεστιν ἱστορῆσαι) about islands and coastal places."[33]

A quasi-natural subject of inquiry is the going-forth and transmigration of souls. Methodius, noteworthy principally for his opposition to Origen on the preexistence of the soul, tells us that "The arrangement of the soul immediately in its going forth may be understood as that of the body in the earth. Now if some phenomenon of having gone to sleep is learned by inquiry (ἱστορεῖται), the like will be seen to be the arrangement which the body has."[34] Ἱστορεῖν is used to indicate inquiring about the gods in the writings of Athanasius, bishop of Alexandria, exiled five times because of his attacks on Arianism in defense of the Nicene Creed. In his apologetic *Oratio contra gentes* (18.3) he argues that the gods cannot be worshiped for having invented the arts, because an identifiable mortal invented each art, "according to those who have inquired (τῶν ἱστορησάντων)." A little further on (23.4) he argues that the variety of idol

---

[32] Theodoretus *Prov. or.* 3 (*PG* 83, 589D).
[33] Basil *Hexaem* 4.6 (*PG* 29, 93B); cf. 4.5 (92A).
[34] Meth. *Resurr.* 3.17.3 (p. 414, 6–9); cf. 3.18.8 (p. 416, 14–16).

cults shows that they are false; and he cites numerous examples, of which one is that, "as those who have inquired (οἱ ἱστορήσαντες) explain," the Pelasgians learned the names of the gods from the Egyptians but do not worship the same gods as the Egyptians.

Among the earliest historians of the new community, ἱστορεῖν is also used in the very ancient sense of firsthand visual inquiring, almost equivalent to seeing. Gelasius, for example, uses it about natural things and social customs.[35] But more often it has to do with social and political events. Thus Eusebius tells us that he "was present and observed (ἱστορήσαμεν)" Christians being tortured and beheaded,[36] and that he "was present and saw (τε παρὼν καὶ ἱστορήσας)" idolatrous cities that had been desolated in accordance with divine providence.[37] And he has Constantine, showing the benefits to the people of his reign and of the Christian God, say that the people "have observed (ἱστόρησαν) battles and have seen (ἐθεάσαντο) the way in which the providence of God assigned the victory to the people."[38] Similarly, Sozomen talks about "those who wanted to see (οἱ ἱστορήσοντες)" Didymus and Paulinus.[39]

The more common meaning of the verb is "to record," as it has been since the Hellenistic Age. Sometimes what is "recorded" concerns natural things or human customs. Basil explains that heat causes the existence of waters all over the earth, as the writers of world travels have recorded (ἱστορήκασιν).[40] Theophilus of Antioch establishes that the Pentateuch is older than the writings of any other nation, according to what Manetho, Menander, and Josephus "have recorded (ἱστορήκασι) about our chronology." For the Pentateuch does not merely include the years from some great war or king, but from the creation of the world, which is not the number of years that Plato alleges, "nor yet 15 times 10,375 years as we have already mentioned that Apollonius the Egyptian recorded (ἱστορεῖν)."[41] What is recorded also sometimes has to do with famous persons or the gods.

---

[35] Gelas. *H.E.* 2.17.29–30; 3.9.4; cf. Eus. *H.E.* 7.18 (*PG* 20, 680C–D).

[36] Eus. *H.E.* 8.9 (*PG* 20, 760B).

[37] Eus. *Or. Const.* 16 (*GCS* 7.176, 30–177, 4).

[38] Ibid. 26 (*GCS* 7.192, 18–20).

[39] Sozom. *H.E.* 3.15.3; 4.28.5. Eus. at *V. Const.* 2.22 (*GCS* 7.50, 8–16) uses ἱστόρησεν in a way that plays on both senses, firsthand visual inquiry and recording, and defies exclusive selection.

[40] Basil *Hexaem.* 3.6 (*PG* 29, 65C); cf. 4.5 (92A) and Sozom. *H.E.* 7.26.3 and (on customs) 1.12.11; 7.18.7.

[41] Theophilus *Autol.* 3.23 (*PG* 6, 1156A); cf. 3.36 (1161A).

Athanasius attacks the divinity of the gods on the grounds that they were mere mortals who "were decreed to be called gods by the order of Theseus, of whom we have been informed (ἱστορουμένου) by the Hellenes." And he defends the divinity of Jesus on the grounds that, although "many wise men and magi have been recorded (ἱστοροῦν-ται) among the Chaldaeans and Egyptians and Indians," none had the power that Jesus has to save people even after his death through his teachings.[42]

Most often, however, the verb used as "record" or "report" has to do with the Sacred Scriptures. Athanasius attacks the disbelief of the Jews, saying, "But the whole Scripture is filled with contradicting the disbelief of the Jews. For who among the just, the holy prophets, and the patriarchs recorded (ἱστορηθέντων) in the divine Scriptures had the birth of his body from a virgin?"[43] Likewise, Theodoretus tells us that the author of Deuteronomy "recorded (ἱστόρησεν) things about the cities, to which he ordered those to flee who had fallen into un-willing murders." He also uses ἱστορεῖν in this way referring to parts of the New Testament. "For also the blessed Matthew has given pro-phetic testimony, recorded (ἱστόρησαν) the mourning of children." And again he quotes Matthew (27:57–60) as to the body of Jesus, and adds, "The thrice-blessed Mark has made the same point; and I shall tell you what he relates (ἱστόρησεν)."[44] Methodius tells us what is recorded about Lazarus;[45] Eusebius tells us what Genesis, Jose-phus, Luke, and a certain Dionysius "relate."[46] And the fifth-century ecclesiastical historian Sozomen uses the verb with an extremely broad scope when he describes a certain Addas who had "great learning of the things that had been recorded (ἱστορημένων) by Greek and by ecclesiastical writers."[47]

---

[42] Athan. *C. gent.* 10.1; cf. *Inc. Verb.* 50.1; Theophilus *Autol.* 2.7 (*PG* 6, 1057A); Sozom. *H.E.* 1.1.16–17; Eus. *Dem. Ev.* 4.16.5 (*GCS* 23.184, 24–27).

[43] Athan. *Inc. Verb.* 35.7; Theophilus [*Autol.* 3.18 (*PG* 6, 1145B)] speaks of "our prophet and the servant of God, Moses giving an account of (ἐξιστορῶν) the origin of the world."

[44] Theodoretus *Q. Deut.* 6.1 (*PG* 80, 408B); cf. *In Zach.* 14.10 (*PG* 81, 1956B); *Dial. 3* (*PG* 83, 257A); Cyr. Al. *In Jo.* (*PG* 73, 166D); Gelas. *H.E.* 2.17.28; Sozom. *H.E.* 8.18.8 (on the O.T.); 2.1.5 (on the N.T.).

[45] Meth. *Resurr.* 3.18.4–5 (p. 415, 13–18); cf. 3.5.8; Theodoretus *Q. Reg.* 3 (*PG* 80, 740).

[46] Sozom. *H.E.* 1.7 (*PG* 20, 92B–93A) on Genesis; 1.8 (105C), 1.10 (112A), 1.11 (116A) on Josephus; 3.4 (220A) on Luke; 3.4 (221A) on Dionysius.

[47] Sozom. *H.E.* 7.21.8; cf. 7.12.4, where ἱστορημένων is the result of φιλοσοφη-σάντων, and Eus. *H.E.* 3.6 (*PG* 20, 229C).

There is another use of the verb by Methodius, which has the added feature that "what is recorded" refers to something other than the literal meaning of the words; for example, on a passage in Judges (9:8–15) in which the trees choose a leader, Methodius comments: "Now it is clear that this was not said about trees that have grown from the earth. For unensouled trees would hardly assemble themselves to elect a ruler, since they are fixed in the ground by roots. Rather this is recorded (ἱστορεῖται) wholly about souls, which, before the Incarnation of Christ, had all grown to wood through their sins."[48] This sort of use becomes increasingly important in Christian writings.

The uses of ἱστορία by the Christian writers of late antiquity still reflect the modal distinction between a kind of account and a kind of literary work; but the latter sense is now very rare. There are some few cases: Sozomen uses ἱστορία quite generally as "narrative" in his Prefatory Address to the emperor Theodosius;[49] and he elsewhere notes the accuracy that is required of history[50] and states that what is fitting in a history (ἱστορία πρέπον), its task, "is only to relate what happened."[51] Theophilus of Antioch refers to what is contained in his own book, no longer extant, *On Histories* and to the *Histories* of Herodotus and Thucydides.[52] Theodoretus refers to the *History* of Josephus and to the "first *History of the Maccabees.*"[53]

Nearly always, however, the noun is used in the older of the two modes of its usage, emphasizing the content rather than the form, as information or an informational account. Among older subjects, it is still used, at least by Basil, about natural things.[54] Sozomen uses ἱστορία for firsthand acquaintance with buildings and places famous for sacred or secular reasons.[55] "History" referring to events is used by John Chrysostom in introducing his account of the provenance of the Septuagint; he says, "But in order that you might learn that the

---

[48] Meth. *Symp.* 10.2 (p. 123, 4–9).
[49] Ibid. Praef. 4.
[50] Ibid. 1.1.16.
[51] Ibid. 3.15.10.
[52] Theophilus *Autol.* 2.30; 3.2; and cf. 3.22.
[53] Theodoretus *In Dan.* 11.28; 11.27; cf. Eus. *H.E.* 1.5 (*PG* 20, 85A); 1.8 (101B, 104B); 3.6 (224C); 3.8 (236C).
[54] Basil *Hexaem.* 4.3 (*PG* 29, 84A); 8.8 (184D); cf. Eus. *V. Const.* 4.7 (*GCS* 7.120, 12–16); Gelas. *H.E.* 2.17.28, and 3.9.3 (about social customs).
[55] Sozom. *H.E.* 2.26.4; 4.5.4; 5.2.19; cf. Eus. *H.E.* 6.11 (*PG* 20, 541C); *Dem. Ev.* 9.1.3 (*GCS* 23.404, 9).

place did not sanctify the books, but rather polluted them, I shall recount to you the ancient history (ἱστορίαν πάλαιαν)."⁵⁶ Theodoretus uses "history" about a famous person, and, of course, it is a person famous for religious reasons. In the beginning of his account of the life of Peter the Ascetic, he says, "I know the sea of his successes, and on account of this I am afraid to approach the history (ἱστορία) of what has been told about him."⁵⁷ And Eusebius gives us the account (ἱστορία) that Julius Africanus had given to explain the apparent inconsistency between Matthew's and Luke's versions of Christ's genealogy.⁵⁸

Among more recent subjects, there are also histories about the gods. The second book of Theophilus' apologetic *Ad Autolycum* takes up the standard attack on belief in the pagan gods. In the introductory section (2.1) he says that he wants to save his audience from vain worship, "but also, I want to make the truth clear to you from a few of your own histories (τῶν κατὰ σὲ ἱστοριῶν) which you read but do not quite understand." He goes on (2.2) to argue that there is a contradiction between imagining the gods as men and then worshiping them as gods, "and this is what happens to you, too, in reading the histories (τὰς ἱστορίας) and genealogies of the so-called gods." He sums up another argument in the same book: "We have shown from their own histories (ἐξ αὐτῶν τῶν ἱστοριῶν) that the names of those who are called gods are found to be the names of men who lived among them."⁵⁹

Of course, an informational account about the events of the new community, the new ἐκκλησία, will be an ἐκκλησιαστικὴ ἱστορία. The founder of the new literary genre called ecclesiastical history is Eusebius, who intends, he tells us, "to write an account of the successions of the holy apostles, as well as of the times which have elapsed from the days of our Saviour to our own; and to relate the many important events which are said to have occurred in the history of the church (κατὰ τὴν ἐκκλησιαστικὴν ἱστορίαν)."⁶⁰ He is aware that of earlier ecclesiastical writers (τῶν ἐκκλησιαστικῶν συγγραφέων)

---

⁵⁶ Io. Chrys. *Adv. Jud.* 1.6 (*PG* 48, 851); Eus. also uses ἱστορία about past events [*H.E.* 1.7 (*PG* 20, 96B); 1.5 (81A–B)] and about current events [*V. Const.* 1.23 (*GCS* 7.19, 10–12), *Pr. Const.* 7.10 (*GCS* 7.215, 8–10)], and opposes ἐξ ἀρχαίων ἱστορίας to τὴν θείαν Γραφήν [*H.E.* 2.1 (137A)].
⁵⁷ Theodoretus *Rel. Hist.* 9 (*PG* 82, 1377D).
⁵⁸ Eus. *H.E.* 1.7 (*PG* 20, 89B–C).
⁵⁹ Theophilus *Autol.* 2.34, trans. Dods (*ANF*).
⁶⁰ Eus. *H.E.* 1.1 (*PG* 20, 48B), trans. Richardson (*NPNF*).

none has done this, and he expects it to be appreciated "by those who have a love of learning about history (περὶ τὸ χρηστομαθὲς τῆς ἱστορίας ἔχουσιν)."⁶¹ The "history" here is certainly an informational account; but there are some new features. Since the ἐκκλησία begins with Christ, the account about it (τῆς ἐκκλησιαστικῆς . . . τὴν ἱστορίαν) must begin with Christ's divine economy.⁶²

Again, Sozomen is aware of the inherent difficulty of writing an ecclesiastical history (ἐκκλησιαστικὴν ἱστορίαν συγγράψαι); yet he is convinced "that since the subject is *not* the achievements of human beings, it might seem almost unbelievable that such a *history* could be written by me; but for God nothing is impossible."⁶³ History's subject matter is in part the doings of divine providence, and the possibility of its being written, therefore, as well as its fidelity, depends on God. It is also clear from the very beginning of ecclesiastical history that the genre has an apologetical function. Eusebius first discusses the Old Testament prophecies and how Jesus existed long before his appearance as a mortal; then he comments, "I have of necessity prefaced my history (πρὸ τῆς ἱστορίας) with these matters in order that no one, judging from the date of his incarnation, may think that our Saviour and Lord Jesus, the Christ, has but recently come into being."⁶⁴

The examination of Christian usage in the first and second centuries suggested, scarcely more, that the Scriptures might be "histories" or at least "historylike." In this later period it is clear that the Scriptures, both the Old and the New Testaments, are thought to be and to contain "histories." There are numerous cases referring to the Testaments. First, in the Old Testament, Theophilus explains the meaning of "firmament" in Genesis: "In the very beginning, therefore, of the history and genesis of the world (τῆς ἱστορίας καὶ γενέσεως τοῦ κοσμοῦ), the holy Scripture spoke not about this (firmament) which we see, but rather about another, heaven, which is invisible to us . . . ." Again, introducing his quotation of the description of Eden, he says, "And Scripture thus relates the words of the sacred history (τῆς

---

⁶¹ Eus. *H.E.* 1.1 (52B).

⁶² Eus. *H.E.* 1.1 (52B–53A). The enterprise is also called a "history" at 8.2 (744C) and an "ecclesiastical history" at 1.5 (80D) and 2.praef. (132C).

⁶³ Sozom. *H.E.* 1.1.11 (italics added). He also calls his work ecclesiastical history at Praef. 17, 1.1.18–19, 1.8.14, and 9.1.23.

⁶⁴ Eus. *H.E.* 1.4 (*PG* 20, 76B–C).

ἱστορίας τῆς ἱερᾶς)."⁶⁵ Likewise John Chrysostom advises us to learn from what happened to David and Absalom: "let the history (ἡ ἱστορία) be a straitening of your life."⁶⁶ Theodoretus refers to the "histories" in the prophets.⁶⁷ Besides these references to particular episodes in the Old Testament, Origen refers to the whole Pentateuch as a history. Having given several examples of passages that contain a "type" or "pattern" of broader or different significance than the text, he asks, "But do you wish to learn, about the rest of the history (ἱστορίας), if it also happened typically (τυπικῶς)?"⁶⁸

In similar ways, the various parts of the New Testament are also called "histories." Eusebius says that his ecclesiastical history must begin "with the main and lordliest events of the whole history about Jesus (τῆς κατ' αὐτὸν ἱστορίας ἁπάσης)" and also uses ἱστορία about the acts of Jesus' disciples.⁶⁹ John Chrysostom explains why Matthew "called the history Good News (Εὐαγγέλιον τὴν ἱστορίαν ἐκάλεσεν)," and distinguishes Matthew's Gospel from John's in that the latter wanted especially to write about the Godhead, "and this is clear both from the history itself (ἐξ αὐτῆς τῆς ἱστορίας) and from the introduction to the Gospel."⁷⁰ Likewise Origen refers to the Gospels of John and Luke as "histories," and insists that the "history" about Jesus is no more improbable than the Old Testament "histories" of Adam, Eve, Cain, Noah, and others;⁷¹ and Methodius mentions how Ananias preached to Paul and baptized him "as the history (ἱστορία) relates in Acts" and refers to the "history" of Lazarus.⁷² It should be clear that the Scriptures are here called "histories" not because they have a particular literary form but, rather, because they consist in a narrative account about persons or events.

There is more to be said about these Scripture "histories." Origen suggests that it is very difficult or even impossible to establish the

⁶⁵ Theophilus *Autol.* 2.13; 2.20; cf. 2.32; 3.19.

⁶⁶ Io. Chrys. *In Psalm.* 3.1 (*PG* 55, 35); cf. *De Dav.* 7 (*PG* 54, 758) and Eus. *H.E.* 1.3 (*PG* 20, 73C).

⁶⁷ Theodoretus *In Jer.* 45 (*PG* 81, 705B); cf. *In Soph.* 2.12 (*PG* 81, 1852A) and Origen *C. Cels.* 1.44.

⁶⁸ Origen *Princ.* 4.1.13 (*PG* 11, 369B). On Origen's exegetical method, see Henri de Lubac, *Histoire et esprit: l'intelligence de Écriture d'après Origène* (Paris, 1950).

⁶⁹ Eus. *H.E.* 1.2 (*PG* 20, 53A–B); 1.12 (117C, 120A).

⁷⁰ Io. Chrys. *In Matth.* 1.4 (*PG* 57, 16); 1.7 (17).

⁷¹ Origen *Luc.* Frs. 223, 17e (*GCS, vol. 9*); *C. Cels.* 1.43 and 1.40 mentions the ἱστορία of the virgin birth and the Gospel as a collection of ἱστορίαι.

⁷² Meth. *Symp.* 3.9.75 (p. 37, 16–19); Meth. *Resurr.* 1.52.1 (p. 307, 8–12); cf. Gelas. *H.E.* 2.17.3–5.

truth of a history. He says, "It is necessary to say that the endeavor to show, with regard to almost any history (σχεδὸν πᾶσαν ἱστορίαν), however true, that it actually occurred, and to produce a cataleptic presentation regarding it, is one of the most difficult undertakings, and is in some instances an impossibility."[73] So that one must judge carefully which ones to assent to (συγκαταθήσεται) and which to accept figuratively (τροπολογήσει). He even admits that "in the Gospels in the literal histories of events (ταῖς τὸ ῥητὸν γεγενημέναις ἱστορίαις) other things are inserted which did not happen."[74] He elsewhere says, "And we have this to say by way of anticipation about the whole history (ἱστορίαν) related in the Gospels concerning Jesus, not as inviting men of acuteness to a simple and unreasoning faith, but wishing to show that there is need of candor in those who are to read, and of much investigation, and, so to speak, insight into the meaning (εἰς τὸ βούλημα) of the writers, that the object with which each event has been recorded may be discovered."[75] The writer of the "history" has some other object of thought (διάνοια) than to inform, some other meaning or purpose (βούλημα).

Similarly, Theodotus relates what happened "according to the history (κατὰ τὴν ἱστορίαν) in Amos," and adds, "but equally, along with these things, others are brought to light."[76] Methodius makes the same point, correcting an interpretation of Paul: "in my estimation it would have been pointless for that wise man who wrote under inspiration—I mean Paul—to apply the union of the first man and woman to Christ and the Church if the Scripture had in view nothing loftier than the words and the history (τῶν ῥητῶν καὶ τῆς ἱστορίας)."[77] History thus means what the actual words say, the literal sense of Scripture,[78] but the Scripture histories communicate something else in addition to or instead of what the actual words say.

There are further instances of "history" used to refer to *kinds* of things the Scriptures might communicate besides their literal ref-

---

[73] Origen *C. Cels.* 1.42.
[74] Origen *Princ.* 4.1.16 (*PG* 11, 377B).
[75] Origen *C. Cels.* 1.42, trans. Crombie (*ANF*); cf. *Luc.* Fr. 125.
[76] Theodoretus *In Am.* 1.2 (*PG* 81, 1668A).
[77] Meth. *Symp.* 3.1, trans. Musurillo (*ACW*).
[78] For ἱστορία as the literal sense, see Cyr. Al. *In Luc.* (*PG* 72, 684D) and *In Jo.* (*PG* 73, 228A–B, 325C, 337A). On Cyril's exegetical method, see A. Kerrigan, "The Objects of the Literal and Spiritual Senses of the New Testament according to St. Cyril of Alexandria," *Studia Patristica* I [= *Texte und Untersuchungen zur Gesch. der altchr. Literatur* 63 (1957)]: 354–74.

erence. In his *Homily on the Hexaemeron*, Basil says (6.2) that "the dogma of theology is sown mystically everywhere in the history (πανταχοῦ τῇ ἱστορίᾳ)," that "the history (ἡ ἱστορία) wishes to exercise our mind" (2.3), and that "in the form of history (ἐν ἱστορίας εἴδει) legislation is given out" (2.8) that the day has priority over night. Similarly, Theodoretus explains that Zachariah's prediction of living waters going forth from Jerusalem refers to Jesus, adding that "it is permitted to discern the prophetic truth in the history (ἱστορίαν) itself."[79] Methodius tells us that "the history (ἱστορία) about Jonah contains a great mystery."[80] John Chrysostom thinks that we should learn and teach the "histories" in order to strengthen our souls.[81] And in Origen's treatise *On First Principles* (4.1.9), the recognition that there are contradictory statements in Scripture histories occasions an extended discussion of the principles of interpretation to be used in such cases. Briefly, the point is that the histories contain certain mysteries that aim at the improvement of our souls; thus they may be understood both figuratively (τροπικῶς) and bodily (σωματικῶς), and the contradictions or things that did not happen which we may find in these histories are put there to force us to see that there is a figurative meaning. Of course, not all the histories did not actually happen. Indeed, most of them are true; but whereas the whole Scripture seems to have a spiritual or figurative sense, the whole does not seem to have a bodily sense.[82]

It is appropriate to conclude this exposition with the Latin Christian usage of the third, fourth, and fifth centuries. For, on the one hand, the fall of the Western empire and the accession of Christianity to a position of cultural dominance in both the West and the East signal the end of that political and cultural organization of the Mediterranean and European world, the career of which we call antiquity. And, on the other hand, it is precisely the Christian thought of these centuries that, because of the growing estrangement of Eastern

[79] Theodoretus *In Zach.* 14.8 (*PG* 81, 1953D); cf. *Q. Reg.* 1, Q. 7 (*PG* 80, 537C), *In Psalm.* 13 (*PG* 80, 949B), *In Isai.* 15.2 (*PG* 81, 340D), *In Ezech.* 31.14 (*PG* 81, 1125C), *In Nah.* 2.1 (*PG* 81, 1797A).
[80] Meth. *Resurr.* 2.25.1 (p. 380, 16–19).
[81] Io. Chrys. *De Dav.* 7 (*PG* 54, 759); cf. *In Psalm.* 46.1 (*PG* 55, 188).
[82] On Scripture speaking ἱστορικῶς, see Theodoretus *In Dan.* 11.41 (*PG* 81, 1532), Origen *Luc.* Fr. 217 (*GCS* 49.321), Cyr. Al. *In Jo.* (*PG* 73, 960C, 961B).

and Western Christendom and because Christianity is the only creative cultural force in the West, provides the intellectual foundations
of the European Middle Ages. Let us consider first the period before
Augustine.

The uses of *historia* in the Latin Christian writings of late antiquity
exhibit the ancient modal distinction between informational account
and literary genre. Although the former is now clearly dominant,
there are some few instances of history as a literary genre. Of all the
Latin Fathers, Jerome was perhaps the most widely educated and
most scholarly; and at a time when the Latin-speaking West was
rapidly losing touch with the Greek-speaking East, he was recognized
as the one person who knew Latin, Greek, and Hebrew. Jerome uses
historia to indicate a written work about events in the public world in
one of his letters (60.12.3). He writes: "Antiquity admired a noble
man, Quintus Fabius, who is the writer of a Roman History (*Romanae
scriptor historiae*) but made a name even more from paintings than
from letters." He also mentions various others who write history,[83]
and even Eusebius' *History of the Church.*[84]

Lactantius, an African rhetor turned Christian and said by
Jerome[85] to have been a student of Arnobius, pursuing the standard
apologetical attack on the pagan gods, relies heavily on a work by
Euhemerus, which is called *historia* and is about the gods. According
to him, "Euhemerus, an ancient author, who was from the city of
Messene, collected the things done (*res gestas*) by Jove and the others
who are considered gods, and composed a *historia* from the titles and
sacred inscriptions which were in the most ancient temples. . . . This
historia Ennius translated and followed."[86]

Historia as a literary genre, at least as regards the gods, is also
distinguished from other genres. Speaking of certain rumors about
the gods, Arnobius, African rhetor turned Christian apologist, says,
"Well, let us grant that all these things have been handed down to
the disgrace of the immortal gods by the jesting poets (*a ludentibus
poetis*). But what about these things which the histories contain (*historiae continent*), weighty, serious, careful, and handed down in hidden

[83] E.g., Hieron. *In Dan.* 2 (on 5:1, 6:1, 7:5), 4 (on 12:1–3); *In Ezech.* 2 (on 5:1
sqq.) [*PL* 25, 52]; *In Isai.* 5 (on 23:6) [*PL* 24, 202]; *Ep.* 22.35.8; also Arn. *Adv. Nat.*
6.6, 1.52.

[84] Hieron. *Vir. Ill.* Prol. (*PL* 23, 634A).

[85] Ibid. 80.

[86] Lact. *Div. Inst.* 1.11.33 (*PL* 6, 174A); cf. 1.11.34, 36, 45, 63, 65; 1.13.2; 1.14.1.

mysteries—are these jokes (*lascivia*) thought up by the poets? If they seemed such absurd fables (*ineptiarum talius fabulae*) you would neither retain them in use nor celebrate then as festivals through the years."[87] Lactantius also distinguishes history from poetry in making the same point about Jove in particular. He writes: "Therefore, not only all the poets, but also the writers of histories and ancient events (*historiarum quoque ac rerum antiquarum scriptores*), who handed down to memory his deeds in Italy, agree that he was a man; the Greeks Diodorus and Thallus, the Latins Nepos, Cassius and Varro."[88] This is the old distinction between poetry and history as narrating, respectively, fables and actual events. It is worthy of note, however, that whereas this distinction earlier entailed the exclusion of accounts of the gods from *historia*, now the distinction is made *among* accounts of the gods, some of which are taken to be true and others not.

However, *historia* far more often refers to an informational account per se than to an explicitly written account or the literary genre. In an older sense, Jerome tells us what the "writers of natural history (*scriptores naturalis historiae*) say," by which he means Aristotle, Theophrastus, and Pliny.[89] And he also uses *historia* about persons, indeed about himself, introducing his famous account of the dream in which he was accused of being a Ciceronian rather than a Christian. He says, "I will relate to you the history of my unhappiness (*meae infelicitatis historiam*)."[90]

A larger group of uses of *historia* indicates an informational account about social and political events. Replying to the charge that Christianity had brought disasters on the world, Arnobius says, "Go through your histories (*historias*) and you will be taught how often a prior age by the same diseases came to the wretchedness of poverty." And he goes on to list other "varieties of turpitude, those which histories of antiquity (*antiquitatis historiae*) supply."[91] Lactantius tells us that "all history (*omnis historia*) is full of examples"[92] of the wicked

---

[87] Arn. *Adv. Nat.* 5.1; cf. 7.38. Sid. Apoll. [*Ep.* 1.2.10] distinguishes *historia* from *epistula*.

[88] Lact. *Div. Inst.* 1.13.8 (*PL* 6, 188B).

[89] Hieron. *In Jer.* 3 (on 17:11) [*PL* 24, 789].

[90] Hieron. *Ep.* 22.29.7 (*PL* 22, 416). This may be the first instance of *historia* as an autobiographical account. It is echoed in the title of Abelard's *Historia calamitatum*. Sid. Apoll. [*Ep.* 7.9.5] relates an anecdote about a certain philosopher which *historia saecularis* relates; and cf. 8.3.4.

[91] Arn. *Adv. Nat.* 1.3, 5.8.

[92] Lact. *Div. Inst.* 6.6.17 (*PL* 6, 655A).

becoming more powerful than the good. Cyprian was another African rhetor turned Christian, and bishop of Carthage during the persecution of Decius. In a letter about the Donatist problem of baptizing heretics, he recounts how it happened that many people were led astray under such circumstances earlier; he says, "I want to set forth to you from history (*de historia*) what was done among us relating to this same thing."[93] In these passages, *historia* has to do with plagues, crimes, the careers of famous people of earlier times. These are like the events with which histories have had to do for a very long time—events in the public, human world. In the first two passages the plural is used, so that they might mean the account of these events. But in the latter two the singular is used, suggesting the meaning "past"; so that Lactantius would be saying that "the past" is full of examples, and Cyprian would be setting forth what happened "from the past."

A second subgroup of uses of *historia* in the sense of "the past" may be marked off, concerning events not in the public, human world, but in the biblical world. In order to understand the nontemporal arrangement of the Psalms, for example, Hilary of Poitiers says that ". . . we should be thoroughly instructed in the history of deeds and times (*in gestorum et temporum historia*). For according to *historia* the third Psalm is later than the fiftieth."[94] So that *historia* means the events of the biblical past. Similarly, Hilary instructs us, in interpreting the psalms, to examine the superscriptions in order to find out which ones have to do with *historia*. He says, "But other superscriptions, which signify either events according to history (*secundum historiam*), or times, or days, or have been composed of something else, show in what a psalm consists either in the interpretation of names, or in a comparison of deeds, or in similarity of kinds . . . e.g., a psalm with 'of David' or 'to David,' or 'Saul' in the title is foreseen to fall under the history of deeds (*sub gestorum historia*)."[95] Similarly, Jerome observes that Paul's statement (Gal. 1:17) that he went to Arabia and returned to Damascus before he went to Jerusalem disagrees with what is related in Acts. "The order of history (*historiae ordo*) does not seem to agree with it, recalling what Luke says in the Acts of the

---

[93] Cyprian *Ep.* 75.10 (*CSEL* 3.816, 17–18); cf. Hieron. *In Dan.* 1 (on 4:1a), *Ep.* 60.5.3 (*PL* 22, 592), *In Ezech.* 3, on 12:3 (*PL* 25, 102D).

[94] Hil. *Ps.* Prologus 9 (*PL* 9, 238B).

[95] Ibid. 22 (246A–B); cf. 5 (235A), 9 (238B), *Ps.* 51 (309A), 54.1 (347C), 63.1 (407C).

Apostles."⁹⁶ And he also tries to straighten out the order of events in Daniel; for he comments on the first dream: "This sketch which we now want to set forth, and which we are about to speak about, is prior, according to history (*iuxta historiam*) to the two above. . . . But in the above ones the order of history (*ordo historiae*) is followed."⁹⁷

The "order of history" does not apply only to events within the biblical world; Jerome is also concerned to correlate events in that world and events in the public world. He comments on the statement (Matt. 2:21) that "after Herod's death the angel of the Lord appeared to Joseph in Egypt," saying, "Many fall into error on account of ignorance of history (*propter ignorantiam historiae*), thinking that it is the same Herod by whom the Lord was ridiculed in his passion, and who is now accounted dead. So that Herod who later on was friendly with Pilate is the son of this Herod."⁹⁸ And similarly, he wants to clarify several statements in Daniel that seem to disagree with the succession of kings in Lydia and Persia.⁹⁹ So that *historia* as informational account about past events or the past may be applied to events either in the public world or in the biblical world, or both, but there was not understood to be any difference in kind between the history of the Jews and Christians and that of the nations, no difference *as history*.

In another large group of uses of *historia*, it indicates an informational account about the gods. The standard apologetical attack on the gods includes the claim that they are not divine. Lactantius argues that Saturn was the son of a mortal, and brings in Hermes Trismegistus as a witness: "And Trismegistus attests the truth of this; for when he said that very few had existed in whom there was perfect learning, he named among these his relatives Uranus, Saturn and Mercury. And because he ignored these things, he gave another history (*historiam*) in another place."¹⁰⁰ Elsewhere he refers to the true history (*vera historia*) of Jupiter.¹⁰¹ If accounts about the gods may be true, they may also be false; Arnobius insists that the *historiae* of the gods' mutilations, frenzies, rapes, and the like are *fictiones* and *falsa*.¹⁰²

---

⁹⁶ Hieron. *In Ep. ad Gal.* 1 (on 1:17) [*PL* 26, 328A].
⁹⁷ Hieron. *In Dan.* 2 (on 7:1).
⁹⁸ Hieron. *In Matth.* 1 (on 2:22) [*PL* 26, 29A].
⁹⁹ Hieron. *In Dan.* 2 (on 5:30–31; 6:1–2a), 4 (on 11:21; 12:8–10).
¹⁰⁰ Lact. *Div. Inst.* 1.11.61 (*PL* 6, 182A).
¹⁰¹ Ibid. 1.14.8–10 (191A).
¹⁰² Arn. *Adv. Nat.* 5.14–15.

Such "histories," furthermore, may mislead. Commodian, the first Latin Christian poet, also makes the apologetic attack on the gods, discussing Saturn's devouring of Jupiter:

> Who sent rain in those times, if Jupiter was dead?
> Moreover, is a god believed to be born of a mortal father?
> Saturn grew old on earth and died on earth.
> No one prophesied him before he came.
> Or, if he thunders, the law would have been given by him.
> The made-up histories (*historiae confectae*) mislead.[103]

Thus there are now understood to be both true and fanciful accounts of the gods, that is, accounts that are properly histories and those that are properly poetry or fable. *Historia* is being used to indicate what, in the opinion of the Christians, is true about those who are popularly esteemed gods, as distinct from myths or fables about them. Arnobius is willing to consider the latter *historiae* too, indeed he repeatedly calls them that in the fifth book of his apologetic discourse *Adversus Nationes*, which is devoted to attacking the gods. He rejects the imagined defense of the accounts as being meant only allegorically,[104] on the grounds that one cannot tell an allegorical story from a nonallegorical one, and insists that all of them are records of actual events (*rerum gestarum conscriptiones*) and hence are damning evidence against their divinity.[105]

In the Latin Christian writings of late antiquity, as in the Greek, history most frequently has to do with an account of something from the Old or New Testament. Most generally, it is suggested that they are or contain histories. Replying to the charge that the Old Testament is false, Arnobius says, "but if that *historia* of events is false, as you say, then how in so short a time has the whole world been filled with that religion?"[106] Rufinus, translating Origen, says that the belief that the world began in time is "one of the ecclesiastical articles that is held principally in accordance with faith in our history (*secundum historiae nostrae fidem*)."[107] And Jerome, quoting Exodus, refers to

---

[103] Commod. *Instr.* 1.6.10–15; cf. 1.9.5–9.
[104] Arn. *Adv. Nat.* 5.8 and 32; cf. 7.44.
[105] Ibid. 5.39; cf. 7.46 and 49.
[106] Ibid. 1.55.
[107] Rufin. *Pr. Orig.* 3.5.1.

the sighing of the Israelites, "according to the history (*iuxta historiam*)."[108] He elsewhere mentions Luke's *historia*, the *historia* that is related in Judges, and what the Gospel's *historia* says.[109]

The later Greek fathers discovered that there were some inconsistencies or even falsehoods within the Scriptures, and solved the problem by supposing that there was some further meaning to such "histories." Among the 156 heresies that Filastrius of Brescia includes in his *Book of Heresies* is that of permitting such an inconsistency: "There are other heretics who allow no small error about the inequality of the psalms, estimating that the whole book of Psalms is not by the most blessed David; and when they investigate the *historia* in order, they find inequality, that is, they discern that what is latest is placed first, and what is first is latest."[110] His solution is that the "inequalities according to history" are to be understood spiritually about Christ.[111] He also points out the heresy of finding ambiguity in Isaiah and being upset because "now investigating *historia*, now scrutinizing intelligible reason, they fall into ambiguity, when both according to the letter there is no small usefulness, and according to intelligible reason the celestial knowledge of Christ resounds."[112]

Similarly, Jerome advises us that "when the history contains either something impossible or a vice, it is transferred to higher things."[113] So that these accounts are called *historiae* and are taken to be capable of or to require being understood about something other than their literal meaning.

As with the Greek, so with the Latin fathers there is a third subgroup of uses of *historia* about events in the Old or New Testament, in which various things are indicated as the alternative meaning of the text. Jerome says that "when a passage does not fit according to history (*iuxta historiam*), it can have another meaning according to analogy."[114] And Prudentius, the greatest early Christian poet, suggests that the "history" of Lot has a prophetic meaning:

---

[108] Hieron. *Ep.* 18^A.2.2 (*CSEL* 54.76, 17).

[109] *In Ep. ad Gal.* 1 (on 1:17) [*PL* 26, 328A], *In Isai.* 17.62 [*PL* 24, 723], *Hom. Or. in Luc.* 27 (*PL* 26, 279D).

[110] Filastr. *Haer.* 130.1 (*CSEL* 38, 97–98); cf. 130.5 (38, 98).

[111] Ibid. 130.3 (38, 98); cf. 130.7 (38, 99).

[112] Ibid. 155.1 (38, 130).

[113] Hieron. *In Matth.* 3 (on 21:4, 5) [*PL* 26, 153A]; cf. *In Ep. ad Gal.* 3 (on 5:13) [*PL* 26, 434C–D], *Hom. Or. in Luc.* 5 [*PL* 26, 242A–B]; Rufin. *Pr. Orig.* 3.5.1.

[114] Hieron. *In Ezech.* 2 (on 7:13) [*PL* 25, 68]; cf. *Ep.* 53.9.4.

Take in the famous monuments of deeds,
in which *historia* gives beforehand a visible sign.[115]

The most usual distinction, however, is between the letter and the spirit of a text, or between *historia* and *intelligentia*. These are taken to be different ways of reading and understanding the Scriptures. About Jesus' sending two of the disciples to take an ass, Jerome says, "Indeed it seems to me to pertain rather to the higher understanding than to simple history (*magis ad altiorem intelligentiam, quam ad simplicem historiam*)."[116] Although they are different, they are usually understood to be coordinate or complementary. Filastrius tells us, "Neither shall we lose *historia*, which makes it 70 years that the people were in Persia, nor shall we spurn spiritual knowledge."[117] Ambrose likewise says, "It seems to you highly exalted if you understand the letter. Cross over to the spiritual understanding, because the law is spiritual . . . for the letter kills, but the spirit vivifies."[118] Jerome, speaking about the prophets, tells us that "everything is to be taken spiritually, after the truth of history (*historiae veritatem*)." And in two different places he says that *historia* is the foundation of spiritual understanding.[119]

The uses of *historicus* by the Christians in late antiquity tend in the same new directions as the uses of *historia*, and show a renascence in the attributive usage. *Historicus* is used substantively to indicate writers of histories about the gods by Lactantius, Arnobius, and Sidonius Apollinaris.[120] Prudentius speaks of "Moses, the historian (*historicus*) of the world's birth."[121] But most often the adjective is used attributively and in relation to what has already been seen as the "historical" dimension of the Scriptures. Of the Scriptures, Ambrose says that Luke is a historian (*historicus*), and adds that "he kept to the historical (*historicum*) order and revealed to us many miracles among the Lord's deeds." And he also observes that the Gospel "is arranged

[115] Prud. *Hamart.* 723–24.

[116] Hieron. *Hom. Or. in Luc.* 37 (*PL* 26, 325C); cf. *In Dan.* 3 (on 11:3–4a, 11:5a), *In Isai.* 1.1 (*PL* 24, 23), *Ep.* 18^A 2.1.

[117] Filastr. *Haer.* 107.8 (*CSEL* 38.67, 9–10).

[118] Ambr. *In Ps.* 36.80 (*PL* 14, 1055C); cf. Hil. *Ps.* 53.2.

[119] Hieron. *In Isai.* Prol. (*PL* 24, 20B), 6.praef. (205C–D), and *Ep.* 129.6; cf. *In Eccl.* 1 (*PL* 23, 1085B–C).

[120] Lact. *Div. Inst.* 5.4.6 (*PL* 6, 563B), 1.8.8 (156A); Arn. *Adv. Nat.* 5.34; Sid. Apoll. *Ep.* 4.1.2, 4.3.8.

[121] Prud. *Hamart.* 339–40.

in historical style (*historico stylo*)."[122] But usually *historicus* is used, not of the Scriptures themselves, but of the way in which we are to deal with them. Cassian tells us that "learning explains the simple order of historical exposition (*historicae expositionis*), in which no more hidden knowledge is contained except what resounds in the words."[123] Jerome, too, mentions this "historical" exposition, and says that he will pass on to the spiritual treatment of Isaiah now that "we have taught the historical interpretation (*historica interpretatione*)."[124]

Augustine is entitled to a separate place in this account no less because of the important modifications of usage that appear clearly in his writings than because he was the preceptor of the Middle Ages and his ideas have thence a currency even in our own times.

Augustine uses *historia* in the sense of the literary genre when he refers to particular written works and when he speaks, more generally, of the "writers of history."[125] He also seems to think that *historia* is a distinct genre, and that it is a part of education, for he insists that "those among the pagans, who, having been educated in the liberal studies, love history, easily recognize" the numerous calamities that befell the Romans before Christianity.[126]

Turning to older subjects, and to *historia* as an informational account, Augustine uses the word in the sense of "natural history"[127] and as an episode in someone's life.[128] There is an occasional use of *historia* as an informational account about the gods,[129] and, like other Latin apologists of the time, he distinguishes among accounts of the gods between true ones, which he calls *historiae*, and false or fabulous ones, *fabulae*.[130]

Like other Christian writers of late antiquity, Augustine understands the Scriptures as *historia*, and as *historia* with some other mean-

---

[122] Amb. *Exp. Luc.* Prol. 1 (*PL* 15, 1607), Prol. 4 (1609B–C), Prol. 7 (1611B); cf. Cass. *Conl.* 8.7.3 (*PL* 49, 732A). But Sid. Apoll. (*Ep.* 7.9.2) says that he avoided the *pondera historica* in his own work.

[123] Cass. *Conl.* 14.8.7 (*PL* 49, 965A–B); cf. 8.3.5–6, 14.8.1–2, 14.10.3.

[124] Hieron. *In Matth.* 1 (*PL* 26, 65B), *In Isai.* 5.prol. (*PL* 24, 154, 183), and 5.23.28 (206B).

[125] Aug. *CD* 2.18, 2.22, 3.17, 3.26, 4.6, 18.40.

[126] Aug. *CD* 2.3; cf. 18.40.

[127] Aug. *CD* 16.8, 16.11.

[128] Aug. *CD* 22.8.

[129] Aug. *CD* 4.31, 7.27.

[130] Aug. *CD* 18.12, 18.13.

ing. *De civitate Dei* is the greatest and most influential of all the Christian apologies.[131] It was written to counter the claim that Christianity caused the fall of Rome. Its basic moves are those of all Christian apologies, and before them of Jewish apologies; one first shows the inferiority of the pagan gods and cults, and then the superiority of Christianity. The device by which Augustine pursues the task is the comparison of the "heavenly" and "earthly" cities. Thus, while the first part of the work (Books 1–10) show how bad things in the earthly city are and always have been, the second part (Books 11–22) is a sustained comparison of the two cities as regards their origins (Books 11–14), their careers (Books 15–18), and their ends (Books 19–22). The examination of their careers is largely an exposition of the Old Testament.

The Scriptures are or contain "histories" on Augustine's view. He responds to the question what "the writer of this history (*scriptor huius historiae*) intended in recording the generations from Adam,"[132] and he insists that we should believe or accept these histories, saying, "Now it seems to me that the *historia* is to be defended, lest Scripture be unbelievable when it says that a city was built by one man at a time when no more than four men, or rather three, after brother killed brother, were seen on earth. . . ."[133] In his essay *On the Character of the Ecclesia*, he is even more vehement. Having just put forward the curious argument that the *ecclesia* must be good because it depends upon good beliefs, he says (29.60) that the only possible objection is to suggest that the writing may be false; but no one would say that, he insists, "For the complete perversion of all literature will follow, and the abolition of all books handed down from the past, if what is

---

[131] Augustine himself so calls it (*Retr.* 2.69.1; and cf. *Ep.* 169.1 and 184A.5). Mommsen ["St. Augustine and the Christian Idea of Progress," *JHI* 12 (1951):346–74] has noted that it makes all the same moves as Tertullian, Lactantius, and Arnobius. Both Altaner [*Patrology*, trans. Hilda C. Graef (New York: Herder and Herder, 1961), p. 503] and Bardenhewer [*Patrology*, trans. Thomas J. Shahen (St. Louis: Herder, 1908), p. 481] consider the work an apology. P. S. Hawkins ["Polemical counterpoint in the *De civitate Dei*," *Augustinian Studies* 6 (1975):97–106] argues that the contrast between the two cities is not a theological or historical one, but an act of polemical evangelism. That it is the best of the early Christian apologies has been recognized by Johannes Geffcken [*Zwei griechischen Apologeten* (Leipzig and Berlin, 1907), pp. 318–21], C. N. Cochrane [*Christianity and Classical Culture* (New York: Oxford University Press, 1944), pp. 359–98], and Olof Gigon [*Die antike Kultur und das Christentum* (Gütersloh, 1966), pp. 123–30].

[132] Aug. *CD* 15.20; cf. 15.8, 18.38, *Util. Cred.* 3.8.

[133] Aug. *CD* 15.8.

supported by such belief of the peoples and founded on such consent of men and of times, is brought into doubt, so that it cannot have the credit and right of even common history (*historiae quidem vulgaris fidem gravitatemque*)." And in the *City of God* he bases the trustworthiness of Bible history on prophecies fulfilled and divine authority:

> For in what narration of past events could we better trust than one which also predicted coming events (*futura*) which we now see before our eyes? For the very disagreement of historians (*historicorum*) among themselves gives us grounds for trusting rather him who does not contradict the divine *historia* that we hold. . . . (The pagans, seeing the contradictions among their historians, know not whom to believe.) But we, relying on divine authority in our religion's history (*in nostrae religionis historia*) are in no doubt that whatever resists that is completely false, whatever other things may be in secular literature, which whether they be true or false, contribute nothing of importance by which we might live rightly or blessedly.[134]

Although, then, we are to trust these histories, Augustine clearly recognizes that they also have other meanings. He says, "I do not condemn those who have been able to carve out a meaning of spiritual understanding (*sensum intelligentiae spiritalis*) for every event there, so long as they have first maintained the truth of history (*historiae veritate*)."[135] And he later goes further, insisting "that we should agree neither with those who will take the history only (*solam historiam*) about the ark and the flood without allegorical significance, nor with those who defend only figures, having rejected historical truth (*historica veritate*)."[136] Likewise, we are taught by the seventy translators "to see a level above *historia* and to seek out those things which the *historia* itself was written to convey (*significanda*)."[137]

A third subgroup of *historia* about the Scriptures expresses and instances Augustine's views on exegesis. He writes:

> All that Scripture, therefore, which is called the Old Testament, is

---

[134] Aug. *CD* 18.40; cf. 18.38, *Vera Rel.* 50.99, *Doct. Chr.* 2.28.44. On Augustine's view of the authority of Scripture and the relation between *historia* and *prophetia* as disclosures of God's purposes, see R. A. Markus, *Saeculum: History and Society in the Theology of St. Augustine* (Cambridge, 1970), p. 187–96.

[135] Aug. *CD* 17.3.

[136] Aug. *CD* 15.27.init.

[137] Aug. *CD* 18.44.

handed down four-fold to them who desire to know it; according to history (*secundum historiam*), according to aetiology, according to analogy, and according to allegory; according to history when there is taught what hath been done; what not done, but only written as though it had been done. According to aetiology, when it is shown for what reason anything hath been done or said. According to analogy, when it is shown that the two Testaments, the Old and the New, are not contrary to one another. According to allegory, when it is taught that certain things which have been written are not to be taken in the letter (*ad litteram*), but are to be understood in a figure (*figurate*).[138]

The same four ways of setting forth the Scripture generally are elsewhere noted.[139] "Jerusalem," he tells us, refers to both the terrestrial Jerusalem according to *historia* and to the celestial Jerusalem in a figure.[140] But he says that the whole book of Genesis should be examined first as *historia* then as prophecy, and where the literal sense is not worthy of God we should take things figuratively.[141]

The latter half of the *City of God* is an extended account of the origin, career, and end of the two cities. In this discussion is found the largest concentration of uses of *historia* anywhere in the early Christian writings. And there is here a fifth group of uses of *historia* as informational account about the past or past events in which the Scriptures, as embodying or containing the *historia* of the Chosen People, is distinguished from and opposed to the *historia* of the non-Judaeo-Christian peoples. On the one hand, there is the sacred (*sacra*) or divine (*divina*) *historia*. In spite of lack of physical evidence for the longevity of people in the Old Testament, he says (15.9) that

---

[138] Aug. *Util. Cred.* 3.5; cf. 3.6.

[139] Aug. *Gen. Imp.* 2.5; examples 3.6.init. For present purposes it is sufficient to show Augustine's use of the idea of history in connection with the literal level of biblical exegesis. For an analysis of his exegetical theory and its development during his career, see R. A. Markus, *Saeculum*. A similar fourfold system of exegesis—*historicus* or *literalis, tropologicus, allegoricus,* and *anagogicus*—is very widely accepted throughout the Middle Ages. See Harry Caplan, "The Four Senses of Scriptural Interpretation and the Medieval Theory of Preaching," *Speculum* 4 (1929):282–90. Henri de Lubac [*Exégèse Médiévale* (Paris: Aubier, 1959–64)] offers an extensive and detailed analysis of the fourfold system with voluminous documentation of patristic through late medieval sources. For Augustine's views of the utility of "history" in biblical exegesis, see *Doct. Chr.* 2.28.42ff.

[140] Aug. *CD* 17.3.

[141] Aug. *Gen. c. Manech.* 2.2.3. The same general principle about literal and figurative passages is laid down in the *De doctrina christiana* (3.10.14 and 3.16.24), but only the general distinction between literal and figurative is operative there.

"faith in this *sacra historia* is not to be withdrawn." The *sacra historia* shows that Nahor, the brother of Abraham, left Chaldaea and settled in Mesopotamia (16.13). Elsewhere we examine what this *sacra historia* says about the son of Seth.[142] And to those who worry about how many people there were when Cain founded his city, he replies (15.8) that "the writer of this *sacra historia* did not have to necessarily name all the people who were then, but only those whom the plan of the work required. For the aim of that writer, through whom the holy Spirit was working, was to come down to Abraham . . . and then to proceed from Abraham to God's people, which was set apart from the other nations (*a ceteris gentibus*) and would serve to prefigure and foretell all things that relate to the city. . . ." So this *sacra historia* has to do with God's people, who are separate from the other *gentes* or peoples.

On the other hand, there is the *historia* of these peoples, the *historia gentium*. The *historia gentium* praises the marvelous construction of Babylon (16.4), but "the *historia gentium* neither Greek nor Latin knew" about the Flood (18.8). It tells, too, about the wondrous works or miracles by which the gods persuaded people to worship them (10.16, 18). And the *historia gentium* also contains numerous portents.[143] When the Scriptures are referred to as *historia* it is with a view more to their content—what kind of account they are, factual or figurative—than to their form. In the opposition between sacred *historia* and the *historia* of the peoples, *historia* seems to indicate a mixture of the meanings informational account about past events and the information itself or "the past," though leaning more toward the former.

There is a final group of uses of *historia* in which the mixture of these two strains leans more toward "the past" per se. The first half of the *City of God* raised the standard apologetic defense against the charge that the fall of Rome was due to the worship of the new God and forgetfulness of the old gods who gave Rome peace and victory. Augustine replies "that for the most part they come about against their will, not only fables, lying about many things and barely indicating or showing anything true, but also Roman history itself (*ipsa Romana historia*) testifies."[144] Again, "both ancient history (*vetus his-*

---

[142] Aug. *CD* 15.17; cf. 17.8, 18.40, 17.24.init.
[143] Aug. *CD* 21.8; cf. 4.6, 12.11, 16.8, *Doct. Chr.* 2.28.42–43.
[144] Aug. *CD* 3.10; cf. 2.3, 18.38.

toria) testifies and the unhappy experience of our own times teaches us" that people are sometimes reduced to cannibalism.[145] And, arguing that the 89th Psalm is a prophecy of Jesus, he says (17.10) that the dire description of the state of the world in lines 39–45 applies to the earthly city, "but of the way in which these things came upon that kingdom, *historia* is the indicator of events (*index rerum gestarum*), if it is read."

Finally, an even clearer example is found in his treatise about the discovery and expression of the meaning of Scripture, *On Christian Doctrine*. The two chief sources of obscurity in Scripture are unknown and ambiguous signs. In the second book he claims that ignorance of signs is to be remedied in part by knowledge of the original languages and contexts and in part by knowledge of things. In the quest for greater knowledge of things he permits the use of *some* profane sources; but profane knowledge may be of either human or divine institution. Some of the former, for example, astrology and divination, are superstitious; but some are not. Among those kinds of knowledge useful for understanding the Scriptures that are not of merely human institution Augustine includes history. He says:

> Whatever, then, informs (us) about the order of past times—that which is called history (*Quidquid igitur de ordine temporum transactorum indicat ea quae appellatur historia*)—assists us very much in understanding the sacred Scriptures, even if it is spoken outside the Ecclesia as a matter of childish instruction.

From it we may learn, for example, the consulship in which Jesus was born so that we are not confused about his age when he was crucified; for "this may be collected more clearly and more certainly from a comparison of the history of the peoples (*historia gentium*) with the Gospel." The usefulness of history (*utilitas historiae*) is also shown by the fact that Ambrose, "having investigated the history of the peoples (*historia gentium*)," proved that Plato learned his philosophy from the prophet Jeremiah (*sic*). He concludes:

> Even when in an historical narration (*narratione historica*) former institutions of men are narrated, the history itself (*ipsa historia*) is not to be numbered among human institutions; for those things which are past

---

[145] Aug. *CD* 22.20; cf. 18.41.

and cannot be undone, belong to the order of times, of which God alone is the author and administrator. For it is one thing to narrate what has been done, another to teach what ought to be done. History narrates what has been done faithfully and usefully; but the books of the haruspices, and the like writings, aim to teach what ought to be done or observed, with the boldness of an adviser, not the fidelity of a reporter (*non indicis fide*).[146]

Of the two passages extracted above, the context of the first does not permit a clear judgment whether *history* means an account of past events or "the past." In the second passage, however, "the past" is clearly meant; for in the first sentence the "history itself" is distinguished from the "historical narration," and the passage following the semicolon virtually defines the "history itself" as "those things which are past and cannot be undone (*quae transierunt, nec infacta fieri possunt*)." And Augustine's point here is that history so defined can be useful in understanding Scripture precisely because it is *not* a human production but, rather, a divine production; it belongs "to the order of times, of which the author and administrator is God." This is the first and only instance in antiquity in which history is said to be an existing entity and/or under the control of God.

Augustine's uses of *historicus*, like the contemporaneous uses by Christian writers, lean toward the attributive usage, and tend to bear out the sorts of shifts that the uses of *historia* suggest. It is used substantively to indicate historians of nature,[147] historians of events,[148] and those who have handed down accurate accounts of the gods.[149] The attributive usage exceeds the substantive; and while it occasionally occurs in the context of investigation of nature,[150] it more often has to do with religious matters. The tendency among the Latin Christian apologists, already noted, to distinguish between true and false accounts about the gods, is repeated here. Augustine contends that the gods were once men, "as not only poetic literature, but also historical (*historicae*) hands down."[151] Similarly, he distinguishes the

---

[146] Aug. *Doct. Chr.* 2.28.42–44. On the *De doctrina christiana*, see my articles, "The Subject and Structure of Augustine's *De doctrina christiana*," *Augustinian Studies* 11 (1980):99–124 and "The Content and Argument of Augustine's *De doctrina christiana*," *Augustiniana*, 31 (1981):165–82.

[147] Aug. *CD* 16.8.

[148] Aug. *CD* 1.5, 2.14, 2.18, 5.12, 18.2, 18.17.

[149] Aug. *CD* 6.7, 18.8.

[150] Aug. *Ench.* 3.9, *CD* 15.9, 16.9.

[151] Aug. *CD* 7.27; cf. 3.31, *Doct. Chr.* 2.28.44.

fabulous (*fabulosa*) from the historical explanation (*historica ratio*) of the name of Athens, and notes that while the account of Minos is accepted as historical truth (*historicae veritati*), that of Jupiter belongs to the emptiness of fables (*vanitati fabularum*).¹⁵² As regards the Sacred Scriptures of his own religion, he says that "some spiritual signification may well be found in the account of paradise, in which the first humans dwelt, agreeable with the historical truth (*vertitate historicae*) of its bodily existence."¹⁵³ And, while pleading ignorance of the reason why certain ancient books are not included in the canon of Scripture, he confesses:

> I think even those men to whom the Holy Spirit certainly revealed matters that properly fell within the authority of religion may have written sometimes as men, by historical investigation (*historica diligentia*), and sometimes as prophets, by divine inspiration; and the two kinds were so different that one kind, such was the verdict, must be credited, as it were, to themselves, the other to God speaking through them. Thus one kind contributed to the increase of knowledge (*ad ubertatem cognitionis*), the other to the authority of religion; and in this authority the canon is guarded.¹⁵⁴

Thus the view that the Scriptures are at least in one aspect "history" or "historylike" is echoed in these statements about their historical truth and the historical investigation that seemingly went into them.

¹⁵² Aug. *CD* 18.10, 18.12; cf. 18.16.
¹⁵³ Aug. *CD* 13.21.init.
¹⁵⁴ Aug. *CD* 18.38, trans. Greene (Loeb).

VI

Conclusion: The Development of the Idea of History and the Cultural Ferment of Late Antiquity

T HE ANCIENT WORD ἴστωϱ either meant someone who was known for a capacity to "see" clearly which of two conflicting accounts of an emotionally charged matter was correct, or, used as an adjective, attributed that capacity to someone. The verb ἱστοϱεῖν seems to have been derived from ἴστωϱ; and in the Hellenic Age it indicated the activity characteristic of the ἴστωϱ, that is, finding out or inquiring the correct account in a case where the matter is both disputed and emotionally charged. The noun ἱστοϱία seems coeval with the verb; of far less frequent occurrence in the Hellenic Age, it meant an instance of the activity indicated by the verb, an inquiring or an inquiry of that sort. After Herodotus published his account of the Persian Wars under the title ἱστοϱίαι, *Histories*, however, the noun came to indicate the results of such inquiring, and these either written or not. What underlies these uses, however, is an activity idea: inquiring for accurate information or the facts about persons, things, or events.

Perhaps because of the authority that the work of Herodotus had already attained, ἱστοϱία in the Hellenistic Age came increasingly to indicate the results of inquiring and these especially as a written account concerned with events; ἱστοϱία as a literary genre. At the same time, ἱστοϱεῖν acquired the meaning "to record, report, or relate" some information, a meaning evidently derived from ἱστορία as a written account and which began to supplant the older meaning. Moreover, the noun was more frequent than the verb. Thus even in uses of the verb the product has begun to dominate the activity, and a gap has begun to appear between the product per se, the facts or information, and the product in writing. What appears in the Greek idea of history appears also in the uses of the Latin transliterations, *historia* and *historicus*: a modal distinction between an accurate factual account about persons, things, or events, and such an account about events and in writing. Both in Greek and in Latin the primary meaning in the Hellenistic Age was that of the account in writing, history as a literary genre with its rules and styles, canons of greatness and social utility. In Philo's use of Greek to talk about the things of the Jewish world, however, history means, rather, a factual account or the facts than a literary genre. And his usage suggests that the facts that history indicates might be signs of something else and that the reliability of the account might be guaranteed not by the publicity of the facts, but by its divine origins.

The changed political conditions and the intensified influence of rhetoric on the educated world produced a relaxation of conceptual boundaries in the Roman Age. A balance seems to have been restored between the two modes, history as a literary genre and as an informational account. Both in Greek and in Latin the range of subjects began to include the gods (what we should call "myths" or "legends") and ordinary mortals, histories in which the truth or accuracy of the account was less important than that it be entertaining or instructive. Thus we have a quite new use of history as story; history thus far approaches poetry. Moreover, and perhaps representing the interaction between poetry and rhetoric, history as information about past events is used occasionally in an apparently collective way, as the past. And in Greek, ideas or opinions can now be subjects of a history. In the early Christian literature of the Roman Age, which was mostly in Greek, the idea of history is very like that of the non-Christian world. As compared with Hellenic or even Hellenistic times, in their usage the limits are relaxed and include accounts of the gods as well as the accounts in the Old and New Testaments. Accuracy or literal truth was not crucial, which suggests that with respect to both Christian and non-Christian matters history was understood for the most part as story. A history in this sense might well have another meaning. The important differences between the Christian and non-Christian ideas of history are that the Christian is almost always applied to matters of religious interest and that it regularly occurs in the context of apologetical attacks on the pagan gods and defenses of Christianity.

Non-Christian Greek and Latin usage during the later empire generally continued the developments of the preceding centuries. The shift away from history as a literary genre to history as an informational account was very marked, and the former became infrequent. The requirement of accuracy or factuality of the account continued on the wane. The Christian usage of the later empire reveals the divergence between East and West in the differing developments that the idea underwent in Greek and in Latin. In both languages it appears most often in two contexts: biblical exegesis and apology. In both languages history is involved in exegesis because scriptural accounts or the Scriptures themselves are considered histories; these histories, however, are capable of bearing another meaning. Literal exegesis is "according to history," as opposed to various kinds of figurative or spiritual exegesis. In the apologetical writings, however, there is a difference between the Greek and the Latin. The Greek Christians carry on the same use of history in the apologies that characterized the earlier period, that is, history as story. But the Latin writers reassert the old requirement of accuracy, and argue that the truth about the gods, the histories about them, show them to be unworthy of worship. Thus what history means to them, their idea of history, is true informational accounts or information about persons, events, and gods, and the relationships between people and their gods; and they even seem to have used history in the collective sense as the past, implicitly distinguishing the history of the Chosen People from that of the non-Christian peoples.

It is in this last usage that Augustine makes his great innovation. For while his usage is in no essential way different from that of his Christian contemporaries, he makes of the distinction that they only implied—the distinction and opposition between the sacred, providential history of the celestial city and the peoples' history of the earthly city—the dominant literary and rhetorical motive of his *City of God*. Although this distinction and opposition is present, history in both cases seems on the evidence to indicate an informational account or the information itself, rather than the hypostatic unity of the past, which our word "history" sometimes means.[1] The opposition,

---

[1] R. A. Markus [*Saeculum: History and Society in the Theology of Saint Augustine* (Cam-

then, might better be expressed by "the sacred or divine account of things" and "the peoples' account of things." The history is, moreover, meaningful both in the sense that besides the literal meaning there may be a "higher" or "spiritual" way in which it is to be understood and in the sense that accounts of earlier events are prophetic of later. What Augustine means by the term "history," then, is true and meaningful informational accounts about the gods and (divinely filled) events of a people.

It follows from all this that the widely accepted account of the idea of history in antiquity is wrong on a number of points. In the first place, history was not a philosophical problem to the Greeks or the Romans. It is nowhere discussed by the philosophers. It came in for some criticism among the pre-Socratics; Plato's Socrates rejected it as philosophically insufficient because it did not explain the causes; the Stoics, Epicureans, and Skeptics scarcely mentioned it. Aristotle said that poetry was more philosophical than history, but he also seemed to think that history in the sense of accurate information about a subject was useful or necessary as a prerequisite to the properly philosophical enterprise of learning the causes. This view survived in the Peripatetic School long after Aristotle's death, and during the renascence of the school in late antiquity even the Master's résumés of earlier opinions about whatever problem he happened to be considering were called histories by Alexander of Aphrodisias and Syrianus. But for all that, history was still not a philosophical problem. And this is not surprising; for history, as has been seen, was not an entity or a category of reality such that one might have difficulty understanding it.

Second, history was not related by ancient writers to the ways in which they understood time. Time did come in for some consideration by philosophers and others; and it is one of Aristotle's categories, at least in some enumerations of them in the corpus. But if time as the "when" of something poses philosophical problems, time as the medium of history does not. Perhaps this reflects a kind of philosophical naïveté about the logical relationship between the ideas of time and history, but it seems unlikely that this problem would occur to someone who did not think about the category or entity "history,"

---

bridge, 1970), pp. 14–15, 231–32] makes the same point while showing the difference between what Augustine and Cullmann mean by "sacred history."

and did not think that history indicated the whole temporal process of a thing. The idea of history, then, is not understood as being dependent on or derivative from the idea of time. At any rate, there is not a single view of time as a circle that all Greeks accepted, as is supposed (see p. 12, n. 34 *supra*).

It is also not the case, third, that either time or history was a great problem from the point of view of Greek or Roman religious thought. So it is a misunderstanding of ancient thought to say that, since time was understood as cyclical, it "must be experienced as an enslavement, as a curse . . . everything keeps recurring. . . . That is why the philosophical thinking of the Greek world labors with the problem of time and also why all Greek striving for redemption seeks as its goal to be freed from this eternal circular course and thus to be freed from time itself."[2] Time may have been a puzzle to certain ancient writers, but there is no evidence of its having been experienced as an "enslavement" or a "curse." Nor is it the case that philosophers "labor" with the problem of time, nor does any Greek striving for redemption seek to be liberated from time. Indeed the striving for redemption is a typically Christian goal, but not Greek or Roman.

History is also not a theological or religious problem for the Christians. It figures in their apologetical and exegetical writings, but in neither case are there problems posed that relate to Christian doctrine. History does not figure in the creeds or in the antiheretical literature in which Christian doctrine was being formulated. There were speculative problems raised and discussed in this early period of Christianity, but history was not one of them.

Fourth, neither Greeks nor Romans nor Christians understood history as having a pattern. No Greek or Roman has been found saying that it is repetitive, nor any Christian saying that it is linear and once and for all. In order for someone to find a pattern in history, history must be taken to be the sort of thing that is capable of exhibiting a pattern; that is, a composite whole, made up of parts capable of being organized in a conceivable pattern. In other words, history must be understood as the collected temporal career or process of a thing. But no one in antiquity understood history in this way: not the Greeks and Romans, and not the Christians. It might be argued that Augustine comes very near or that he creates

---

[2] Cullmann, *Christ and Time* (trans. Filson), p. 53.

the conditions for understanding history in this new way; but this is to read Augustine from the point of view of later tradition.

Finally, while history does, as is widely believed, become meaningful in Christian thought, this does not seem to be due to reflection on their religious beliefs, or for any theological reasons. Rather, the Jews and, following them, the Christians suppose that their Scriptures were or contained histories. In this they conformed to contemporary usage, which allowed that a history might be about gods or divine acts and that it need not be true in the older sense of conformity to observed fact. In the apologies these histories were used to show how bad the popular religion was and how much better Christianity was. And in the exegetical works apparent inconsistencies or immoralities were explained by the use of nonliteral exegesis. Nonliteral exegesis was a Greek invention, dating back to the fifth century at least. So there was nothing new in the Christians applying nonliteral exegesis to their Scriptures. What is new is that the same account that is called a history is also said to have some other meaning. This is a regular feature of the Christian exegetical literature, so that history acquires the capacity to bear some other meaning in connection with religion and through the agency of Christian thought, but for reasons that are not so much theological as apologetical and exegetical. Put somewhat differently, the widely accepted account finds the vast difference between the Graeco-Roman and Judaeo-Christian ideas of history to be religious or, more precisely, theological; according to the evidence examined here, the rather slight differences are rhetorical and literary. It is, again, only from the standpoint of the later tradition, and reading ancient texts retrospectively, that the changes appear to be related to Christian doctrine; for it is typically modern to suppose that history is the essence of Christianity. Cullmann may be correct when he argues that "All Christian theology in its innermost essence is Biblical history,"[3] but he is not correct in supposing that the Christians saw themselves and their faith in that way in the early centuries. Nor is he correct in supposing that the Christian view of history is fundamentally different from and opposed to the Graeco-Roman.

The account that has been accepted by scholars for such a long time traditionally claims the authority of early Christian thought. The essentials of this account are: (1) the circular pattern of time and

[3] Ibid.

history (as world process) in Greek thought vs. the rectilinear patterns of them for Judaeo-Christian thought; (2) the repetition and eternal recurrence predicated by the Graeco-Roman view vs. the innovation and renovation predicated by the Judaeo-Christian view; and (3) the hopelessness, meaninglessness, and enslavement of the soul entailed by the Graeco-Roman view vs. the hopefulness, meaningfulness, and liberation possible on the Judaeo-Christian view. Something resembling all of these themes is already found in Augustine's *City of God*.

The second half of the work is an extended comparison of the two cities, devoted to showing that we should dwell in the celestial city and avoid the earthly city. It is divided into three parts of four books each, which treat, respectively, of the origins, careers, and ends of the two cities. Book 11 shows how the cities originated in the separation of the good and bad angels, and discusses, incidental to that, the scriptural account of the creation of the world. Book 12 begins with a discussion of the goodness of the good angels, the badness of the bad, and the reasons for both. Then, since the two cities are populated by both angels and humans, the argument proceeds to the creation of man. This discussion, which occupies the remainder of the book, is a sustained argument against the view, attributed to certain "philosophers of this world," that the question of the eternity of the world is to be solved by the introduction of "cycles of times (*circuitus temporum*) in which, according to them, the same things have always been renewed and repeated in the nature of things (*in rerum natura*); there will likewise be hereafter an uninterrupted series of revolving ages coming and going; either these cycles took place in a permanent world or else the world, arising and dying at certain intervals, always displayed the same things as if new which were completed and come to pass."[4]

This doctrine of "false cycles" of temporal things is repeatedly contrasted with "the straight path of sound doctrine," and Psalm 12:4 is dubiously quoted: "The wicked shall walk around in circles." Among the various grounds on which the theory of cosmic cycles is rejected are (1) that it entails that nothing new ever happens—wrong because it denies the omnipotence of God—and (2) that according to it the soul is enslaved without hope of liberation. By contrast, the "straight way" of Christian doctrine offers the assurance that something new

[4] Aug. *CD* 12.14.1–2.

can happen and therefore the possibility that the soul might be liberated. The creation of man is thence affirmed against the objections
of the "philosophers."

Augustine does not claim that this is a "pagan" view, that it is
common to Graeco-Roman culture, but that it is a view expressed by
some "philosophers." Still, in the context of the rhetorical alternation
between Christianity and the culture of the Graeco-Roman world,
which is the mainspring of the early Christian apologies, and here
between the city of God and the city of man, the "philosophers of this
world" belong to the city of this world, the city of man. Augustine
does not attribute to these philosophers the view that history goes in
cycles, but that times (*tempora*), temporal things (*res temporalia*), or
events (*res gestae*) do. But if one understood by history—as it has been
argued that Augustine himself did not—the whole temporal process
of the world, then this discussion and other similar discussions elsewhere in the work would seem to instantiate the widely accepted
account of the opposition between Christian and pagan ideas of history. And they are so interpreted by scholars. But there is no single
or simple Greek or Graeco-Roman view of time or of history in the
sense of the whole temporal process of the world—indeed history is
not used in that sense in antiquity—to which such a univocal Judaeo-
Christian view of time or history might be opposed.

It seems, rather, that the attractiveness of the usual account is to
be attributed to precisely that same spirit of Christian apology that
first formulated it in the *City of God*. Not only was it the rhetorical or
apologetical motive which recommended the differentiation of sacred
and profane history in the first place, but it is the same motive and
the same apology that has recommended the scholarly analysis of the
sources and meaning of that distinction. The Christian revision of the
idea of history is rhetorical and partisan, and so is the accepted account of it.

Several observations might be made at this point. Rather than the
radical change that is widely believed, the development of the idea of
history in antiquity displays considerable continuity both in the subjects that a history might be about and in the kinds of thing or entity
that a history might be. The earliest subjects, events of social or political importance, natural things, and the particularly dramatic use
about episodes in the lives of persons of great cultural stature, re-

mained the primary subjects throughout antiquity for Christians and non-Christians alike. History about natural things or human customs was never a prominent usage, but also never forgotten. History about persons moved out of the dramatic context in the Roman Age and after; and the stature in the cultural community of the persons involved also declined, although the Christian use of history about the characters in the Old and New Testaments represents a return to the original culturally great stature, since these figures are the heroes and archetypal figures of the Judaeo-Christian world-view. Also in the later period, gods and divine acts came to be considered subjects for history, and this, again, by Greeks, Romans, and Christians alike.

The kinds of beings or entities to which "history" referred or for which it was a name varied somewhat by addition, deletion, or change of emphasis, but remained substantially the same throughout antiquity. The earliest reference, to inquiring or inquiry, became moribund in Greek after the beginning of the Hellenistic Age, and never occurred in Latin. For this reason, too, the early reference to results of inquiring changed into the less activity-oriented informational account. A certain species of informational accounts was enshrined in the reference to the literary genre. The general distinction in kinds of entities between informational account and literary genre remained a fundamental distinction throughout antiquity (and has remained so to the present day, though in an attenuated form). Besides this fundamental distinction, there is a distinction within "informational account" between the account per se and the information itself, the facts. In later antiquity there came to be an added species of the former, story, and an added species of the latter, the past.

If there is substantial continuity in the development of the idea there are also two changes found in the Christian writings and not elsewhere. The first is that history is here understood to be capable of bearing a meaning other than the literal one. This note had wide currency in Christian writings both in Greek and in Latin; and there were disputes about the extent to which Scripture should be read literally, that is, "according to history," or figuratively, allegorically, typically, etc. The second new note, implicit in the later Latin fathers, but explicit in Augustine, is the differentiation between Christian and Gentile history. History is supposed to be something different for Jews and Christians from what it is for other peoples.

These two changes are characteristic of Christian writers. But the training and profession of the writers, the kinds of literature in which the changed usage of history is found, and the kind of role played by the term in these works suggest, as a second observation, that the changes are due to literary and rhetorical, rather than theological, considerations.

It has already been noted that the Christian writers of the first two centuries were rhetoricians by training.[5] The fathers of the later period, too, were trained rhetors. Among the Greeks, the Cappadocian Fathers, Basil the Great, Gregory of Nazianzus, and Gregory of Nyssa were all not only trained in rhetoric, but also were rhetors by profession for some time.[6] Gregory of Nazianzus was known as the "Christian Demosthenes" to the Byzantine scholars, and his *Orations* were a subject of commentary down to the sixteenth century.[7] Among the Antiochenes, famed for their literal or "historical" exegesis, Theodore of Mopsuestia was a student of the eminent pagan orator Libanius, as well as of the Christian Diodorus of Tarsus.[8] And Diodorus' other famous pupil was John, called Chrysostom, that is, Golden-mouthed, for his eloquence from the pulpit, which vied with that of Libanius in the Council.[9] Among the Latin fathers, Cyprian, Arnobius, Lactantius, and Augustine, all Africans, were all rhetors by training and profession before turning their talents to the service of Christianity.[10] Lactantius was named by Diocletian professor of rhet-

---

[5] Pp. 86–87, above. Ferdinand Lot [*La fin du monde antique et la début du moyen âge* (Paris, 1926), p. 158] observes that before 350, Christian writers were "first and foremost apologetical writers fighting against paganism" and that they were all trained in rhetoric (p. 165). On the question of Irenaeus' knowledge of philosophy, William R. Schoedel ("Philosophy and Rhetoric in the *Adversus haereses* of Irenaeus," *Vigiliae Christianae* 13 (1959):22–32) concludes that it "was confined largely to doxographical material [and] . . . for the most part was employed in a sceptical fashion for the sole purpose of refuting the Gnostics" (p. 32). Cf. R. M. Grant, "Irenaeus and Hellenistic Culture," *Harvard Theol. Rev.* 42 (1949):41–51.

[6] On Basil: Berthold Altaner, *Patrology*, trans. Hilda C. Graef (New York: Herder and Herder, 1961), p. 336; Johannes Quasten, *Patrology* (Utrecht-Antwerp: Spectrum, 1962) 3:204. On Gregory Nazianzus; Altaner, p. 346; Quasten, 3:236. Rosemary Radford Ruether [*Gregory of Nazianzus: Rhetor and Philosopher* (Oxford: Clarendon, 1969)] shows how, in Gregory, the ancient rivalry between philosophy and rhetoric is transformed into a conflict between "two modalities of thought which form his mind and underlie his writings" (p. ix). On Gregory of Nyssa: Altaner, p. 351; Quasten, 3:254.

[7] Altaner, *Patrology*, p. 347; Quasten, *Patrology* 3:236.

[8] Altaner, *Patrology*, p. 370; Quasten, *Patrology* 3:401.

[9] Altaner, *Patrology*, p. 373; Quasten, *Patrology* 3:424–25. Harry M. Hubbell ["Chrysostom and Rhetoric," *CP* 19 (1924):261–76] examines his transformation of the classical encomium.

[10] On Cyprian: Altaner, *Patrology*, p. 193; Quasten, *Patrology* 2:341. On Arnobius: Altaner, p. 205; Quasten, 2:383. On Lactantius: Altaner, p. 208; Quasten, 2:392–93.

oric at Nicomedia, but was forced to resign the office when he became a Christian.[11] Hilary, Ambrose, and Jerome, though not professional rhetors, were at least partially so educated. In his famous dream, Jerome is accused of being more interested in literary achievement than religious, of being a Ciceronian, not a Christian. If these famous and influential fathers of the Church are Christians from the standpoint of religion, they are rhetoricians from the standpoint of education, training, and early profession.

The nature of the writings in which the changed idea of history is found also points to the influence of rhetoric on the development. The passages examined in the preceding chapters came from three kinds of works: apologies, homilies, and commentaries or expositions. Apologies and homilies are frankly rhetorical works, written respectively for non-Christians and Christians.[12] They aim at persuasion, not understanding; the enterprise in which the writers are engaged in such works is not inquiry, but exhortation. This is shown not only by the persuasive form in which the works are cast, but also by the reasoning that characterizes them, exclusive alternations. Either this or that. Either God or the Devil. Either Salvation or Damnation.

The commentaries and expositions, on the other hand, are attempts to explain the meaning of the Scriptures, especially to explain apparent inconsistencies, immoralities, or falsehoods. They are not exhortations except insofar as the reader is encouraged to find an acceptable reading of the text rather than to suppose that the Scriptures are flawed. The widely accepted way of escape from these difficulties was nonliteral exegesis of one kind or another, and there is discussion of the proper sort or extent of nonliteral exegesis to be employed; but it was *literal* exegesis that was "according to history." The origin of Christian nonliteral exegesis is usually traced back to the Alexandrian tradition, which, through the mediation of Philo, ultimately derived from the nonliteral interpretations of Homer's accounts of the gods as far back as Xenophanes. Textual exegesis comprised a large part of the standard Graeco-Roman education, of which the Christian fathers were products.[13] Although, therefore, the literature of commentary and exposition had a religious motive, the

---

[11] Altaner, *Patrology*, p. 208; Quasten, *Patrology* 2:393.

[12] Of Theophilus, for example, Robert M. Grant shows ["Scripture, Rhetoric and Theology in Theophilus," *Vigiliae Christianae* 13 (1959):35–45] that "scriptural sources are employed in a rhetorical manner for theological purposes" (p. 33).

[13] Cf. Marrou, *History of Education in Antiquity*, pp. 165–70.

enterprise itself should be seen as literary. Another kind of early Christian literature, the antiheretical, is more concerned with matters of doctrine; for it was usually on matters of doctrine that there was difference of opinion severe enough to warrant separation. In this literature, however, scarcely any use of history has been found.

Moreover, the uses themselves are rhetorical and literary. In the apologetical literature, history is continually used to show the inferiority of popular religion and the superiority of Christianity. Disagreement among the histories about Homer showed that they were false and that Homer (= Greek culture) is not as old as Moses (= Judaeo-Christian culture).[14] Histories of the gods show them to have been mortals and unworthy of worship. Histories about the popular cults show them to be either ridiculous or reprehensible. Histories about events show that the world is no worse off with Christianity than it was without it. In all this, history is involved in the polemic, but not in an examination of Christian doctrine; for, from their own point of view, the writers are not engaged in an examination of doctrine, but in its defense. The discussions appear theological to the eyes of the modern reader because the terms and ideas utilized for the defense, whether borrowed from the "pagan" culture or devised for the occasion, have become familiar features of the literary terrain of early Christian literature, of patrology, and the essentially controversial nature of the writings is easily overlooked.

Nor is history involved in theological discussion in the homiletic and exegetical literature. In these works non-literal exegesis was used for edification, moral exhortations, and explanation of apparent inconsistencies or immoralities, and history indicated the literal level of the texts involved. But while history as the letter or literal level of Scripture here acquires the capacity to be the bearer of some other meaning, this is in connection with examining the Scriptures, not Christian doctrine.

The circumstances in which the Christians changed the idea of history thus suggest that the influence of Christianity as a distinctly intellectual phenomenon has more to do with rhetoric than is ordinarily supposed. A history of rhetoric in later antiquity and in early Christian thought would be required to clarify the nature and extent of such influence;[15] but it is worth mentioning that early Christian

---

[14] Paul Ciholas ["Plato: The Attic Moses?" *Classical World* 72 (1978–79)] correctly reminds us that the fathers often contrasted Plato with Moses, arguing for "the dependence of Plato on Old Testament prophets and especially on Moses" (p. 222).

[15] In 1924 Harry Hubbell ("Chrysostom") wrote that little was known of the early

history writing was also a largely rhetorical or polemical enterprise. Beginning with Eusebius, the founder of Christian historiography, the historical writings of the Christians are attempts to establish the truth of their religion. Despite divergences of emphasis, "the Church historians' task had a basic unity, for all the historians and their readers would agree that church history was properly and essentially a record of the power of God and of the action of God in human affairs. Thus church history was a test of the truth of the faith."[16] This task, as distinct from that of the Greek or Roman writer of history—which was to (investigate and) relate the facts, to inform—is

---

history of Christian rhetoric, but that by the fourth century rhetoric was in complete control of preaching. In 1928 and 1929 Aimé Puech published a nine-part study of "L'Éloquence chrétienne au IVᵉ siècle" in the *Revue des Cours et Conférences* [29:1 (1928), 421–31, 481–93, 673–88; 29:2 (1928), 177–87, 633–45; 30:1 (1928–29), 75–86, 223–35, 443–54, 565–76]. More recently, in addition to the articles cited earlier in this chapter, Jaeger [*Early Christianity and Greek Paideia* (Cambridge: Harvard University Press, 1961), Chaps. 1 and 2] has discussed the early fathers' adoption of classical rhetoric as part of their transformation of Greek *paideia*. On the rhetoric of the New Testament itself, see Amos N. Wilder, *Early Christian Rhetoric. The Language of the Gospel* (London: SCM Press, 1964). There are also several very detail-oriented pieces by Antonio Quacquarelli: *La retorica antica al bivio* (Rome: Edizioni Scientifiche Romane, 1956); *Retorica e liturgia antenicena* (Rome, 1960); *Saggi Patristici* (Bari, 1971 = *Quaderni di "Vetera Christianorum"* 5), Chap. 1 "I presupposti filosofici della retorica patristica," and "Inventio ed elocutio nella retorica cristiana antica," *Vet. Chr.* 9 (1972):191–218. Michael McGee ["Thematic Reduplication in Christian Rhetoric," *Quarterly Journal of Speech* 56 (1970):196–204] argues that "The Christian world view . . . changed the *meaning* . . . rather than the *form* of rhetorical theory" (p. 201). And there have been a couple of interesting studies of Lactantius' debt to Cicero: P. Monat ["Lactance et Cicéron. A propos d'un fragment de l'*Hortensius*," *Revue des Études Latines* 53 (1975):248–67]; and E. Gareau ["*Bene et vere loqui*: Lactance et la conception cicéronienne de l'orateus idéal," *Revue des Études Latines* 55 (1977):192–202]. George Kennedy ["The Present State of the Study of Ancient Rhetoric," *CP* 70 (1975)] has promised (p. 281) a third volume in his history of rhetoric and oratory that will take us to A.D. 800 and concludes by saying that "the most open frontier now seems to lie in examination of the relationships between the classical tradition and its variants or alternatives within Judaism, Christianity, Islam, or the cultures of Africa or Asia." The brief study of "Judaeo-Christian Rhetoric" in his *Classical Rhetoric and Its Christian and Secular Tradition from Ancient to Modern Times* (Chapel Hill: University of North Carolina Press, 1980), pp. 120–60, is the best to date; see my review in the *Journal of the History of Philosophy*, forthcoming. But at present there is still no thorough study of early Christian rhetoric or of rhetoric's place in the cultural history of late antiquity. Heinrich Kuch's study of the idea of philology is part of the work that needs to be done: *Philologus* (Berlin, 1965), see especially the résumé, pp. 122–28.

[16] Glanville Downey, "The Perspective of the Early Church Historians," *GRBS* 4 (1965):69. Similarly, James T. Shotwell ["Christianity and History," *J. of Philosophy, Psychology, and Scientific Method* 17 (1920):85–94, 113–20, 141–50] sees the spread and triumph of Christianity as a calamity for historiography and claims that in Eusebius "history is the reservoir not of argument, but of proof" (p. 147).

the task of ecclesiastical historiography throughout the Middle Ages.[17] And it is interesting to note that it was pursuant to this persuasive task, to which history writing was turned by the early Christians, that history writing first came to rely upon extensive use of documentary evidence.[18] What had first been the tool of the Jewish apologetical historian Josephus became the tool of the Christians and thence a regular feature of the discipline called history. Eusebius is famous for this, but it is also characteristic of the less famous church historians Socrates and Sozomen.

Such changes as were made in the idea of history under the impact of Judaeo-Christianity, then, were rhetorical, and it would be appropriate to say that the idea, so altered, is a rhetorical idea. But more important, and notwithstanding the detail into which these pages have gone, the idea of history in antiquity was not an important idea, not one of the formative and widely influential ideas either in the Graeco-Roman or in the Judaeo-Christian culture. There are such ideas in both cultures. In the Graeco-Roman culture, nature (φύσις, *natura*), wisdom (σοφία, *sapientia*), and the good (ἀγαθόν, *bonum*) continue to be objects of inquiry and action throughout antiquity and in all facets of culture. Similarly, the Christians began in the third century an examination of their beliefs, in which the ideas of love (ἀγάπη, *charitas*), faith (πίστις, *fides*), and the tri-unity and perfection of God (Θεός, *Deus*) figured prominently. One might give other lists of the important ideas; there are other matters frequently discussed.

The relationships between the two cultures with respect to such ideas are many. Sometimes an idea important in Graeco-Roman culture is taken over whole cloth into Judaeo-Christian culture; sometimes an idea originally formulated in Graeco-Roman culture is carried over and reformulated in Judaeo-Christian culture. And there are differences between the two cultures as to the importance attached to various ideas. The idea of God, for example, is found in both cultures. The interpretations given by the two cultures are quite different; but in addition to that it does not seem to be the case that anywhere near as much importance is attached to the idea by the Greeks and Romans as by the Christians. This is not to say that the

[17] Cf. Floyd Seward Lear, "The Medieval Attitude toward History," *Rice Institute Pamphlet* 20 (1933):156–77.

[18] Arnaldo Momigliano, "Pagan and Christian Historiography in the Fourth Century A.D.," in *Paganism and Christianity in the Fourth Century*, ed. Momigliano (Oxford: Clarendon Press, 1963), p. 92.

Greeks and Romans did not have or did not attend to their gods and their religious duties as they conceived them; but rather, that they did not experience them as great mysteries, puzzles, or problems to be discussed and analyzed. In the remains of Greek and Roman literature, discussions of the nature of the Godhead are relatively infrequent and seldom of first-rate importance. It is a measure of the retrospective misunderstanding of these discussions that they are often excerpted and examined by modern writers as though the ideas were as important to ancient civilization as they are to modern. On the other hand, there are ideas which are prominent in Greek and Roman thought but which, carried over into early Christian thought, have little importance. Such, for example, is the idea of nature.

Given these different kinds of relationships between the cultures as regards ideas, and given the prominence that the idea of history has had in Western culture for the past three or four centuries, it is all the more interesting to observe that the idea of history was not an important idea in antiquity. History does not pose any theoretical or speculative problems. History neither explains anything nor itself needs explanation. In fact, the opposition between history and reason or explanation lasts throughout antiquity and provides the basis for the continuing rejection of history as philosophically insufficient.[19] When history was discussed by the Greeks and Romans, the literary genre was meant and the discussions were carried on by rhetoricians. The problems that history posed for them were problems of art, not problems of science or knowledge. There was "natural history" and, in the later period, "history of opinions"; but history here was just accurate information, the facts, or an account thereof. Such knowledge as this indicated was knowledge by acquaintance. History was discussed by the Christians not directly but, rather, in the context of Bible criticism. Here history, similarly, was the literal or somatic level or dimension of Scripture, and it was to be understood straightforwardly. There was no problem about understanding "according to history"; the problems in exegesis had to do with nonliteral exegesis. The Christians had a history, found in the Scriptures, which served them as their equivalent of the histories of the Greeks and Romans and which they accepted on faith. But here too there were no specu-

---

[19] It was rejected as early as Heraclitus; cf. p. 25, *supra.* The opposition between history and reason or explanation was reiterated in the exegetical distinction between historical and intellectual interpretation.

lative or scientific problems; one needed only to be acquainted with the facts.

If the idea of history was not important in ancient culture, it certainly became so later on. Augustine set up the opposition between sacred and gentile history as different histories, with different beginnings and ends, going on at the same time and in the same place. The two cities are side by side in this world and in the universe. But the history of the celestial city is providential and its end is salvation; its meaning and end are not those of the history of the terrestrial city. The great authority enjoyed by Augustine and the uninterrupted availability of the *City of God* during the succeeding centuries established the distinction between sacred and profane history as a fundamental (metaphysical) distinction in Western thought.[20] But sacred and profane history were not only understood to be different. It came to be understood also that the sacred history, which began with the creation of the world and would end with the second coming of the messiah,[21] which depended for its reliability upon the divine authority of inspired authorship rather than upon the merely human authority of observation and inquiry, was the measure of all other histories. If there was a conflict between what was found in the sacred history and what was said somewhere else, the latter had to be considered incorrect. Likewise, since the sacred history began with the creation of the world, any local or national history was understood as taking place within the time continuum established thereby. The histories written during the Middle Ages were, for the most part, ecclesiastical histories, telling about the progress of the celestial city, the kingdom of God on earth, and proceeding from creation.[22] It was

---

[20] Augustine, however, considered the distinction more mystical than metaphysical. He says (*CD* 15.1): 'I speak of these branches (of mankind) also mystically (*mystice*) as two cities, that is two societies of human beings, of which one is predestined to reign eternally with God and the other to undergo eternal punishment with the devil."

[21] The practice of commencing historical accounts with creation seems to have begun with the *Chronographia* of Julius Africanus, which devoted two books to the period from creation to Moses. This was followed by Eusebius in the construction of his *Chronicle*, which was a historical sourcebook for the next thousand years. Cf. Milburn, *Early Christian Interpretations of History*, pp. 58–60.

[22] For example, Prosper of Aquitaine's *Chronicum integrum* proceeds from Adam to A.D. 455. Gregory of Tours' *Historia Francorum* begins with the creation. Isidore of Seville's *Chronica maiora* is a universal chronicle from creation to A.D. 615. The works of Otto of Freising and Vincent of Beauvais both proceed from creation to the end of time.

left for the Renaissance to rediscover the value of knowing something about the history of the terrestrial city.[23] Even when national histories were being written once again, since all history was still understood to begin with creation and with Adam, writing a national history required that one show the national lineage from the offspring of Noah.[24] And since the national histories derive from the providential history, they characteristically proceed upon the notion that that nation has some particular role to play in the providential history.

Criticism of this view of history as differentiated into a sacred and a profane part began as a reaction against the excesses of millenarianism and as one facet of the skeptical crisis of sixteenth- and seventeenth-century France, and particularly as a result of the transformation of Bible criticism which these movements of thought precipitated.[25] The Scriptures were found to be fallible; the history of the world was found to be somewhat longer than that of the Old Testament peoples; it was argued that there were men before Adam; the lineages from Noah were found to be undocumentable. When the framework of the sacred history—that is, the events from creation to Jesus Christ and the projected Second Coming—dropped out of the picture, the continuity between sacred and profane history was broken. David Hume's *History of England* makes no mention of the sacred history or of the then customary evangelization of England by St. Peter but, rather, begins with the earliest documentable events. The exclusion of that part of history which was called sacred and the rejection of the distinction between sacred and profane brought into being something entirely new, history as a quasi-science (in contemporary terminology, a *social* science) and as part of the educational curriculum of Western civilization. Insofar as the subject matter is

[23] Cf. Louis Green, "Historical Interpretation in the Fourteenth Century Florentine Chronicles," *JHI* 28 (1967):161–78; Constantinos Patrides, *The Phoenix and the Ladder* (Berkeley: University of California Press, 1964), Chap. 6; John Baillie, *The Belief in Progress*, Chap. 3; Wallace K. Ferguson, *The Renaissance in Historical Thought*, Chap. 1.

[24] See Don Cameron Allen, *The Legend of Noah* (Urbana: University of Illinois Press, 1963), Chap. 6, especially pp. 117ff.

[25] Accounts of these historiographical developments during the Renaissance may be found in: Grace E. Cairns, *Philosophies of History* (New York: Philosophical Library, 1962), Part 2 Chap. 5; Frank Manuel, *Shapes of Philosophical History* (Stanford: Stanford University Press, 1965), Chap. 3; Patrides, *Phoenix and Ladder*, Chaps. 5–8, a more detailed study; Winston H. F. Barnes, "On History. I.—Historical Inquiry," *Durham University Journal* 8 (1946–47):89–97; S. G. F. Brandon, "B.C. and A.D.: The Christian Philosophy of History," *History Today* 15 (1965):198–99; Beatrice Reynolds, "Shifting Currents in Historical Criticism," *JHI* 14 (1953), especially pp. 480–92.

concerned, this constitutes a return to the ancient Greek and Roman idea of history as an account of events in the human world, distinct from myth and fable in that it excludes accounts of gods, miracles, and the like. But while the biblical beginning and end of the historical continuum and the miraculous events of the sacred history dropped out of the later view, the providential meaning attributed to events has proved more persistent. Even though the Judaeo-Christian beginning and end of history were relegated to the status of "mythology," the notion that history is moving toward some goal or end has survived. Bayle, Voltaire, and others of the *encyclopédistes* may not have believed that history was going anywhere, but the German Romantics did. If the providential meaning of history was removed by seventeenth- and eighteenth-century French thinkers, it was put back by eighteenth- and nineteenth-century German philosophers of history—with the difference that for them the development is immanent rather than transcendent. Thus history has become a matter of sustained philosophical and theological interest in the modern world.

All of these developments—and this is, of course, only a sketch of the later fortunes of the idea of history—are based on Augustine's distinction between the two histories and the attribution to the sacred history of a providential or salvational meaning. In order for there to be philosophies or theologies of history, however, history must first be understood to be the sort of thing about which there can be a philosophy or a theology. That is to say, history must be understood to indicate the whole temporal process or career of a thing taken collectively. History in this sense is something rather different from the various senses of the term that have been examined in the preceding chapters. In Greek and Roman and Christian writings alike, history meant an informational account or accurate information about various sorts of things. There was a general distinction between uses in which the form was emphasized and those in which the content was emphasized; that is, between history as a literary genre and history as informational account. The latter genus came to have some modified senses in later antiquity; an informational account in which accuracy was less important than entertainment or instruction, history as story, and the information about something or someone taken as a collective whole, history as the past. This last sense most nearly approximates history in the sense required for philosophy or theology of history. But in antiquity and even in Augustine this does not seem to be quite the same sort of history, for all the ancient histories are human productions.

Written works called "histories" are, of course, the products of human art; and history as a literary genre is largely concerned with the rules and styles for producing them. History as informational account is also a human product, both in the earliest sense that it is the result of someone's inquiring and in the later sense that an account of the information about something is possessed by or known to someone, handed down or reported by someone. Here a very great difference between ancient and modern ideas of history appears. For while in the ancient world there is no history apart from human thought and art, in the modern world there is such history, and it is this to which human thought and art are applied. The difference is between (1) someone giving, writing, or knowing the history of something, and (2) something *having* a history, which someone might attempt to learn or to communicate. The difference may be described as one of independent existence or subsistence. In modern thought there is history independent of any knower or writer as an aspect or dimension of the subject thing, person, or nation whose history it is. History thus has become a category of reality, and in that sense a subsistent entity. And just as one may theorize or speculate about time, space, and number, so one may speculate about history.

But history is not this sort of thing for late antiquity or for Augustine. Their usage of history as the past is closely connected to the notion of information or the facts as human productions and possessions, not as possessions of the subjects of the history. Augustine may want to talk about the history of the two cities in this later sense as the whole temporal process or career, but he never uses *historia* or any cognate word for this purpose. His words are *cursus, excursus,* and *procursus*.[26] The inquiry thus comes to a second significant negative observation about the idea of history in antiquity: that history was not understood as a subsistent entity. But Augustine's rhetorical and apologetic differentiation between the two histories and the notion

[26] Augustine speaks of the "course (*cursus*) of the most glorious city" (15.15) and the "courses (*cursus*) of the two cities" (15.27), of the "origin and career (*excursus*) and final end of the two cities" (11.1), and their "career (*excursus*) . . . until human beings cease to reproduce" (15.1), their "origin and progress (*procursus*) and final end" (1.35). The very first sentence of the work declares Augustine's intention to defend "the most glorious city of God both in this course of times (*in hoc temporum cursus*)" and in eternity (1. praef.); similarly 10.15. See also *De Genesim ad Litteram Imperfectam* 5.4 and *De Doctrina Christiana* 2.16.25.

that each had its own beginning, course, and end provide the starting point for that particular phase in the development of the idea of history from which it emerges as, in one sense, this subsistent entity. So that the later idea of history as a subsistent entity, which is the idea involved in modern philosophies and theologies of history, develops from—and only develops from—the rhetorical interpretation which Augustine adumbrated in his *City of God*.

An objection might be raised at this point, and responding to it provides an occasion to recapitulate the argument of this book. The accepted account has been that the Judaeo-Christian idea of history was something entirely new and essentially opposed to the Graeco-Roman, which it superseded. The latter was history as circular, repetitive, and meaningless, but the former made it linear, once and for all, and meaningful. Thus Christians invented the philosophy of history, a branch of philosophy that is of great interest in the modern period, which first came to expression in Augustine's *City of God*. The essentials of this account are innovation, opposition, and supersession, and it characterizes not only studies specifically of the idea of history in antiquity, but also general studies of the relation between "pagan" and "Christian" in the cultural history of the ancient world. I have been arguing, on the contrary, that what the early Christian writers meant by history was not something essentially new and different, that there were not widely accepted patterns of circles vs. lines, repetition vs. uniqueness, and so forth, and that neither culture invented philosophy of history or philosophized about history at all, because neither understood history to be the whole temporal process of a thing taken collectively and understood to be a possession or attribute of that thing (i.e., as independently subsisting) which is prerequisite to any theorizing or philosophizing about it.

Given that argument, the objection is this: if I say that although Augustine does not use *historia* for this, he might seem (or may have wanted) to talk about history as the whole course of a people's career, am I not admitting, in effect, that something radically new *is* found in Augustine's thought, and thus that the accepted account of the idea of history in antiquity can be defended in a modified form? The argument would be that there really is a new and opposed idea of history here, but that it is not connected with *historia* and its cognates until later in the Western tradition.

There are several different answers to this objection. To begin with, when Augustine seems, from our point of view, to be talking about the whole temporal process, he uses (as I have pointed out above), the words *cursus, excursus,* and *procursus.* All of them derive from *curro,* to run; thus *cursus* means basically a running or course as the way, path, or passage run, and thus it comes to be used figuratively for the course (direction, way) of honors,[27] battles,[28] life,[29] or, more vaguely, of things[30] and of times, the *cursus temporum,*[31] which is precisely the phrase that Augustine himself uses at the outset of the *City of God* (1.praef.). *Procursus,* again, basically means a running forth or forward, as in an army's charge, and figuratively the outbreak or first appearance of something. Thus Valerius Maximus speaks of "the origin and first manifestations *(initia procursusque)* of virtue."[32] But when Augustine uses the same phrase *(CD* 1.35) to apply to the two cities, translators are tempted to render *procursus* as "progress."[33] I shall not dispute that translation. But there are two points to be noted about uses of these words that allegedly refer to the whole temporal process: first, they come from the traditional language and culture—they are not Judaeo-Christian neologisms—so that if they indicate the whole temporal process as a conceived unity in Augustine, there is no *prima facie* reason why they should not have in the non-Christian tradition. There would be nothing radically new on that account. In fact, in their contexts the words do not carry such a burden but, rather, only refer, and rather vaguely, to the successions of events; second, in Augustine as in the previous tradition, these words do not have any particular associations with history either as a literary genre or as an informational account, nor are they words that deliberately refer to processes that might be analyzed for such features as goal-directedness or patterns of any sort. They are not, in short, part of the analytical, philosophical, or theoretical vocabulary at all. So if they refer to the whole temporal process—which I think they do not—it would be misleading to suppose that they deliberately refer to it in any philosophically serious way.

[27] Cic. *Fam.* 3.11.2; Tac. *Hist.* 1.48.

[28] Tac. *Agr.* 27.

[29] Cic. *Cael.* 17.39; *Off.* 1.4.11, 1.32.117; *Phil.* 2.19.47; *Sest.* 21.47. Macrob. *Sat.* 1.2.3.

[30] Cic. *Fam.* 4.2.3; Tac. *Agr.* 39; *Hist.* 4.34.

[31] Cic. *Fam.* 6.5.2.

[32] Val. Max. 3.2.init.; cf. *procursus irae,* 7.3.

[33] See, e.g., the translations by M. Dods, G. Wilson, and J. J. Smith in *Basic Writings of Saint Augustine,* ed. Whitney J. Oates (New York: Random House, 1948), Vol. 1, p. 40, and G. G. Walsh, D. B. Zema, G. Monahan, and D. J. Honan in *Saint Augustine. The City of God,* ed. Vernon J. Bourke (New York: Image Books, 1958), p. 64.

Next, if it is admitted that neither the language of *historia* nor that of *cursus* and the like reveals anything radically new and different in Augustine's idea of history, still, it might be argued, the *City of God* as a whole seeks to show the providential meaning of the course of celestial and terrestrial events, and this (logically) implies a conception of history as a whole. To this, too, I would like to make two replies: first, as with *cursus* and its derivatives, if Augustine's enterprise "implies" such an idea, then no less does that of Vergil, for whom "history is something more than a panorama, a glittering pageant which is yet without significance. To him it embodies a hidden meaning which, while it may be dimly forecast in the utterances of seers and prophets, is to be fully disclosed only with the culmination of secular process in the evolution of Eternal Rome."[34]

This suggests the second reply,[35] that there is a fallacy involved in basing one's judgments in the history of culture on ideas supposedly "implied" but not directly discovered in the texts that one is interpreting. The same fallacy underlies the objection being considered here that derives from my earlier statement that "Augustine may want to talk about the history of the two cities in this later sense as the whole temporal process or careers." Such a statement is metaphorical, as are statements about "forerunners," "anticipations," "foreshadowings," and the like in the history of ideas.[36] From a later point of view, and looking backward, we can see how earlier views might have or did provide foundations upon which (or in opposition to which) later views were constructed. We human beings are always mining our physical and spiritual past for materials to build with in the present. But the past was not somehow obscurely "trying" to be

[34] C. N. Cochrane, *Christianity and Classical Culture* (New York: Oxford University Press, 1944), p. 68. Such a view is not, however, restricted to intellectual historians of a past generation. Brooks Otis [*Virgil. A Study in Civilized Poetry* (Oxford: Clarendon Press, 1964), p. 389] observes that Virgil ". . . saw in Rome the paradigm and goal of all historical activity." Cf. R. D. Williams, "Virgil," *Greece & Rome. New Surveys in the Classics* No. 1 (Oxford: Clarendon Press, 1967), p. 27.

[35] The critique sketched here is developed at length by Quentin Skinner, "Meaning and Understanding in the History of Ideas," *H & Th.* 8 (1969):3–53. See also John Dunn, "The Identity of the History of Ideas," *Philosophy* 43 (1968):85–104; Louis O. Mink, "Change and Causality in the History of Ideas," *Eighteenth Century Studies* 2 (1968–69):7–25; and Alfred Soman, "Methodology in the History of Ideas: The Case of Pierre Charron," *Journal of the History of Philosophy* 12 (1974):7–25. Already in 1945 Harold Cherniss had diagnosed a similar fallacy in Platonic scholarship as "retrojection"; see *The Riddle of the Early Academy* (Berkeley: University of California Press, 1945; reissued, New York: Russell and Russell, 1962), pp. 61ff.

[36] See Skinner, "Meaning and Understanding in History of Ideas," pp. 10–12.

the future, and earlier writers were not trying to say or saying badly what later writers finally did say.[37] Writers say what they mean as best they can; we must be careful not to confuse the two valuable but different tasks of understanding what an author's statements mean in their own context and understanding what was made of them by later interpreters.

Thus the objection brings us back to an important point, already premised in Chapter I, of methodology in the history of ideas: that writers, texts, and ages are to be interpreted and understood not in the inherited terms and categories of the interpreter's own age and circumstances—however familiar and unquestionable these may seem—but, rather, in their own terms. As Quentin Skinner observes, "The essential question which we therefore confront, in studying any given text, is what its author, in writing at the time that he did write for the audience he intended to address, could in practice have been intending to communicate by the utterance of this given utterance."[38]

Augustine was not trying to invent the philosophy of history, nor was he "anticipating" eighteenth- and nineteenth-century speculations on the pattern and meaning of history; because for him as for the ancient Graeco-Roman and Judaeo-Christian traditions generally, history was not the sort of thing that could exhibit a pattern and meaning. What Augustine was trying to do was to defend the religion he had adopted with the weapons at his command. That the rhetorical motif of two cities and two histories was used by later writers in such a way that history came to be that sort of thing, came to be conceived as a subsistent entity, does not mean he himself actually did or "must" have had such an idea.

Finally, a comment on the cultural ferment of late antiquity is in order. The linear-cyclic version of the idea of history in antiquity, I have argued, reflects an accepted account of the cultural developments of late antiquity: that the Graeco-Roman and Judaeo-Christian cultures are fundamentally different and opposed. So that the analyses and interpretations of the period that are offered tend to focus on either what came before or what came after and to interpret

---

[37] Notwithstanding Aristotle's treatment of his predecessors' statements as imperfect and partial answers to his own questions; on which, see Chap. 4, n. 85, *supra*.

[38] Skinner, "Meaning and Understanding in History of Ideas," pp. 48–49.

the whole period either in terms of classical civilization or in terms of medieval civilization. Discussions have tended to be either of the decline of the ancient world or of the classical heritage of the Middle Ages.

This study of the idea of history, to the contrary, suggests that there was extensive continuity of ideas and that, at least as regards the ideas which are the tender of communication within the community of users of a language, there is more continuity than change. If this is true, then in order to understand this cultural ferment we must approach it not in terms only of its origins or of its influence and later impact, but in terms of what in fact went on in it; that is, in its own terms. It seems to be the case with the accepted account of late antiquity generally, as it was with the accepted account of the idea of history, that the popularity of the view is to be traced back to the early Christian apologists themselves, whose stock in trade was the opposition between Christianity and "paganism." But what was for them a political necessity in their struggle for survival against ridicule, slander, or persecution has become for modern thought a pair of distorting glasses through which this part of our common past is seen.

The opposition between Judaeo-Christian and Graeco-Roman thought as a pattern for understanding the cultural history of late antiquity is not corroborated in these pages. The pervasiveness of the pattern itself in historical studies is a measure, even in our time, of the hold that early Christian thought has upon our understanding of our past. What would seem to be called for in the future is historical investigation of late antiquity not based on a presumption of opposition and difference—which amounts to a presumption of the Christian apologetical framework—but, rather, investigation that can recognize where there is more of tradition than of innovation, more continuity than change.

It is appropriate to conclude with an example of the difficulty and the alternative. In 1923 Ernest Sihler wrote a book entitled *From Augustus to Augustine*, in which he undertook "to give voice to those utterances which were made in the generation presented, making due allowance for the differences, antipathies and sympathies of minds as presented by themselves, and without intruding any thesis or prejudice of my own."[39] At the beginning of the third chapter he criticizes

---

[39] Ernest G. Sihler, *From Augustus to Augustine. Essays and Studies Dealing with the Con-*

a fashion, established by Gibbon, of supposing that life under the Antonine emperors was happy; for really, according to Sihler, things were very bad, and worst of all in religion. "After all," he comments, "religion is the core and substantial element in any given civilization—and the passing of pagan religion was the passing of paganism."[40] The supposition to which I want to draw attention is that religion is the essence of civilization. For it is not a Graeco-Roman supposition. In fact the one striking difference that has turned up in these pages between Graeco-Roman and Judaeo-Christian culture is the almost obsessive interest of the latter in religious matters, and in matters of broader social, political, and cultural concern only insofar as they relate to religion. If there is a fundamental change in Western culture brought about by the triumph of Christianity, it is this: that the leading motive of all culture *became* religion.[41]

---

tact and Conflict of Classic Paganism and Christianity (Cambridge: Cambridge University Press, 1923), p. viii.

[40] Ibid., p. 54.

[41] A. D. Nock [*Conversion* (London: Oxford University Press, 1933; 1961), pp. 160–63], realized the fundamental difference between what "religion" meant to the Greeks and Romans and what it means to Judaeo-Christianity. Augustine is the crucial figure in the cultural history of late antiquity because he both created and legitimized the synthesis of the Graeco-Roman and Judaeo-Christian cultures that directly formed medieval European culture and thus indirectly forms our own. In H.-I. Marrou's *Saint Augustin et la fin de la culture antique* (Paris: Bocard, 1938), the most influential modern study of Augustine's thought in relation to classical culture, it is repeatedly observed that all culture is to be religious; e.g., "the rigid subordination of all manifestations of spirit to the religious end that dominates the entire doctrine of culture" (p. 510) or "the care to subordinate all culture to the only necessary, the religious end" (p. 518). But the religiocentrism in Christian culture was not invented by Augustine; it may appear to us special in his thought because he is the first to explicitly accept, in the *De doctrina christiana*, the "pagan" arts and sciences and to claim for them an essential function in the propagation of Christianity.

Appendix: Bibliography of Works on the Accepted View of the Idea of History in Antiquity

A. GENERAL

Armstrong, A. H., and Markus, R. A. *Christian Faith and Greek Philosophy*. New York: Sheed and Ward, 1964.

Baillie, John. *The Belief in Progress*, especially Chap. 2. New York: Scribner's, 1950.

Chroust, Anton-Hermann. "The Relation of Religion to History in Early Christian Thought." *The Thomist* 18 (1955):61–70. A particularly thorough and succinct statement of the accepted view.

Connolly, James M. *Human History and the Word of God*, Chap. 1. New York: Macmillan, 1963–64.

Daniélou, Jean. "The Conception of History in the Christian Tradition." *Papers of the Ecumenical Institute* 5 (1950), pp. 67–79; reprinted, *Journal of Religion* 30 (1950):171–79.

Dawson, Christopher. "The Christian View of History." *Blackfriars* 32 (1951):312–27.

Green, William M. "Augustine on the Teaching of History." *University of California Publications in Classical Philology*, Vol. 12, No. 18, pp. 315–32.

Guthrie, Harvey H. *God and History in the Old Testament*, New York: Seabury Press, 1960.

Harbison, Elmore Harris. *Christianity and History*. Princeton: Princeton University Press, 1964. An excellent summary of the recent discussion is found in Chap. 2, pp. 35–52.

Hardy, E. R., Jr. "Christianity and History." *Theology* 40 (1940): 14–25, 104–11.

Holborn, Hajo. "Greek and Modern Concepts of History." *Journal of the History of Ideas* 10 (1949):3–13.

Johnston, E. I. "How the Greeks and Romans Regarded History." *Greece and Rome* 3 (1933–34):38–43.

Laberthonnière, Lucien. "Dieu d'Aristote, Dieu de l'école, Dieu des Chrétiens." *Archivio di Filosofia* 2 (1933):3–36.

LaPiane, George. "Theology of History." In *The Interpretation of History*, edited by Joseph R. Strayer, pp. 149–86, Princeton: Princeton University Press, 1943.

McIntyre, John. *The Christian Doctrine of History*. Edinburgh: Oliver and Boyd, 1957.

Musurillo, H. "History and Symbol." *Theological Studies* 18 (1957):357–86.

Papaioannou, Kostas. "Nature and History in the Greek Conception of the Cosmos." *Diogenes* No. 25 (1959):1–27.

Priess, T. "The Vision of History in the New Testament." *Papers of the Ecumenical Institute* 5 (1950):48–66.

Quispel, G. "Zeit und Geschichte im antike Christentum." In *Man and Time, Papers from the Eranos Yearbooks*, pp. 85–107. London, 1958.

Reinhardt, Karl. "Philosophy and History among the Greeks." *Greece and Rome* N.S. 1 (1954):82–90.

Roberts, Tom A. *History and Christian Apologetics*. London: S.P.C.K., 1960.

Shinn, Roger L. "Augustinian and Cyclical Views of History." *Anglican Theological Review* 31 (1949):133–41.

B.   THE JUDAEO-CHRISTIAN VIEW OF HISTORY AS MORIBUND, IF NOT DEFUNCT

Patrides, Constantinos A. *The Phoenix and the Ladder*. University of California Studies in English Literature, No. 29, 1964.

White, Lynn. "Christian Myth and Christian History." *Journal of the History of Ideas* 2 (1942):145–58.

C.   ON THE IDEA OF TIME ESPECIALLY

Armstrong, A. MacC. "The Fulness of Time." *Philosophical Quarterly* 6 (1956):209–22.

Bury, J. B. *The Idea of Progress*. London: Macmillan, 1920.

Chroust, Anton-Hermann. "The Metaphysics of Time and History in Early Christian Thought." *The New Scholasticism* 19 (1945): 322–52.

Cullmann, Oscar. *Christ and Time. The Primitive Christian Conception of Time and History.* Translated by Floyd Filson. Philadelphia, 1950.

Cushman, Robert E. "Greek and Christian Views of Time." *Journal of Religion* 33 (1953):254–65.

Lovejoy, Arthur O. "The Entangling Alliance of Religion and History." *Hibbert Journal* 6 (1907):258–76.

———. "Religion and the Time-Process." *American Journal of Theology* 6 (1903):439–72.

Muilenberg, James. "The Biblical View of Time." *Harvard Theological Review* 54 (1960):225–52.

Munz, P. "History and Myth." *Philosophical Quarterly* 6 (1956):1–16.

North, C. R. *The Old Testament Interpretation of History.* London: Epworth, 1946.

D.   On the Philosophy of History Especially

Brandon, S. G. F. "B.C. and A.D.: The Christian Philosophy of History." *History Today* 15 (1965):191–99.

———. "The Jewish Philosophy of History." *History Today* 11 (1961):155–64.

Bréhier, Émile. Quelques traits de la philosophie de l'histoire dans l'antiquité classique." *Revue d'histoire et philosophie religieuse* 14 (1934): 38–40.

Cairns, Grace E. *Philosophies of History.* New York: Philosophical Library, 1962.

Case, Shirley Jackson. *The Christian Philosophy of History.* Chicago: University of Chicago Press, 1943.

Curtis, J. Briggs. "A Suggested Interpretation of the Biblical Philosophy of History." *Hebrew Union College Annual* 34 (1963):115–23.

Löwith, Karl. *Meaning in History.* Chicago: University of Chicago Press, 1957.

———. "The Theological Background of the Philosophy of History." *Social Research* 13 (1946):51–80. An earlier version of the thesis that the philosophy of history is an essentially Christian enterprise, for which the *locus classicus* is the preceding citation.

Manuel, Frank. *Shapes of Philosophical History.* Stanford: Stanford University Press, 1965.

Pittenger, Norman. "The Earliest Philosophy of History." *Anglican Theological Review* 29 (1947):238–41.

E. On Historiography Especially

Collingwood, Robin George. *The Idea of History,* especially Pt. I, paras. 3 and 4, and Pt. II, paras. 1 and 2. Oxford: Clarendon Press, 1946.

Den Boer, W. "Some Remarks on the Beginnings of Christian Historiography." *Studia Patristica* 4:348–62.

Downey, Glanville. "The Perspective of the Early Church Historians," *Greek, Roman, and Byzantine Studies* 6 (1965):57–70.

Milburn, R. L. P. *Early Christian Interpretations of History.* London: A. and C. Black, 1954.

Shotwell, James T. "Christianity and History." *Journal of Philosophy, Psychology and Scientific Method* 18 (1920):85–94, 113–20, 141–50.

F. For the Accepted View from the Jewish Standpoint

Polish, David. *The Eternal Dissent,* especially Chap. 9. London: Abelard–Schuman, 1961.

Index Locorum

T HE EVIDENCE for the thesis developed in this study consists principally of actual uses of ἱστορεῖν, ἱστορία, *historia*, and the like by
ancient authors. The Index that follows tabulates all passages cited in
this study. It is divided into Greek and Latin authors. Every passage
indexed is cited at least once; some more than once. Citations followed
by an asterisk (*) do not contain occurrences of ἱστορεῖν, ἱστορία, *historia*,
and so forth.

GREEK AUTHORS

Aesch.	Aeschylus.
Ag.	*Agamemnon* 676–80
Eum.	*Eumenides* 455.
PV	*Prometheus Vinctus* 632.
Aet.	Aetius.
Plac.	*Placita* 5.7 [*DG* 419, 12–18].
Alex. Aph.	Alexander of Aphrodisias.
In Metaph.	*In Aristotelis Metaphysica Commentaria* [*CAG* Vol. I] 9, 6; 16, 18; 23, 12; 41, 17; 42, 22; 42, 25; 51, 12; 52, 10; 60, 8; 120, 1; 120, 6; 120, 15–17.
In Mete.	*In Aristotelis Meteorologicorum libros Commentaria* [*CAG* Vol. III, Pars II] 31, 7–8; 31, 21–22; 32, 11–18; 37, 5–9; 40, 23–24; 57, 2–3; 57, 25–28.
In Sens.	*In librum de Sensu Commentarium* [*CAG* Vol. III, Pars I] 4, 13–17; 12, 8–12; 72, 3–4.
Antig.	Antigonus of Carystus [ed. Beckmann], pp. 6, 27, 80, 169, 180, 192, 194, 197, 199, 202, 205, 207.
Ap.	Appollonides Fr. 2 [*TrGF²* ed. A. Nauck].
App.	Appian.
BCiv.	*Bella Civilia* 9.67.284.
Hist.	*Historiae* 12.103.
Praef.	*Praefatio* 12.
Arist.	Aristotle.
APr.	*Analytica Priora* 46a24–27.
Cael.	*De Caelo* 298b2.

Cyr. Al.	Cyril of Alexandria.
In.Luc.	*Commentarius in Lucam* [*PG* 72] 684D.
In Jo.	*Commentarium in Evangelium Ioannis* [*PG* 73] 166D; 228A, B; 325C; 337A; 684D; 960C; 961B.
D.C.	Dio Cassius 7.25.1; 7.25.6; 37.17.4; 40.63.4; 54.23.1; 56.18.1; 57.24.6; 59.22.5; 66.9.4; 67.8.1; 72.4.7; 72.7.2; 72.18.3; 72.23.2.
Dem.	Demosthenes.
Cor.	*De Corona* 144.
Democr.	Democritus [D–K⁷] Fr. (68) B299.
D.H.	Dionysius of Halicarnassus.
Amm. 1, 2	*Epistula ad Ammaeum 1, 2* 1.3; 1.4; 1.11; 2.2; 2.15.
Ant. Rom.	*Antiquitates Romanae* 5.17.3; 5.17.4; 5.56.1.
Pomp.	*Epistula ad Pompeium* 3.4; 3.6; 3.8; 3.13; 3.14.
Rh.	*Ars Rhetorica* 11.2.
Th.	*De Thucydide* 2, 5, 7, 9, 16, 24, 41.
Did.	Didymus.
In D.	*Commentary on Demosthenes* [ed. Diels and Schubart (Berlin, 1904)] 12, 47.
Dion. Thr.	Dionysius Thrax, *De Arte Grammatica* [ed. Uhlig (Leipzig, 1883) = *Grammatici Graeci*, Vol. I] Para. 1.
Sch.	Scholia *in Dionysii Thracis Artem Grammaticam* [ed. Hilgard (Leipzig: Teubner, 1901) = *Grammatici Graeci*, Vol. I, Pars III] 14, 19; 303, 4; 470, 4.
D.L.	Diogenes Laertius 8.6; 5.46–50.
Eur.	Euripides.
Ion.	*Ion* 1547.
IT	*Iphigenia Taurica* 1431.
Hel.	*Helena* 1371.
Or.	*Orestes* 380.
Tr.	*Troades* 261.
Eus.	Eusebius of Caesarea.
Dem. Ev.	*Demonstratio Evangelica* 9.1.3.
H.E.	*Historia Ecclesiastica* 1.1; 1.2; 1.3; 1.4; 1.5; 1.7; 1.8; 1.10; 1.11; 1.12; 2.praef.; 2.1; 3.4; 3.6; 3.8; 6.11; 7.18; 8.2; 8.9.
Or. Const.	*Oration of Constantine* 16, 26.
Pr. Const.	*Praise of Constantine* 7.10.
VConst.	*Vita Constantini* 1.23, 2.22, 4.7.

Gal.   Galen [in Karl Deichgräber, *Die Griechische Empirikerschule* (Berlin: Weidmann, 1930)].

αἱρής.   περὶ αἱρήσεων τοῖς εἰσαγώγοις 3.2.2 [95, 15–20].

ἀρίστ.   περὶ τῆς ἀρίστης αἱρήσεως [97, 9–11; 126, 23–127,1; 127, 9–10, 11–14, 21, 25, 28, 31, 35; 128, 1, 20].

εἰσαγ.   εἰσαγώγη ἢ ἰατρός [91, 29–33; 100, 17–20].

'Ιππ.' Επιδ.   εἰς τὸ Ἱπποκράτους ἐπιδημίων ὑπόμνημα [237, 16–18].

'Ιππ.φύσ. ἀνθ.   εἰς τὸ Ἱπποκράτους περὶ φύσεως ἀνθρώπου ὑπόμνημα [128, 12–20].

συνθ. φαρμ.   περὶ συνθέσεως φαρμάκων [147, 27–31].

Gelas.   Gelasius.

H.E.   *Historia Ecclesiastica* 2.17.3–5, 28, 29–30; 3.9.3; 3.9.4.

Hdn.   Herodian.

Hist.   *Histories* 1.1.1; 1.11.1; 1.11.15; 2.1.1; 2.15.6; 2.15.7 fin.; 3.7.3; 3.7.6.

Hdt.   Herodotus 1.1.1; 1.24.7; 1.56.1–2; 1.61.2; 1.122.1; 2.19.3; 2.29.1; 2.34.1; 2.99.1; 2.113.1; 2.118.1; 2.119.3; 3.51.1; 3.77.2; 4.192.3.

Heracl.   Heraclitus.

Q.Hom.   *Quaestiones Homericae* [ed. Oelmann (Leipzig: Teubner, 1910)] 39, 15–40; 63, 5–13; 69; 9–17; 77, 9–19; 80, 20–81, 9; 84, 11–16; 89, 2–15.

Heraclit.   Heraclitus Philosophus (D-K, *Vors.*[7]) Frr. (22) B35, B40, Bl29.

Hes.   Hesiod.

Op.   *Opera et Dies* 793.

Hom.   Homer.

Il.   *Iliad* 18.499–501; 23.485–487.

h.Hom.   *Hymni Homerici* 32.2.

Iamb.   Iamblichus.

VP   *De Vita Pythagorica* [ed. A. Nauck (Leipzig, 1884)] 11, 3; 22, 4; 23, 9; 25, 11; 30, 15–16; 41, 12; 66, 9–12; 68, 13; 99, 7; 105, 12; 106, 11; 136, 13; 169, 5.

Io. Chrys.   Ioannes Chrysostomus (John Chrysostom).

Adv. Jud.   *Adversus Judaeos* 1.6 [*PG* 48, 851].

De Dav.   *Homiliae de Davide et Saule* 7 [*PG* 54, 758, 759].

In Matth.	*Homiliae in Mattheum* 1.4 [*PG* 57, 16]; 1.7 [*PG* 57, 17].
In Psalm.	*Expositio in Psalmos* 3.1 [*PG* 55, 35]; 46.1 [*PG* 55, 188].
Isoc.	Isocrates.
Pan.	*Panathenaicus* 246.
J. Mart.	Justin Martyr.
Apol.	*Apology* 1.21.4; 1.22.4; 1.53.1; 1.53.8.
Dial.	*Dialogue with Trypho* 62.2; 69.2.
John Chrysostom	*See* Io. Chrys.
Lucian	
Alex.	*Alexander* 1.
Hipp.	*Hippias* 2.67.
Hist. conscr.	*Quomodo historia conscribenda sit* 2, 4, 5, 6, 7, 8, 9, 10, 16, 17, 39, 42, 55, 63.
Im.	*Imagines* 4.
Laps.	*Pro Lapsu inter Salutandum* 7.
Scyth.	*Scytha* 8.
Syr. D.	*De Syria Dea* 11.
Max. Tyr.	Maximus of Tyre.
Diss.	*Dissertationes* [cited by enumeration of F. Dübner (Paris: Didot, 1840)] 28, 5; 28, 5–6.
Meth.	Methodius of Olympus (ed. Bonwetsch).
Resurr.	*De Resurrectione* 1.52.1; 2.25.1; 3.17.3; 3.5.8; 3.18.4–5; 3.18.8.
Symp.	*Symposium* 3.1; 3.9; 10.2.
Nausiph.	Nausiphanes [D–K, *Vors.*7] *Fr.* (75) B2.
Olymp.	Olympiodorus.
In Alc.	*In Platonis Alcibiadem commentarium* [ed. L. G. Westerink (Amsterdam: North Holland, 1956)] 43, 12; 50, 8; 154, 9–10; 155, 16–17; 167, 23–24; 218, 14–15.
Origen	
C. Cels.	*Contra Celsum* 1.40; 1.42; 1.43; 1.44.
Luc.	*In Lucam* Frr. 17e, 125, 217, 223.
Princ.	*De Principiis* 4.1.13; 4.1.16.
Phld.	Philodemus.
Rh.	*Volumina Rhetorica* [ed. Sudhaus, 2 vols. (Leipzig: Teubner, 1892, 1896)] 1.28, 34–29, 14; 44, 16–21; 200, 18–30; 299, 1–7; 345, 1–8; 2.19, 1; 105 (Fr. XII), 5ff.

Philo   Philo Judaeus Alexandrinus.
  Abr.   *De Abrahamo* 1*, 65.
  Aet. Mundi   *De Aeternitate Mundi* 120, 139.
  Cher.   *De Cherubim* 105.
  Congr.   *De congressu quaerendae Eruditionis gratia* 14, 15,
                            23, 44, 74.
  In Flacc.   *In Flaccum* 43*.
  Praem. et Poen.   *De Praemiis et Poeniis* 1–2.
  Sacr. Ab.   *De Sacrificio Abrahami* 78.
  Somn.   *De Somniis* 1.52; 1.205; 2.302.
  Spec. Leg.   *De Specialibus Legibus* 1.342; 2.146.
  V. Mos.   *De Vita Mosis* 2.46–48; 2.53*; 2.59; 2.143, 2.263*.
Philostr.   Philostratus [ed. Kayser (Leipzig, 1879)].
  Im.   *Imagines* 2.9.7.
Pl.   Plato.
  Cra.   *Cratyulus* 406B, 407C.
  Phd.   *Phaedo* 96A.
  Phdr.   *Phaedrus* 244C–D.
  Sph.   *Sophist* 267D–E.
Plb.   Polybius 1.1.1–2; 1.3.8; 1.14.5–6; 1.35.9–10; 1.37.3;
                          1.63.7; 2.14.1–2, 7; 2.16.13–14; 2.17.2; 2.35.5–6;
                          2.37.3, 6; 2.61.3–6; 2.62.2, 6; 2.71.2; 3.4.8; 3.5.9;
                          3.20.5; 3.38.2–3; 3.48.12; 3.57.4–5; 3.61.2–3;
                          3.118.12; 4.2.2; 4.8.4; 4.28.4; 4.40.3; 4.47.2; 5.31.6;
                          5.33.2–3; 5.75.5–6; 6.2.2–3; 6.49.2; 6.54.6; 8.9.2;
                          8.11.2; 9.19.3–4.
Plu.   Plutarch.
  Alex. Fort.   *De fortuna Alexandri* 330A, 331F.
  Curios.   *De curiositate* 515D; 516C, D; 517F; 518C.
  Fort. Rom.   *De fortuna Romanorum* 320B.
  Gen.   *De genio Socratis* 575B–C, 578D.
  Glo. Ath.   *De gloria Atheniensium* 347D–E.
  Malign.   *De malignitate Herodoti* 855B–F.
  Mus.   *De musica* 1135F; 1136B, C; 1140C, F.
  Non Poss.   *Non posse suaviter vivi secundum Epicurum* 1092F–
                            1095A.
  Prof. Virt.   *De profectu in virtute* 440E.
  Q. Conv.   *Quaestiones convivales* 7.701C, 715E; 8.724D, 728E,
                            733B, C; 9.738F, 741A.
  Q. Gr.   *Quaestiones Graecae* 292F, 293B, 301F.

Q. Rom.	*Quaestiones Romanae* 264D; 267B–C; 268D; 269A; 272D, F; 278F; 285E.
Porph.	Porphyry [ed. Nauck (1886)].
Abst.	*De Abstinentia* 1.25; 2.49.
Antr.	*De Antro Nympharum* 2 (p. 55, 14–18).
V. Pyth.	*De Vita Pythagorica* 2 (p. 18, 10–12); 5 (19, 15–17); 44 (40, 20–23); 55 (47, 20–22); 61 (52, 7–9).
Procl.	Proclus.
In Crat.	*In Platonis Cratylum commentaria* [ed. Pasquali (Leipzig: Teubner, 1908)], p. 34, 24.
Pseudo-Lucian	
Erot.	*Erotes* 8.406; 15.414.
S.E.	Sextus Empiricus.
Math.	*Adversus Mathematicos* 1.43; 1.272; 1.278; 2.96; 7.140; 7.190; 8.14; 8.290; 9.32; 9.57; 9.366; 11.191.
Pyr.	*Outlines of Pyrrhonism* 1.84; 3.225; 3.232.
Simp.	Simplicius.
In Cael.	*In Aristotelis de Caelo commentaria* (*CAG* Vol. VII) 510a41.
In Phy.	*In Aristotelis Physica commentaria* (*CAG* IX, X) f. 25ʳ16.
Soph.	Sophocles.
El.	*Electra* 850, 1101.
OT	*Oedipus Tyrranus* 1150, 1156, 1484.
Trach.	*Trachiniae* 415.
Sozom.	Sozomen.
H.E.	*Historia Ecclesiastica* Praef. 4, 17; 1.1.11, 16, 17, 18–19; 1.8.14; 1.12.11; 2.1.5; 2.26.4; 3.15.3, 10; 4.5.4; 4.28.5; 5.2.19; 7.12.4; 7.18.7; 7.21.8; 7.26.3; 8.18.8; 9.1.13.
Stob.	Stobaeus.
Flor.	*Florilegia* 67.6.
Strabo	15.1.30; 15.1.34.
Tatian	
Ad Gr.	*Oratio ad Graecos* 1.1; 31.1; 31.4; 36.2; 37.1; 39.1.
Them.	Themistius.
In de An.	*In libros Aristotelis de Anima paraphrasis* (*CAG* Vol. V, Pars III) 14, 4–6.

Theodoretus
Dial.	*Dialogus* III [*PG* 83, 257A].
In Am.	*In Amos* 1.2 [*PG* 81, 1668A].
In Dan.	*In Danielis* 11.27; 11.28; 11.41.
In Ez.	*In Ezechielis* 31.14 [*PG* 81, 1125C–D].
In Isai.	*In Isaiae* 15.2 [*PG* 81, 340D].
In Jer.	*In Jeremiae* 9.45 [*PG* 81, 706B].
In Nah.	*In Nahum* 2.1 [*PG* 81, 179A].
In Ps.	*In Psalmis* 13 [*PG* 80, 949B].
In Soph.	*In Sophoniae* 2.12 [*PG* 81, 1852A].
In Zach.	*In Zachariae* 14.8 [*PG* 81, 1953B]; 14.10 [*PG* 81, 1956B].
Prov.	*De Providentia* III [*PG* 83, 589D].
Q. Deut.	*Quaestiones in Deuteronomion* 6.1 [*PG* 80, 408B].
Q. Reg.	*Quaestiones in Libros Regum I, Q.* 7 [*PG* 80, 537C]; III, Q. 66 [*PG* 80, 740A].
Rel. Hist.	*Religiosa Historia* 9 [*PG* 82, 1377D].

Theophilus
Autol.	*Ad Autolycum* 2.7; 2.13; 2.20; 2.30; 2.32; 2.34; 3.18; 3.22; 3.23; 3.36.
Thphr.	Theophrastus [Diels, *DG*] Frr. 1 [475, 10–13]; 8 [484, 17–18]; 9 [484, 19–485, 4]; 12 [486, 17–21].

Latin Authors

Ambr.	Ambrose.
Exp. Luc.	*Expositio Evangelii secundum Lucam,* Prol. 1 [*PL* 15, 1607A]; Prol. 4 [*PL* 15, 1609B–C]; Prol. 7 [*PL* 15, 1611B].
In Ps.	*Enarrationes in Psalmos* 36.80 [*PL* 14, 1055C].
Amm. Marc.	Ammianus Marcellinus 21.10.6; 23.4.10; 24.2.16; 26.1.1; 27.2.11.
Apul.	Apuleius.
Apol.	*Apologia* 30.
Flor.	*Florida* 9, 16, 20.
Met.	*Metamorphoses* 2.12; 6.29; 7.16; 8.1.
Plat.	*De Dogmate Platonis* 1.4.7.
Arn.	Arnobius.
Adv. Nat.	*Adversus Nationes* 1.3; 1.52; 5.1, 5.8, 5.14–15; 5.18; 5.30; 5.32; 5.34; 6.6; 7.38; 7.44; 7.46; 7.49.

Index Indicum

To determine what any author means by a word, one needs to examine its uses in their contexts. A study of the sort undertaken here—which considers several related words in different languages over a period of nearly a thousand years—requires the examination of as many uses by as many authors as possible. It is therefore dependent on the use of dictionaries and indexes of individual authors. Unfortunately there is no current, comprehensive, and annotated list of such works for either Greek or Latin. P. Faider's *Repertoire des index et lexique d'auteurs latines* (Paris, 1926 = *Collection d'études latines* [serie scientifique], 3) to my knowledge has never been updated. Harald and Blenda Riesenfeld's *Repertorium Lexicographicum Graecum* (Stockholm: Almqvist & Wiksell, 1954) is a model of what such a book should be, briefly assessing the completeness and reliability of most of the books mentioned. It should be updated for the last twenty-five years.

What follows is a list of the dictionaries and indexes consulted for this study. I have not included word-lists found in volumes of series such as the *Corpus Aristotelicum Graecum*, *Corpus Scriptorum Ecclesiasticorum Latinorum*, *Patrologia Graeca*, and *Patrologia Latina*. Entries with an asterisk(*) showed no uses of ἱστορεῖν, ἱστορία, *historia*, and so forth.

Greek Authors

*1. Aeschines. Sigmund Preuss. *Index Aeschineus*. Leipzig: Teubner, 1926. Reprint. Amsterdam: Hakkert, 1965.

2. Aeschylus. Gabriel Italie. *Index Aeschyleus*. Leiden: Brill, 1955.

*3. Alciphron. *Alciphron. Epistularum libri iv*. Edited by M. A. Schepers. Leipzig: Teubner, 1905.

*4. Alcman. *Alcman. The Parthenion.* Edited by D. L. Page. Oxford: 1951.

5. Alexander of Aphrodisias. *Commentaria in Aristotelem Graeca,* I–IV.

*6. Anacreon. *Carmina Anacreonta.* Edited by C. Priesendanz. Leipzig: Teubner, 1912.

*7. Andocides. Ludovico Leaming Forman. *Index Andocideus, Lycurgus, Dinarchus.* Amsterdam: Hakkert, 1962.

8. Antigonus of Carystos. *Antigonni Carystii Historiarum Mirabilium.* Edited by Beckmann. Leipzig: Kummer, 1791.

*9. Antiphon. F. L. van Cleef. *Index Antiphonetus.* Ithaca, N.Y., 1895. Reprint. Hildesheim: Olms, 1965.

*10. Apollonius of Rhodes. *Apollonii Rhodii Argonautica.* Edited by A. Wellauer. Leipzig, 1828.

11. Apologists. Edgar J. Goodspeed. *Index Apologeticus sive clavis Iustinus Martyris Operum aliorumque Apologetarum Pristinorum.* Leipzig: Hinrich's, 1912.

12. Appian. *Appiani Alexandrini Romanarum Historiarum quae supersunt.* Edited by Johann Schweighaeuser. Leipzig: Weidmann, 1785.

13. Archimedes. *Opera omnia cum commentariis Eutochii.* Edited by J. L. Heiberg. Leipzig: Teubner, 1910–15.

*14. Aristophanes. O. J. Todd. *Index Aristophaenus.* Cambridge: Harvard University Press, 1932. Reprint. Hildesheim: Olms, 1962.

15. Aristotle. Hermann Bonitz. *Index Aristotelicus.* Berlin, 1870.

16. Artemiodorus Daldianus. *Artemiordori Daldiani Onirocriticon libri v.* Edited by Roger Pack. Leipzig: Teubner, 1963.

17. Athanasius. Guido Muller. *Lexicon Athanasianum.* Berlin: de Gruyter, 1952.

*18. Callimachus. *Callimachea.* Edited by O. Schneider. Leipzig, 1870–73.

*19. Chrysippus. A. Gercke. "Chrysippea." *Jahrbücher für das Philologie,* Suppl. 14 (1885):688–780.

20. Clement of Alexandria. *Clemens Alexandrinus, Opera.* Edited by Otto Stählin. Leipzig: Hinrich's, 1936.

21. Comic Poets. *Fragmenta Comicorum Graecorum.* collected by Augustus Meineke. Berlin: Reimer, 1857; *Comicorum Graecorum Fragmenta.* Edited by G. Kaibel. Berlin, 1899; *Supplementum Comicum.* Edited by Ioannes Demianczuk. Cracow, 1912. Reprint. Hildesheim: Olms, 1962.

*22. Democritus. P. Natorp. *Die Ethika des Demokritos.* Marburg, 1893.

23. Demosthenes. Sigmund Preuss, *Index Demosthenicus.* Leipzig, 1892. Reprint. Hildesheim: Olms, 1963.

*24. Didymus. *Didymus. Kommentar zu Demosthenes.* Edited by H. Diels and W. Schubart. Berlin, 1904 = *Berliner Klassikertexte* 1.

*25. Dinarchus. (See Andocides).

26. Dio Cassius. *Casii Dionis Cocceiani Historiarum quae supersunt.* Edited by U. P. Boissevain. Berlin: Weidmann, 1931.

27. Dionysius Periegetes. *Dionysius Periegetes.* Edited by G. Bernhardy. Leipzig: 1828 = *Geographici Graeci Minores* 1.

28. Dionysius Thrax. *Dionysii Thracis Ars Grammatica.* Edited by G. Uhlig. Leipzig: Teubner, 1883. Reprint, 1965; *Scholia in Dionysii Thracis Artem Grammaticam.* Edited by A. Hilgard. Leipzig: Teubner, 1901. Reprint, 1965.

29. Doxographers. Hermann Diels. *Doxographi Graeci.* 4th ed. Berlin: de Gruyter, 1965.

30. Epictetus. *Epicteti Dissertationes ab Arriano Digestae.* Edited by H. Schenkl. Leipzig: Teubner, 1916.

31. Heraclitus Ephesius. *Heracliti Ephesii Reliquiae.* Edited by I. Bywater. Oxford, 1877.

32. Heraclitus Grammaticus. *Heracliti Quaestiones Homericae.* Edited by Societatis Bonnensis sodales. Leipzig: Teubner, 1910.

*33. Herodes Atticus. *Herodes Atticus. Opera.* Edited by E. Drerup. Paderborn, 1908 = *Studien zur Geschichte und Kultur des Altertums* 2:1.

34. Herodian Historicus. *Historiarum libri octo.* Edited by T. W. Irmisch. Leipzig, 1789 1805.

35. Herodian Technicus. *Herodiani Technici reliquiae.* Collected by Augustus Lenz. Leipzig: Teubner, 1867 = *Grammatici Graeci*, Pars iii, Vol. I, II.

36. Herodotus. J. E. Powell. *Lexicon Herodoteum.* Cambridge: Cambridge University Press, 1938.

*37. Herondas. *Herondas, The Mimes and Fragments.* Edited by A. D. Knox. Cambridge, 1922.

38. Hesiod. Johannes Paulson. *Index Hesiodeus.* Lund, 1890. Reprint. Hildesheim: Olms, 1962.

*39. Hierocles Stoicus. *Ethische Elementarlehre (Pap. 9780) nebst den bei Stobäus erhaltenen ethischen Excerpten aus Hierocles.* Edited by H. von Arnim. Berlin, 1906 = *Berliner Klassikertexte* 4.

40. Homer. Augustus Gehring. *Index Homericus.* Leipzig: Teubner, 1891.
41. Iamblichus. Gustavus Panthey. *Iamblichi De Mysteriis Liber.* Amsterdam: Hakkert, 1965; Hermengild Pistelli. *Iamblichi Protrepticus.* Stuttgart: Teubner, 1967; Augustus Nauck. *Iamblichi De Vita Pythagorica Liber.* St. Petersburg, 1884. Reprint. Amsterdam: Hakkert, 1965.
*42. Isaeus. Jean-Marc Denommé, *Index Isaeus.* Hildesheim: Olms, 1968; W. A. Goligher and W. S. Maguiness. *Index to the Speeches of Isaeus.* Cambridge, Eng.: Heffer, 1962 = *Hermathena* 51 (1938).
43. Isocrates. Sigmund Preuss. *Index Isocrateus.* Stuttgart: Teubner, 1904. Reprint. Hildesheim: Olms, 1963.
44. Lucian. C. C. Reitz. *Index verborum ac phrasium Luciani.* Utrecht, 1746.
45. Lycurgus. (See Andocides).
46. Lyric Poets. Georgios Fatouros., *Index Verborum zur Frühgriechischen Lyrik.* Heidelberg: Universitätsverlag, 1966.
*47. Lysias. D. H. Holmes. *Index Lysiacus.* Bonn, 1895. Reprint. Amsterdam: Hakkert, 1965.
*48. Maximus Astrologus. *Maximi et Ammonis carminum de actionum auspiciis reliquiae.* Edited by A. Ludwich. Leipzig: Teubner, 1877.
49. Maximus of Tyre. *Maximi Tyrii Dissertationes.* Edited by F. Dübner. Paris: Firmin-Didot, 1877.
*50. Menander. *Menandrea ex papyris et membranis vetustissimis.* Edited by A. Koerte. Leipzig: Teubner, 1912.
51. New Testament. J. H. Thayer, *A Greek-English Lexicon of the New Testament.* New York: Harper, 1889.
*52. Nicomachus. *Introductionis arithmeticae libri ii.* Edited by R. Hoche. Leipzig: Teubner, 1866.
53. Olympiodorus. *Olympiodorus. Commentary on the First Alcibiades of Plato.* Edited by L. G. Westerink. Amsterdam: North Holland, 1956.
54. Patres Graeci. Edgar J. Goodspeed. *Index Patristicus sive clavis Patrum Apostolicorum.* Leipzig: Hinrich's, 1907.
55. Peripatetics. F. R. Wehrli. *Die Schule des Aristoteles.* Basel: Schwabe, 1944–59.
56. Philo Judaeus Alexandrinus. *Index verborum ad Philonis Alexandrini Opera.* Compiled by Ioannes Liesegang. Vol. 7, Pt. 2 of

Opera quae supersunt, edited by Cohn and Wendland. Berlin: Reimer, 1915–30; Günter Mayer. *Index Philoneus.* Berlin: de Gruyter, 1974.

57. Philostratus. *Philostrati Imagines.* Edited by Seminariorum Vindobonensum sodales. Leipzig: Teubner, 1893.

58. Pindar. Johann Rumpel. *Lexicon Pindaricum.* Stuttgart: Teubner, 1883. Reprint. Hildesheim: Olms, 1961.

59. Plato. Friedrich Ast. *Lexicon Platonicum.* Leipzig: Weidmann, 1835–38. Reprint. New York: Franklin, 1969; Leonard Brandwood. *Index to Plato.* Leeds: Maney, 1976.

60. Plutarch. D. A. Wyttenbach. *Lexicon Plutarcheum. Plutarchi Moralia Index Graecitatis.* Oxford, 1830. Reprint. Hildesheim: Olms, 1962.

61. Polybius. A. Mauersberger. *Polybios-Lexicon.* Berlin, 1956–.

62. Porphyry. *Porphyrii Opuscula selecta.* Rec. Augustus Nauck. Leipzig: Teubner, 1886. Reprint. Hildesheim: Olms, 1963.

63. Pre-Socratic Philosophers. Hermann Diels. *Die Fragmente der Vorsokratiker.* 6th ed., rev. Walther Kranz. Berlin, 1952.

*64. Ptolemy. E. Düring. *Die Harmonienlehre des Klaudios Ptolemaios.* Göteborg, 1930.

65. Sextus Empiricus. *Sexti Empirici Opera.* Edited by H. Mutschmann and J. Mav. Leipzig: Teubner, 1962.

66. Sophocles. Heinrich Ebeling. *Griechisch-Deutsches Wörterbuch zu Sophocles.* Leipzig: Hahn'sche, 1860; F. Ellendt. *Lexicon Sophocleum.* Berlin, 1872. Reprint. Hildesheim, Olms, 1965.

*67. Soranus Medicus. *Soranus Medicus. Gynaeicorum libri iv.* Edited by J. Ilberg. Leipzig, 1927 = *Corpus Medicorum Graecorum* 4.

68. Stoics. H. von Arnim. *Stoicorum Veterum Fragmenta.* Leipzig: Teubner, 1903–24.

69. Themistius. Wilhelm Dindorf. *Themistii Orationes.* Leipzig, 1832. Reprint. Hildesheim: Olms, 1961; *Commentaria in Aristotelem Graeca,* Vols. V, VI.

*70. Theocritus. Johannes Rumpel. *Lexicon Theocriteum.* Leipzig: Teubner, 1879.

*71. Theognis. *Theognis Reliquiae.* Edited by J. Sitzler. Heidelberg, 1880.

*72. Theophrastus. *Theophrasti Characteres.* Edited by Hermann Diels. Oxford: 1909. Reprint, 1961; *Theophrasti Metaphysica.* Edited by W. D. Ross and F. H. Fobes. Oxford, 1929. Reprint. Hildesheim: Olms, 1967.

*73. Thucydides. E.-A. Bétant. *Lexicon Thucydideum.* Ganf, 1847. Reprint. Hildesheim: Olms, 1961; M. H. N. von Essen. *Index Thucydideus.* Berlin: Wiedmann, 1887.

74. Tragic Poets. Augustus Nauck. *Tragicorum Graecorum Fragmenta.* Leipzig: Teubner, 1889. Reprint. Hildesheim: Olms, 1964.

*75. Xenophon. Catharina Maria Gloth and Francisca Kellogg. *Index in Xenophontis Memorabilia.* Ithaca, N.Y.: Cornell University Press, 1900; F. W. Sturz. *Lexicon Xenophonteum.* Leipzig, 1802. Reprint. Hildesheim: Olms, 1964.

Latin Authors

1. Ammianus Marcellinus. *Ammiani Marcellini Rerum Gestarum Libri qui supersunt.* Edited by V. Gardthausen. Leipzig: Teubner, 1847.

2. Apuleius. W. A. Oldfather, H. V. Canter, and R. Perry. *Index Apuleianus.* Middletown, Conn.: American Philological Association Publication, 1934.

3. Arnobius. Lucille Berkowitz. *Index Arnobianus.* Hildesheim: Olms, 1967.

4. Augustine. F. David Lenfant. *Concordantiae Augustinianae.* Paris, 1656.

*5. Avienus. *Rufi Festi Avieni carminum.* Rec. A. Holder. Innsbruck: Wagner, 1882.

*6. Julius Caesar. H. Merguet. *Lexicon zu den Schriften Cäsars.* Jena, 1886. Reprint. Hildesheim: Olms, 1963.

*7. Cato. H. Merguet. *Index Verborum in Catonis De re rustica.* Leipzig: Teubner, 1897.

*8. Catullus. M. N. Wetmore. *Index Verborum Catullianus.* New Haven, 1912. Reprint. Hildesheim: Olms, 1961.

9. Celsus. *A. Cornelii Celsi quae supersunt.* Rec. F. Marx. Leipzig: Teubner, 1919 = Corpus Medicorum Latinorum 1.

10. Cicero. H. Merguet. *Lexicon zu den Reden des Ciceros.* Jena, 1877. Reprint. Hildesheim: Olms, 1962. Merguet. *Lexicon zu Ciceros philosophischen Schriften.* Jena, 1887. Reprint. Hildesheim: Olms, 1961; Merguet. *Handlexicon zu Cicero.* Leipzig,

1905–6. Reprint. Hildesheim: Olms 1962. W. Abbot, W. A. Oldfather, and H. V. Canter. *Index Verborum Ciceronis Epistularum.* Urbana, 1938. Reprint. Hildesheim: Olms, 1965. Abbot, Oldfather, Canter. *Index in Ciceronis Rhetorica*; John W. Spaeth. *Index Verborum Ciceronis Poeticorum Fragmentorum.* Urbana: University of Illinois Press, 1955.

*11. Claudian. *Claudii Claudiani quae exstant Omnia Opera.* Edited by N. L. Artaud. Paris: Lemaire, 1824.

 12. Curtius Rufus. Otto Eichert. *Vollständiges Wörterbuch zu dem Geschichtswerk des Quintus Curtius Rufus.* Hildesheim: Olms, 1967.

*13. Dares Phrygius. *Daretis Phrygii De Excidio Troiae Historia.* Edited by F. Meister. Leipzig: Teubner, 1873.

*14. Dictys Cretensis. *Dictys Cretensis. Ephemeridos Belli Troiani.* Rec. F. Meister. Leipzig: Teubner, 1872.

*15. Favonius. *Favonii Eulogii Disputatio de Somnio Scipionis.* Edited by A. Holder. Leipzig: Teubner, 1901.

 16. Festus Pompeius. *Pompeius Festus, De Verborum Significatu.* Edited by W. Lindsay. Leipzig: Teubner, 1913.

 17. Firmicus Maternus. *Iuli Firmici Materni De Errore Profanorum Religionum.* Edited by K. Ziegler. Leipzig: Teubner, 1907.

 18. Frontinus. Gerhard Bendz. *Index verborum Frontinianus.* Lund: Gleerup, 1939.

 19. Granius Licinianus. *Grani Liciniani quae supersunt.* Edited by Michael Flemisch. Leipzig: Teubner, 1904.

 20. Horace. Dominicus Bo. *Lexicon Horatianum.* Hildesheim: Olms, 1965; G. A. Koch. *Vollständiges Worterbuch zu den Gedichten des Q. Horatius Flaccus.* Hannover, 1879.

*21. Hyginus. *Hygini Astronomica.* Rec. Bernhard Bunte. Leipzig: Weigel, 1875.

 22. Juvenal. *Iuvenal.* Edited by L. Friedländer. Leipzig, 1895; Lucille Kelling. *Index verborum Iuvenalis.* Chapel Hill: University of North Carolina Press, 1951.

*23. Livy. August Wilhelm Ernesti. *Glossarium Livianum sive Index Latinitatis exquisitores.* Leipzig, 1804. Reprint. Hildesheim: Olms, 1966.

 24. Lucilius. Lucille Berkowitz and Theodore F. Brunner. *Index Lucilianus.* Hildesheim: Olms, 1968.

*25. Lucretius. Johannes Paulsen. *Index Lucretianus.* Darmstadt: Wissenschaftliche Buchgesellschaft, 1961.

*26. Manilius. *M. Manili Astronomicon*. Rec. F. Jacob. Berlin: Reimer, 1846.

*27. Marcellus. *Marcelli De Medicamentis*. Edited by George Helmreich. Leipzig: Teubner, 1889.

28. Martial. *Martialis*. Edited by L. Friedländer. Leipzig: Teubner, 1886.

29. Ovid. R. J. Deferrari, M. I. Barry, and R. P. McGuire. *A Concordance of Ovid*. Washington, D.C.: Catholic University Press, 1939.

30. Patres Latini. J.-P. Minge. *Patrologiae cursus completus, Series Latina.*

*31. *Persius*. Dominicus Bo. *Auli Persii Flacci Lexicon*. Hildesheim: Olms, 1967.

32. Petronius. Johann Segebade and Ernest Lommatzsch. *Lexicon Petronianum*. Leipzig: Teubner, 1898.

33. Phaedrus. Adolf Cinquini. *Index Phaedrianus*. Milan, 1905. Reprint. Hildesheim: Olms, 1964.

34. Plautus. G. Lodge. *Lexicon Plautinum*. Leipzig: Teubner, 1924.

35. Pliny. O. Schneider. *In C. Plini Secundi Naturalis Historiae Libros Indices*. Gotha, 1857. Reprint. Hildesheim: Olms, 1967.

36. Pomponius Porphyrio. *Pomponi Porphyrionis Commentum in Horatium Flaccum*. Edited by Alfred Holder. Innsbruck: Wagner 1889. Reprint. Hildesheim: Olms, 1967.

37. Propertius. J. S. Phillimore. *Index Verborum Propertianus*. Oxford: Clarendon Press, 1905.

38. Quintilian. Eduard Bonell. *Lexicon Quintilianeum*. Leipzig: Teubner, 1834. Reprint. Hildesheim: Olms, 1962.

39. Rhetoricians. Johann C. T. Ernesti. *Lexicon Technologiae Latinorum Rhetoricae*. Leipzig, 1797. Reprint. Hildesheim: Olms, 1962.

40. Sallust. Alva Walter Bennett. *Index verborum Sallustianus*. Hildesheim: Olms, 1970.

*41. Seneca. P. Grimal. *L. Annaei Senecae Operum Moralium Concordantia*. Paris: Presses Universitaires, 1965–67; W. A. Oldfather, H. V. Canter, and A. St. Pease. *Index Verborum quae in Senecae Fabulis Necnon in Octavia Praetexta Reperiuntur*. University of Illinois Studies in Language and Literature, Vol. IV, Nos. 2–4. Urbana: University of Illinois Press, 1918.

*42. Silius Italicus. N. D. Young. *Index Verborum Silianus.* Iowa Studies in Classical Philology, 8. Iowa City: Athens Press, 1939.

43. Suetonius. A. A. Howard and C. N. Jackson. *Index Verborum C. Suetoni Tranquilli.* Cambridge, Mass., 1922. Reprint. Hildesheim: Olms, 1963.

44. Syrus. *Publius Syrus.* Edited by O. Friedrich. Berlin: Grieben, 1880.

45. Tacitus. D. Barends. *Lexicon Aeneium.* A Lexicon and Index to Aeneas Tacitus' Military Manual on the Defense of Fortified Positions. Assen: Vangorcum, 1955. A. Gerber and A. Greef. *Lexicon Taciteum.* Leipzig: Teubner, 1897–1903.

*46. Terence. E. N. Jenkins. *Index Verborum Terentianus.* Chapel Hill: University of North Carolina Press, 1932. Reprint. Hildesheim: Olms, 1962; P. McGlynn. *Lexicon Terentianum.* London: Black, 1963.

47. Tertullian. *Quinti Septimi Florentis Tertulliani Ad Nationes Libri Duo.* Edited by J. G. Ph. Borleffs. Leiden: Brill, 1929; P. Henen. *Index Verborum quae Tertulliani Apologetico continentur.* Louvain, 1910; J. H. Waszink. *Index Verborum et Locutionum quae Tertulliani De Anima continentur.* Bonn: Hanstein, 1935; J. J. Thierry. *Tertullianus, De fuga in persecutione.* Hilversum, 1941. *Tertullien. De paenitentia, De pudicitia.* Edited by Pierre de Labriolle. Paris: Picard, 1906; *Tertullien. De praescriptione Haereticorum.* Edited by Pierre de Labriolle. Paris: Picard, 1907; E. Witters. *Tertullian, De spectaculis. Index verborum omnium.* Louvain, 1943; J. G. Ph. Borleffs. "Q. Sept. Flor. Tertulliani De baptismo ad fidem Trecensis veterumque editionum." *Mnemosyne,* Ser. 2, 59 (1931), "Index Verborum," p. 50–102; Borleffs. "Index verborum quae Tertulliani de paenitentia libello continentur." *Mnemosyne,* Ser. 2, 60 (1932):254–316.

*48. Tibullus. Edward N. O'Neil. *A Critical Concordance of the Tibullan Corpus.* Ithaca, N.Y.: American Philological Association Publication, 1963.

*49. Valerian. William H. Schulte. *Index Verborum Valerianus.* Hildesheim: Olms, 1965.

50. Varro. H. P. Lodge. *Index Verborum in Varronis Rerum Rusticarum.* Leipzig: Teubner, 1902. Vol. 3, Fasc. 2 of Keil ed.

51. Vegetius. *Flavi Vegeti Renati Epitoma Rei Militaris.* Edited by Carolus Lang. Leipzig: Teubner, 1885.

52. Vergil. G. A. Koch. *Vollständiges Wörterbuch zu den Gedichten des P. Vergilius Maro.* Hannover, 1875; J. B. Wetmore. *Index Verborum Vergilianus.* New Haven: Yale University Press, 1911; H. Merguet. *Lexikon zu Vergilius.* Leipzig: Kommissionsverlag, 1907.

53. Vitruvius. Hermann Nohl. *Index Vitruvianus.* Leipzig: Teubner, 1876. Reprint. Stuttgart: Teubner, 1965.

Index of Names and Subjects

(References in italics indicate pages on which an author is quoted.)